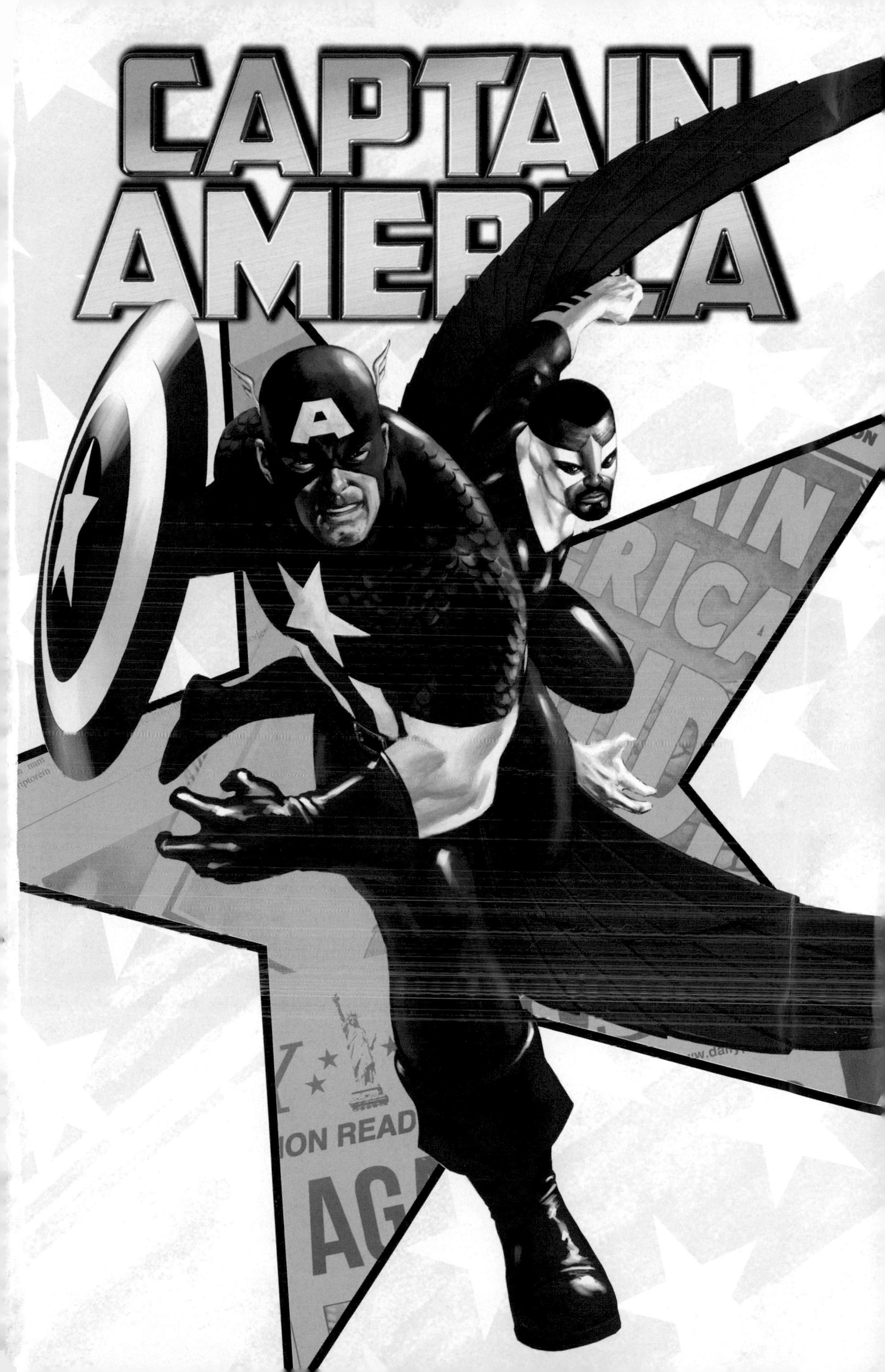
CAPTAIN
AMERICA

DURING THE DARK DAYS OF THE EARLY 1940S, A COVERT MILITARY EXPERIMENT TURNED STEVE ROGERS INTO AMERICA'S FIRST SUPER-SOLDIER, CAPTAIN AMERICA. THROUGHOUT THE WAR, CAP AND HIS PARTNER BUCKY FOUGHT ALONGSIDE OUR INFANTRY AND WITH A GROUP OF HEROES KNOWN AS THE INVADERS. IN THE CLOSING MONTHS OF WWII, CAPTAIN AMERICA AND BUCKY WERE BOTH PRESUMED DEAD IN AN EXPLOSION OVER THE ENGLISH CHANNEL.

DECADES LATER, A FIGURE WAS FOUND TRAPPED IN ICE, AND CAPTAIN AMERICA WAS REVIVED. HAVING SLEPT THROUGH THE MAJORITY OF THE 20TH CENTURY, STEVE ROGERS AWAKENED TO A WORLD HE NEVER IMAGINED, A WORLD WHERE WAR HAD MOVED FROM THE BATTLEFIELD TO THE CITY STREETS...A WORLD IN DIRE NEED OF...

CAPTAIN AMERICA

THE TERRORIST ORGANIZATION HYDRA IS UNDER NEW LEADERSHIP. THE RECENTLY ASCENDED HYDRA QUEEN, ALONG WITH HER HUSBAND CODENAME BRAVO, HAS BEGUN A PROGRAM OF VIOLENCE AND DESTRUCTION THAT SEEMS TO BE CENTERED ON CAPTAIN AMERICA. AFTER BRAINWASHING FORMER GOVERNMENT AGENT HENRY GYRICH AND CAP'S FRIEND AND ONE-TIME ALLY D-MAN, HYDRA MADE D-MAN INTO THE NEW VERSION OF THE VIGILANTE SCOURGE. NOW D-MAN IS DEAD, GYRICH IS IN A COMA, CAP'S FORMER LOVER DIAMONDBACK WAS BRUTALLY BEATEN AND CAP WANTS ANSWERS...AND IT SEEMS HYDRA'S MACHINATIONS ARE FAR FROM OVER.

CAPTAIN AMERICA BY ED BRUBAKER VOL. 4. Contains material originally published in magazine form as CAPTAIN AMERICA #15-19. First printing 2013. Hardcover ISBN# 978-0-7851-6077-9. Softcover ISBN# 978-0-7851-6078-6. Published by MARVEL WORLDWIDE, INC., a subsidiary of MARVEL ENTERTAINMENT, LLC. OFFICE OF PUBLICATION: 135 West 50th Street, New York, NY 10020. Copyright © 2012 and 2013 Marvel Characters, Inc. All rights reserved. Hardcover: $24.99 per copy in the U.S. and $27.99 in Canada (GST #R127032852). Softcover: $19.99 per copy in the U.S. and $21.99 in Canada (GST #R127032852). Canadian Agreement #40668537. All characters featured in this issue and the distinctive names and likenesses thereof, and all related indicia are trademarks of Marvel Characters, Inc. No similarity between any of the names, characters, persons, and/or institutions in this magazine with those of any living or dead person or institution is intended, and any such similarity which may exist is purely coincidental. **Printed in the U.S.A.** ALAN FINE, EVP - Office of the President, Marvel Worldwide, Inc. and EVP & CMO Marvel Characters B.V.; DAN BUCKLEY, Publisher & President - Print, Animation & Digital Divisions; JOE QUESADA, Chief Creative Officer; TOM BREVOORT, SVP of Publishing; DAVID BOGART, SVP of Operations & Procurement, Publishing; RUWAN JAYATILLEKE, SVP & Associate Publisher, Publishing; C.B. CEBULSKI, SVP of Creator & Content Development; DAVID GABRIEL, SVP of Publishing Sales & Circulation; MICHAEL PASCIULLO, SVP of Brand Planning & Communications; JIM O'KEEFE, VP of Operations & Logistics; DAN CARR, Executive Director of Publishing Technology; SUSAN CRESPI, Editorial Operations Manager; ALEX MORALES, Publishing Operations Manager; STAN LEE, Chairman Emeritus. For information regarding advertising in Marvel Comics or on Marvel.com, please contact Niza Disla, Director of Marvel Partnerships, at ndisla@marvel.com. For Marvel subscription inquiries, please call 800-217-9158. **Manufactured between 11/12/2012 and 12/31/2012 (hardcover), and 11/12/2012 and 7/1/2013 (softcover), by R.R. DONNELLEY, INC., SALEM, VA, USA.**

10 9 8 7 6 5 4 3 2 1

DURING THE DARK DAYS OF THE EARLY 1940S, A COVERT MILITARY EXPERIMENT TURNED STEVE ROGERS INTO AMERICA'S FIRST SUPER-SOLDIER, CAPTAIN AMERICA. THROUGHOUT THE WAR, CAP AND HIS PARTNER BUCKY FOUGHT ALONGSIDE OUR INFANTRY AND WITH A GROUP OF HEROES KNOWN AS THE INVADERS. IN THE CLOSING MONTHS OF WWII, CAPTAIN AMERICA AND BUCKY WERE BOTH PRESUMED DEAD IN AN EXPLOSION OVER THE ENGLISH CHANNEL.

DECADES LATER, A FIGURE WAS FOUND TRAPPED IN ICE, AND CAPTAIN AMERICA WAS REVIVED. HAVING SLEPT THROUGH THE MAJORITY OF THE 20TH CENTURY, STEVE ROGERS AWAKENED TO A WORLD HE NEVER IMAGINED, A WORLD WHERE WAR HAD MOVED FROM THE BATTLEFIELD TO THE CITY STREETS...A WORLD IN DIRE NEED OF...

CAPTAIN AMERICA

THE TERRORIST ORGANIZATION HYDRA IS UNDER NEW LEADERSHIP. THE RECENTLY ASCENDED HYDRA QUEEN, ALONG WITH HER HUSBAND CODENAME BRAVO, HAS BEGUN A PROGRAM OF VIOLENCE AND DESTRUCTION THAT SEEMS TO BE CENTERED ON CAPTAIN AMERICA. AFTER BRAINWASHING FORMER GOVERNMENT AGENT HENRY GYRICH AND CAP'S FRIEND AND ONE-TIME ALLY D-MAN, HYDRA MADE D-MAN INTO THE NEW VERSION OF THE VIGILANTE SCOURGE. NOW D-MAN IS DEAD, GYRICH IS IN A COMA, CAP'S FORMER LOVER DIAMONDBACK WAS BRUTALLY BEATEN AND CAP WANTS ANSWERS...AND IT SEEMS HYDRA'S MACHINATIONS ARE FAR FROM OVER.

A BY ED BRUBAKER VOL. 4. Contains material originally published in magazine form as CAPTAIN AMERICA #15-19. First printing 2013. Hardcover ISBN# 978-0-7851-6077-9. Softcover ISB lished by MARVEL WORLDWIDE, INC., a subsidiary of MARVEL ENTERTAINMENT, LLC. OFFICE OF PUBLICATION: 135 West 50th Street, New York, NY 10020. Copyright © 2012 and 2013 Marvel ed. Hardcover: $24.99 per copy in the U.S. and $27.99 in Canada (GST #R127032852). Softcover: $19.99 per copy in the U.S. and $21.99 in Canada (GST #R127032852). Canadian Agreement # ured in this issue and the distinctive names and likenesses thereof, and all related indicia are trademarks of Marvel Characters, Inc. No similarity between any of the names, characters, pers magazine with those of any living or dead person or institution is intended, and any such similarity which may exist is purely coincidental. Printed in the U.S.A. ALAN FINE, EVP - Office of the Presid EVP & CMO Marvel Characters B.V.; DAN BUCKLEY, Publisher & President - Print, Animation & Digital Divisions; JOE QUESADA, Chief Creative Officer; TOM BREVOORT, SVP of Publishing; DAVID B curement, Publishing; RUWAN JAYATILLEKE, SVP & Associate Publisher, Publishing; C.B. CEBULSKI, SVP of Creator & Content Development; DAVID GABRIEL, SVP of Publishing Sales & Circulation Brand Planning & Communications; JIM O'KEEFE, VP of Operations & Logistics; DAN CARR, Executive Director of Publishing Technology; SUSAN CRESPI, Editorial Operations Manager; ALEX ins Manager; STAN LEE, Chairman Emeritus. For information regarding advertising in Marvel Comics or on Marvel.com, please contact Niza Disla, Director of Marvel Partnerships, at ndisla@m tion inquiries, please call 800-217-9158. Manufactured between 11/12/2012 and 12/31/2012 (hardcover), and 11/12/2012 and 7/1/2013 (softcover), by R.R. DONNELLEY, INC., SALEM

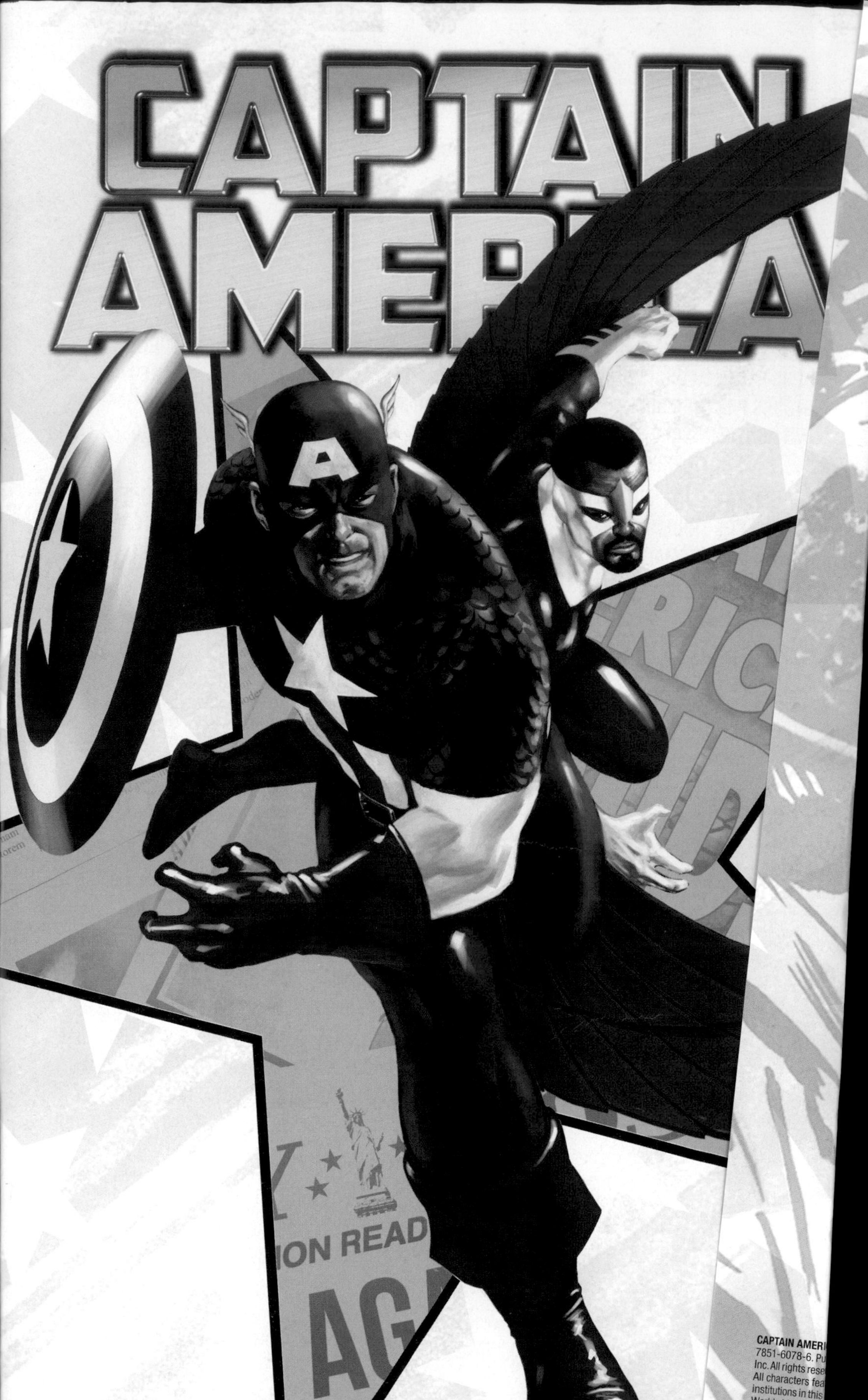
CAPTAIN
AMER
ION READ

CAPTAIN AMERI
7851-6078-6. Pu
Inc. All rights rese
All characters fea
institutions in this
Worldwide, Inc. an
of Operations & Pr
PASCIULLO, SVP o
Publishing Operati
For Marvel subscri

10 9 8 7 6 5 4 3 2

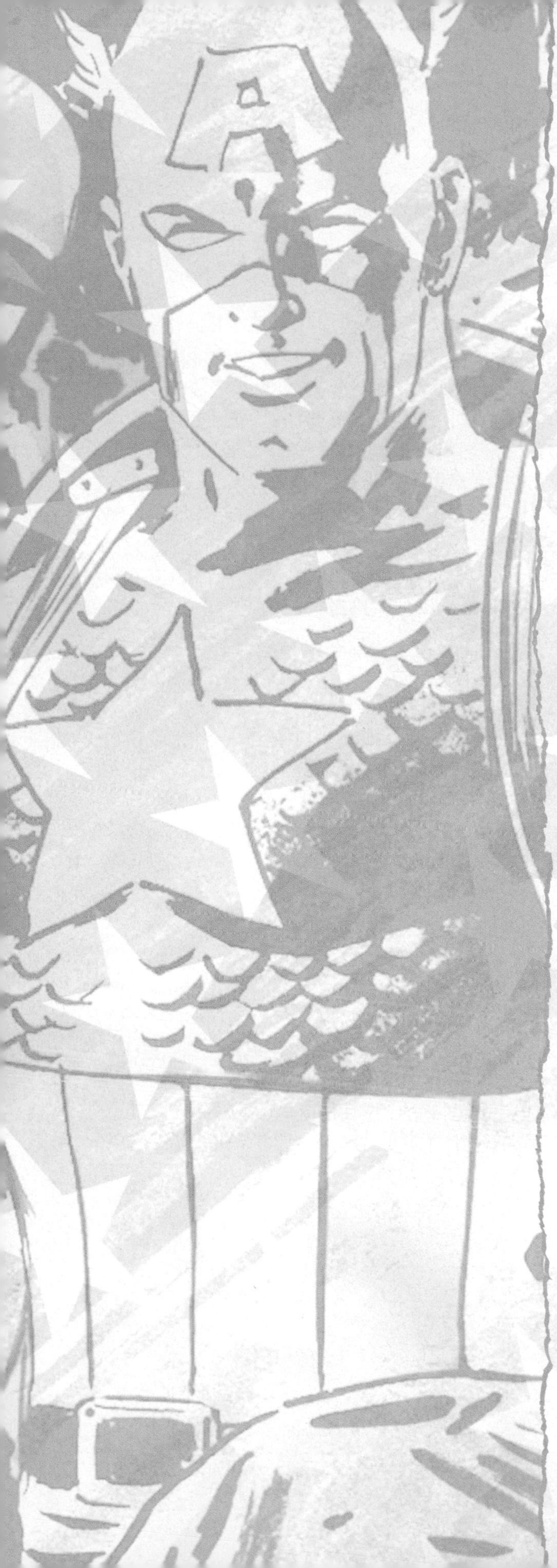

ISSUES #15–18

WRITERS
ED BRUBAKER & CULLEN BUNN

PENCILER
SCOT EATON

INKERS
RICK MAGYAR
WITH **RICK KETCHUM & MARK PENNINGTON** (#16)

COLORIST
GURU-eFX

ISSUE #19

WRITER
ED BRUBAKER

ARTIST
STEVE EPTING

COLOR ARTIST
FRANK D'ARMATA

LETTERS
VC'S JOE CARAMAGNA

COVER ART
STEVE EPTING

ASSISTANT EDITOR
JAKE THOMAS

EDITORS
TOM BREVOORT WITH **LAUREN SANKOVITCH**

CAPTAIN AMERICA CREATED BY
JOE SIMON & JACK KIRBY

COLLECTION EDITOR
JENNIFER GRÜNWALD
ASSISTANT EDITORS
ALEX STARBUCK & NELSON RIBEIRO
EDITOR, SPECIAL PROJECTS
MARK D. BEAZLEY
SENIOR EDITOR, SPECIAL PROJECTS
JEFF YOUNGQUIST
SENIOR VICE PRESIDENT OF SALES
DAVID GABRIEL
SVP OF BRAND PLANNING & COMMUNICATIONS
MICHAEL PASCIULLO
BOOK DESIGN
JEFF POWELL

EDITOR IN CHIEF
AXEL ALONSO
CHIEF CREATIVE OFFICER
JOE QUESADA
PUBLISHER
DAN BUCKLEY
EXECUTIVE PRODUCER
ALAN FINE

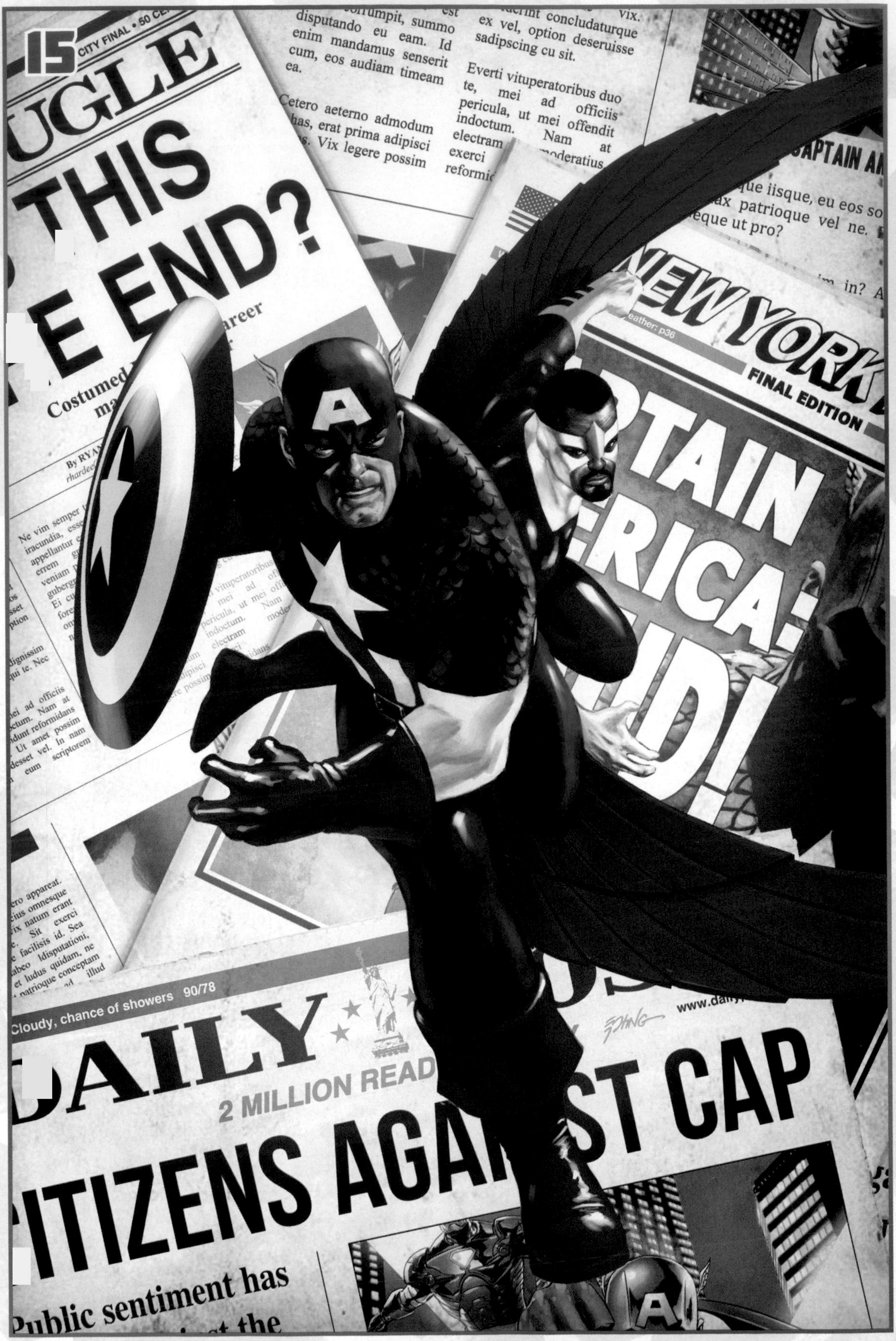
15
CITY FINAL • 50 CE
UGLE
THIS
E END?
Costumed
disputando eu eam. Id
enim mandamus senserit
cum, eos audiam timeam
ea.
Cetero aeterno admodum
has, erat prima adipisci
Vix legere possim
ex vel, option deseruisse
sadipscing cu sit.
Everti vituperatoribus duo
te, mei ad officiis
pericula, ut mei offendit
indoctum. Nam at
APTAIN AM
que iisque, eu eos so
ax patrioque vel ne.
eque ut pro?
NEW YORK
FINAL EDITION
eather: p36
PTAIN
ERICA:
Cloudy, chance of showers 90/78
DAILY
2 MILLION READ
www.daily
CITIZENS AGA ST CAP
Public sentiment has

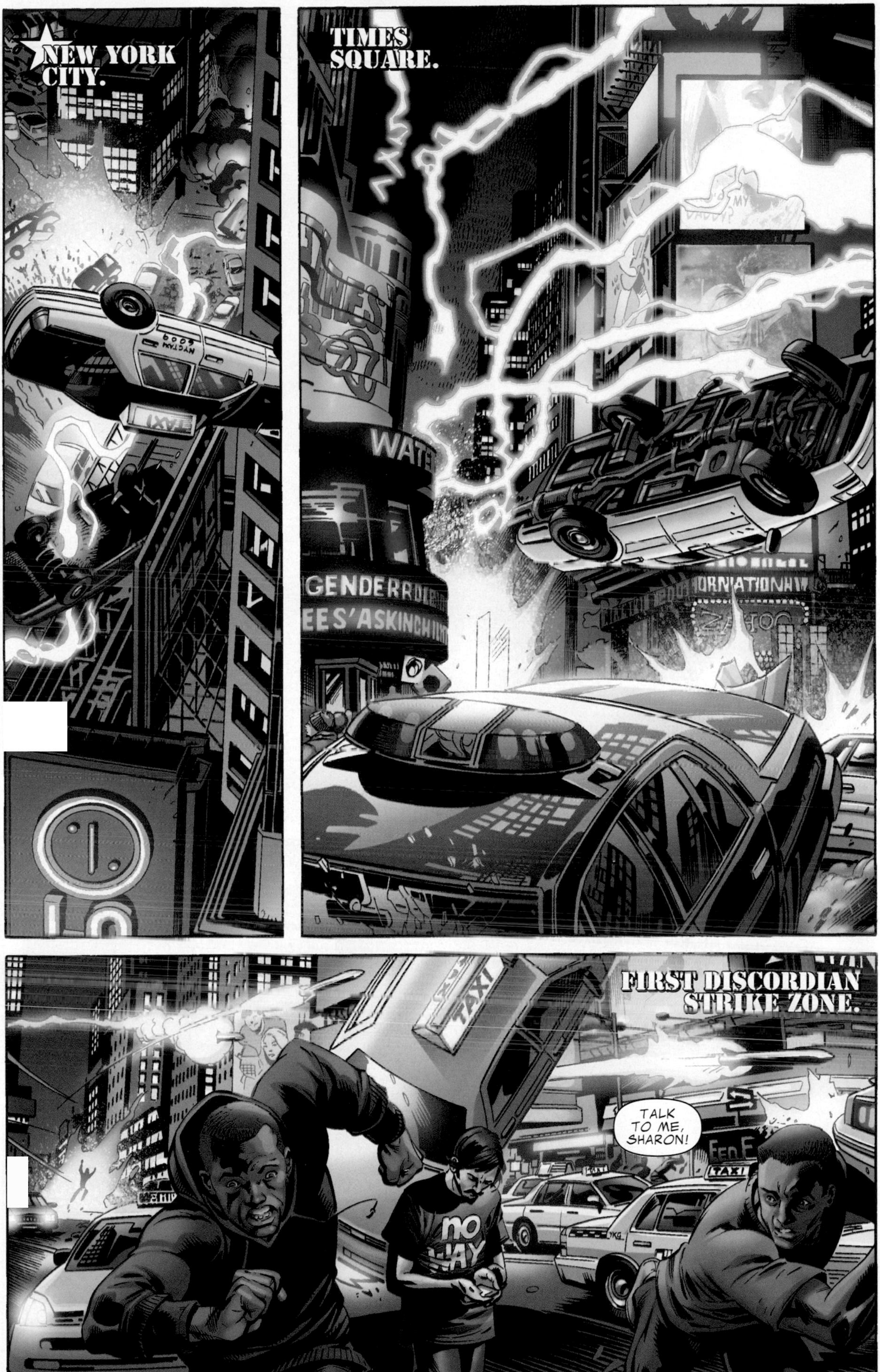
NEW YORK CITY.
TIMES SQUARE.
FIRST DISCORDIAN STRIKE ZONE.
TALK TO ME, SHARON!

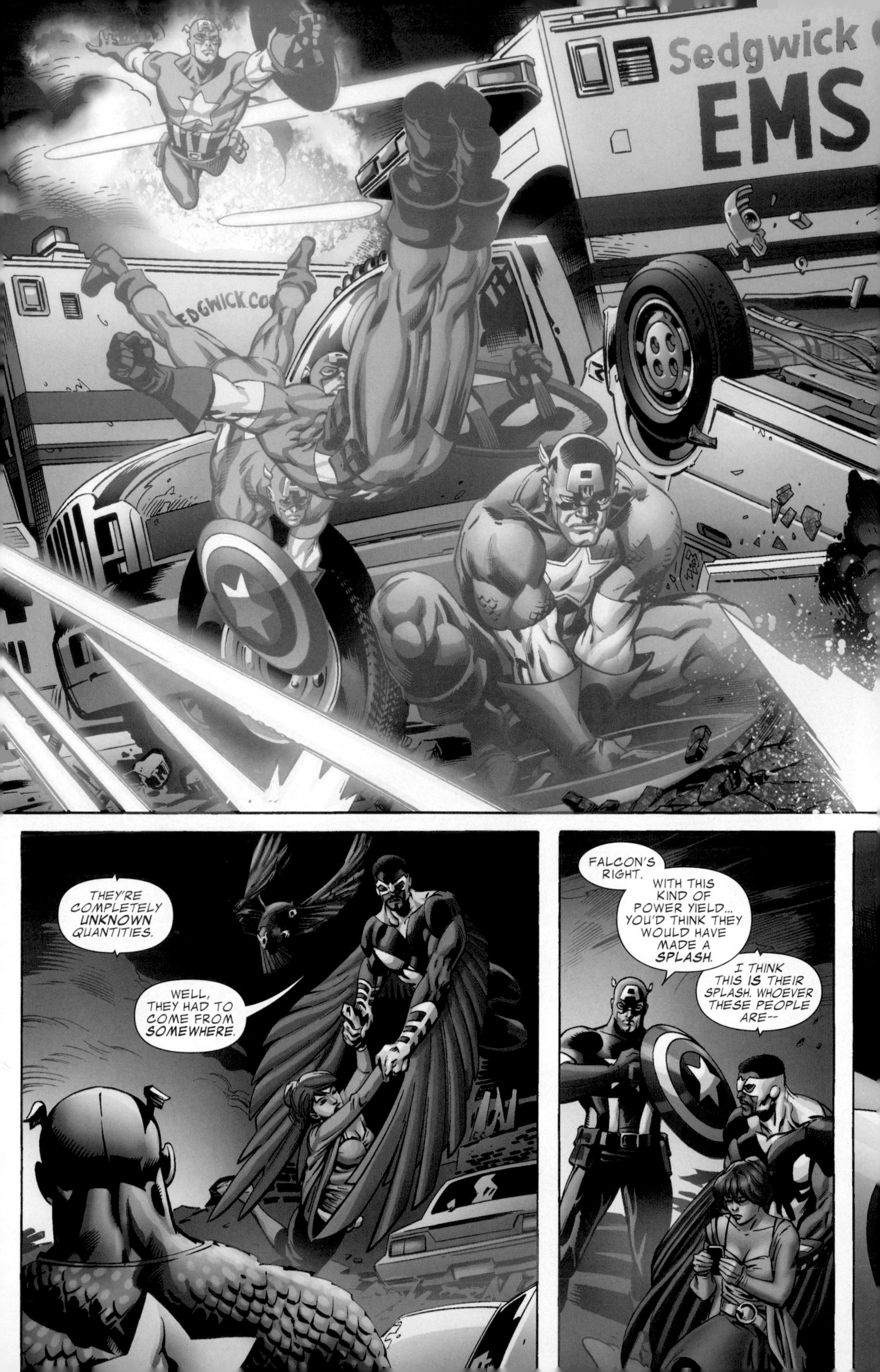
Sedgwick
EMS
SEDGWICK CO
THEY'RE COMPLETELY UNKNOWN QUANTITIES.
WELL, THEY HAD TO COME FROM SOMEWHERE.
FALCON'S RIGHT.
WITH THIS KIND OF POWER YIELD... YOU'D THINK THEY WOULD HAVE MADE A SPLASH.
I THINK THIS IS THEIR SPLASH. WHOEVER THESE PEOPLE ARE--

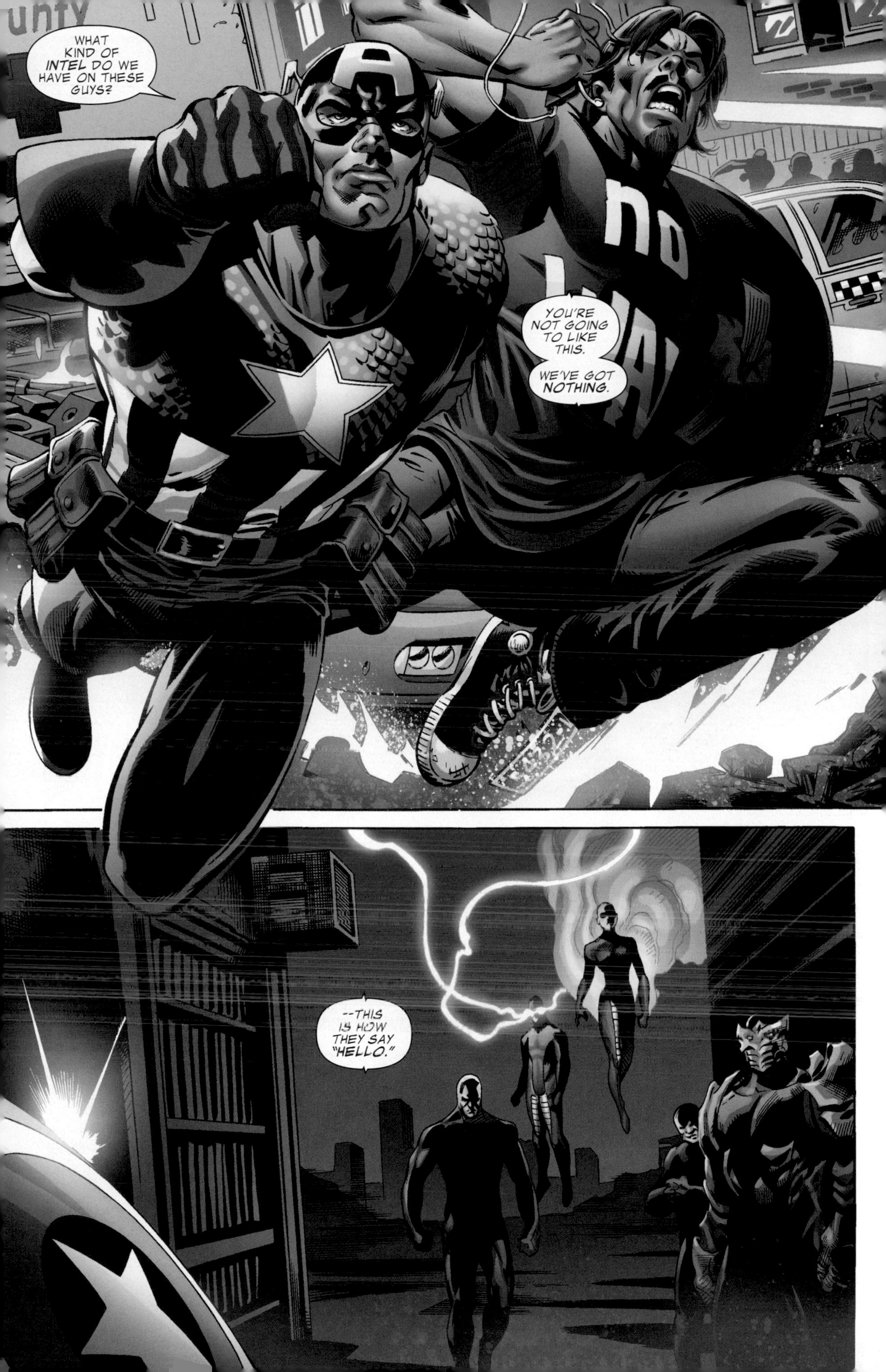
WHAT KIND OF INTEL DO WE HAVE ON THESE GUYS?
YOU'RE NOT GOING TO LIKE THIS.
WE'VE GOT NOTHING.
--THIS IS HOW THEY SAY "HELLO."

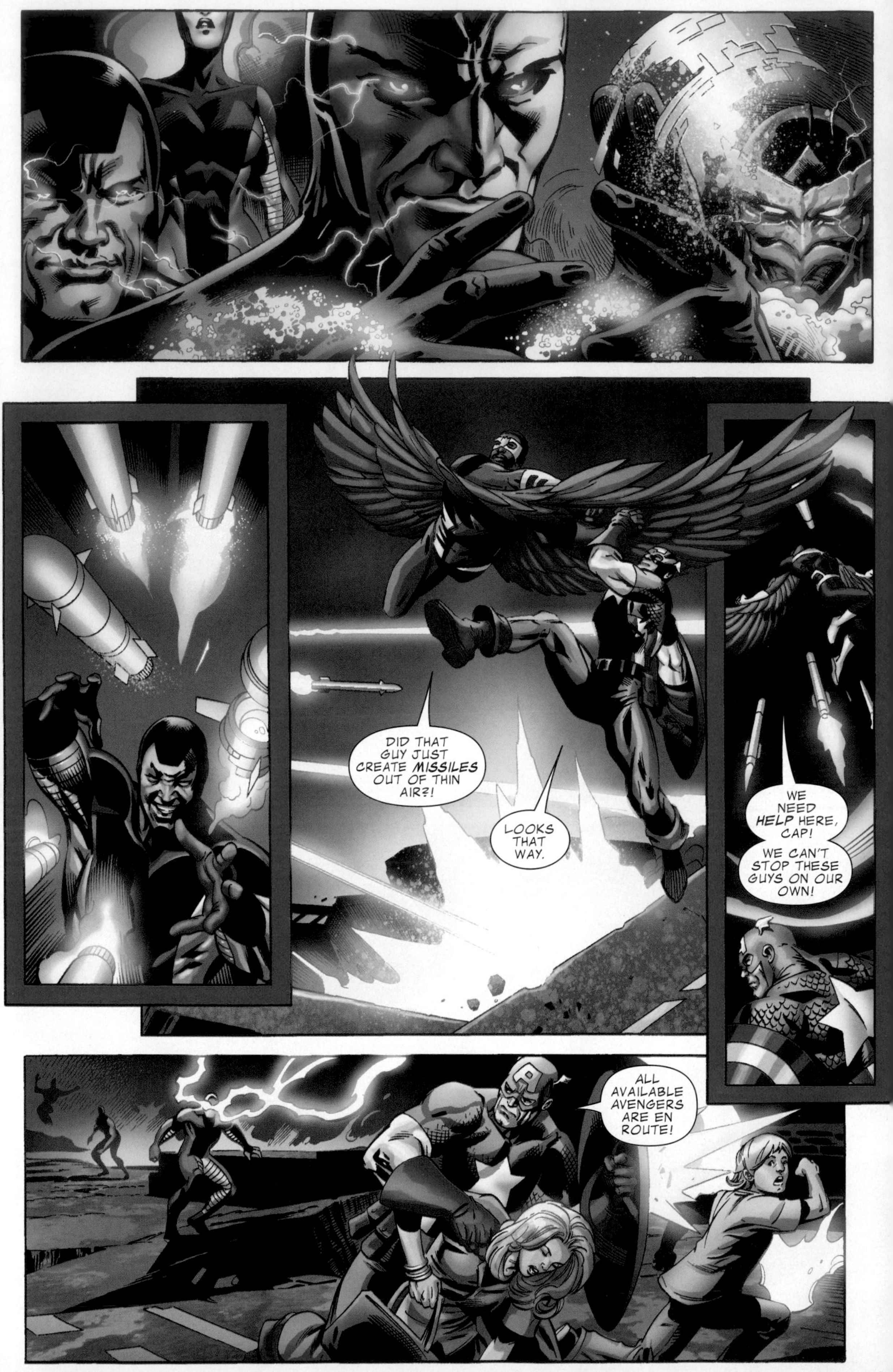
DID THAT GUY JUST CREATE MISSILES OUT OF THIN AIR?!
LOOKS THAT WAY.
WE NEED HELP HERE, CAP!
WE CAN'T STOP THESE GUYS ON OUR OWN!
ALL AVAILABLE AVENGERS ARE EN ROUTE!

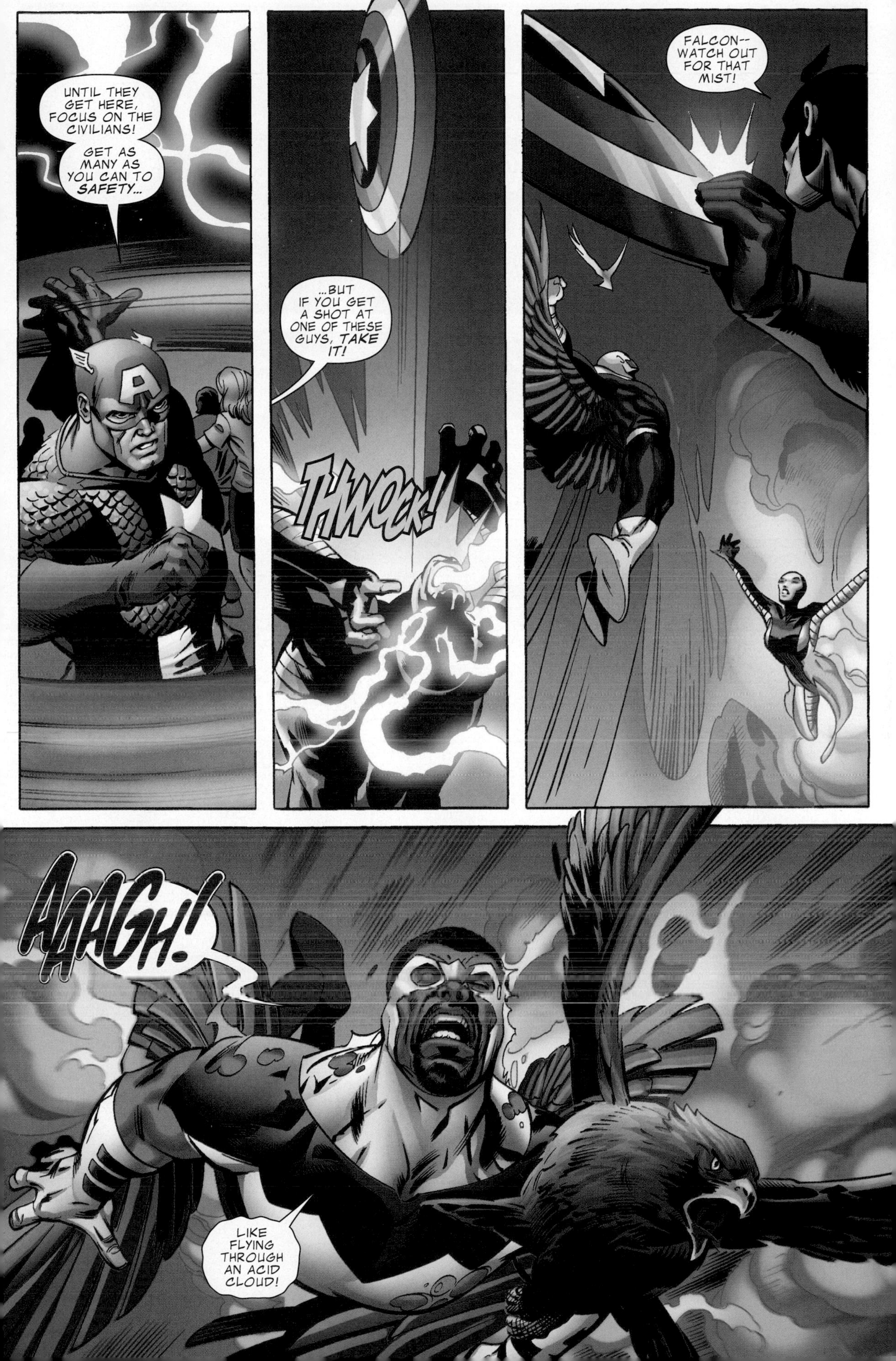
UNTIL THEY GET HERE, FOCUS ON THE CIVILIANS!
GET AS MANY AS YOU CAN TO SAFETY...
...BUT IF YOU GET A SHOT AT ONE OF THESE GUYS, TAKE IT!
THWOCK!
FALCON-- WATCH OUT FOR THAT MIST!
AAAGH!
LIKE FLYING THROUGH AN ACID CLOUD!

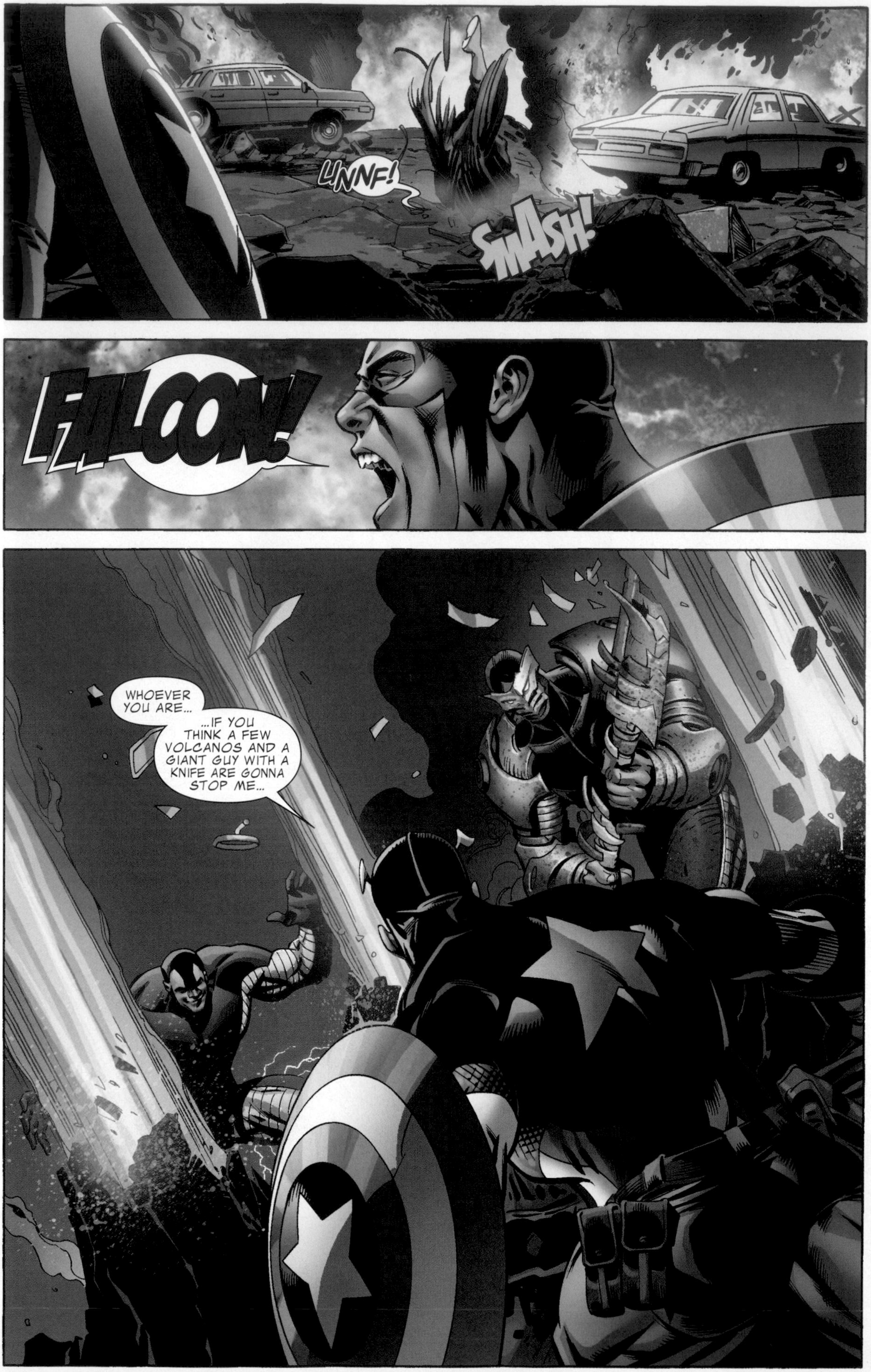
UNNF!
SMASH!
FALCON!
WHOEVER YOU ARE...
...IF YOU THINK A FEW VOLCANOS AND A GIANT GUY WITH A KNIFE ARE GONNA STOP ME...

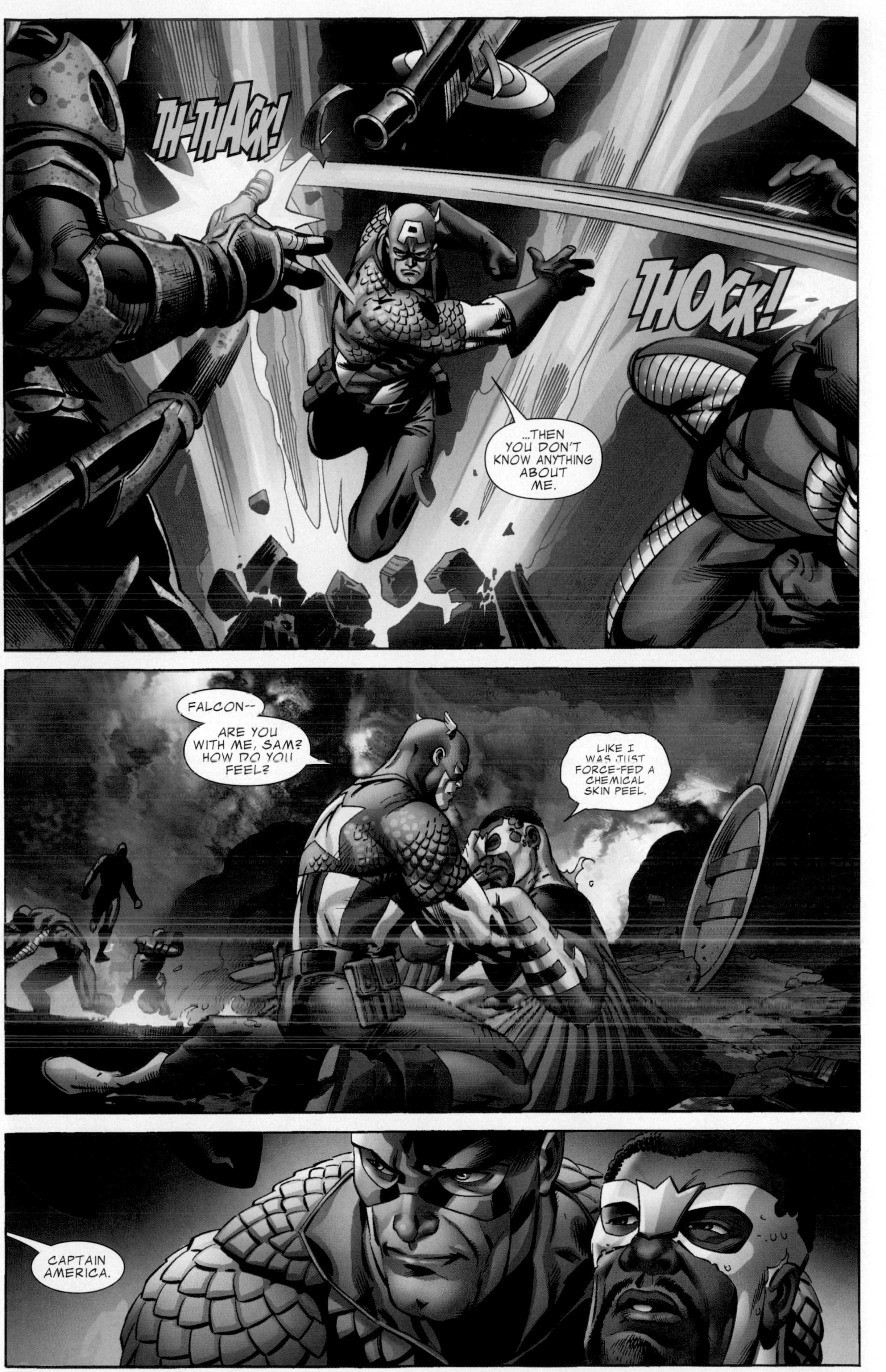
TH-THACK!
THOCK!
...THEN YOU DON'T KNOW ANYTHING ABOUT ME.
FALCON--
ARE YOU WITH ME, SAM? HOW DO YOU FEEL?
LIKE I WAS JUST FORCE-FED A CHEMICAL SKIN PEEL.
CAPTAIN AMERICA.

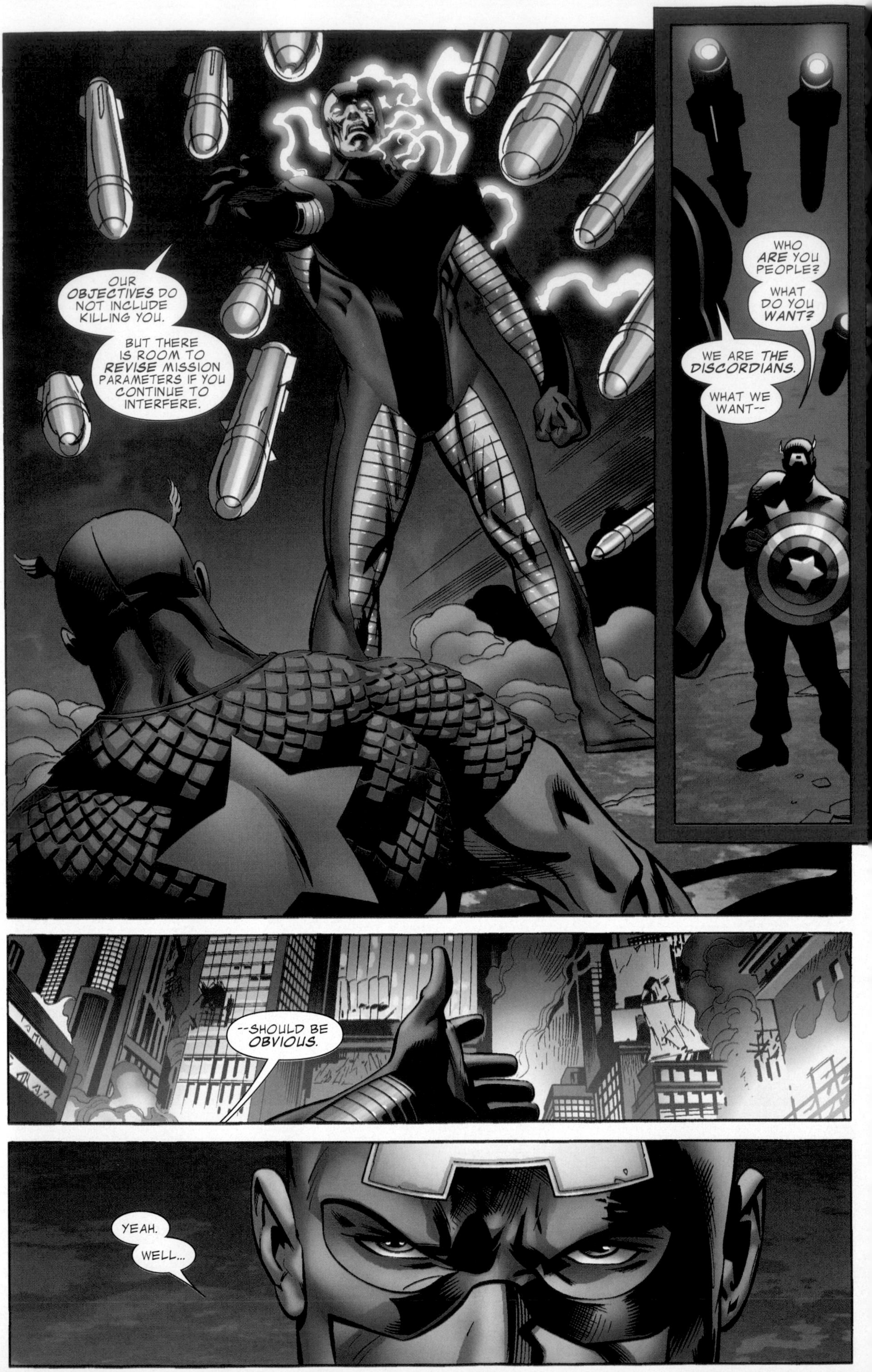
OUR OBJECTIVES DO NOT INCLUDE KILLING YOU.
BUT THERE IS ROOM TO REVISE MISSION PARAMETERS IF YOU CONTINUE TO INTERFERE.
WHO ARE YOU PEOPLE?
WHAT DO YOU WANT?
WE ARE THE DISCORDIANS.
WHAT WE WANT--
--SHOULD BE OBVIOUS.
YEAH.
WELL...

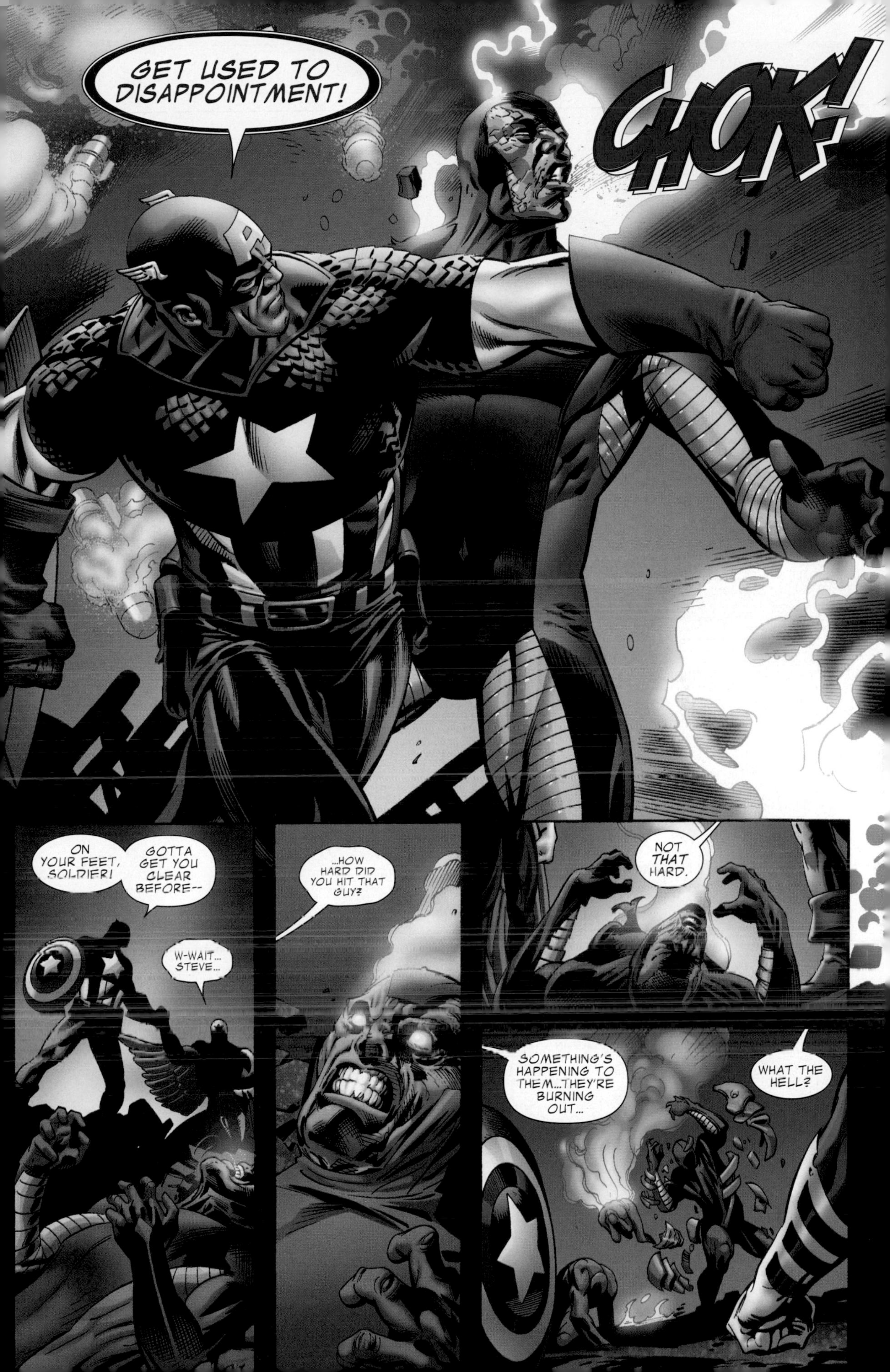
GET USED TO DISAPPOINTMENT!
CHOK!
ON YOUR FEET, SOLDIER!
GOTTA GET YOU CLEAR BEFORE--
W-WAIT... STEVE...
...HOW HARD DID YOU HIT THAT GUY?
NOT THAT HARD.
SOMETHING'S HAPPENING TO THEM...THEY'RE BURNING OUT...
WHAT THE HELL?

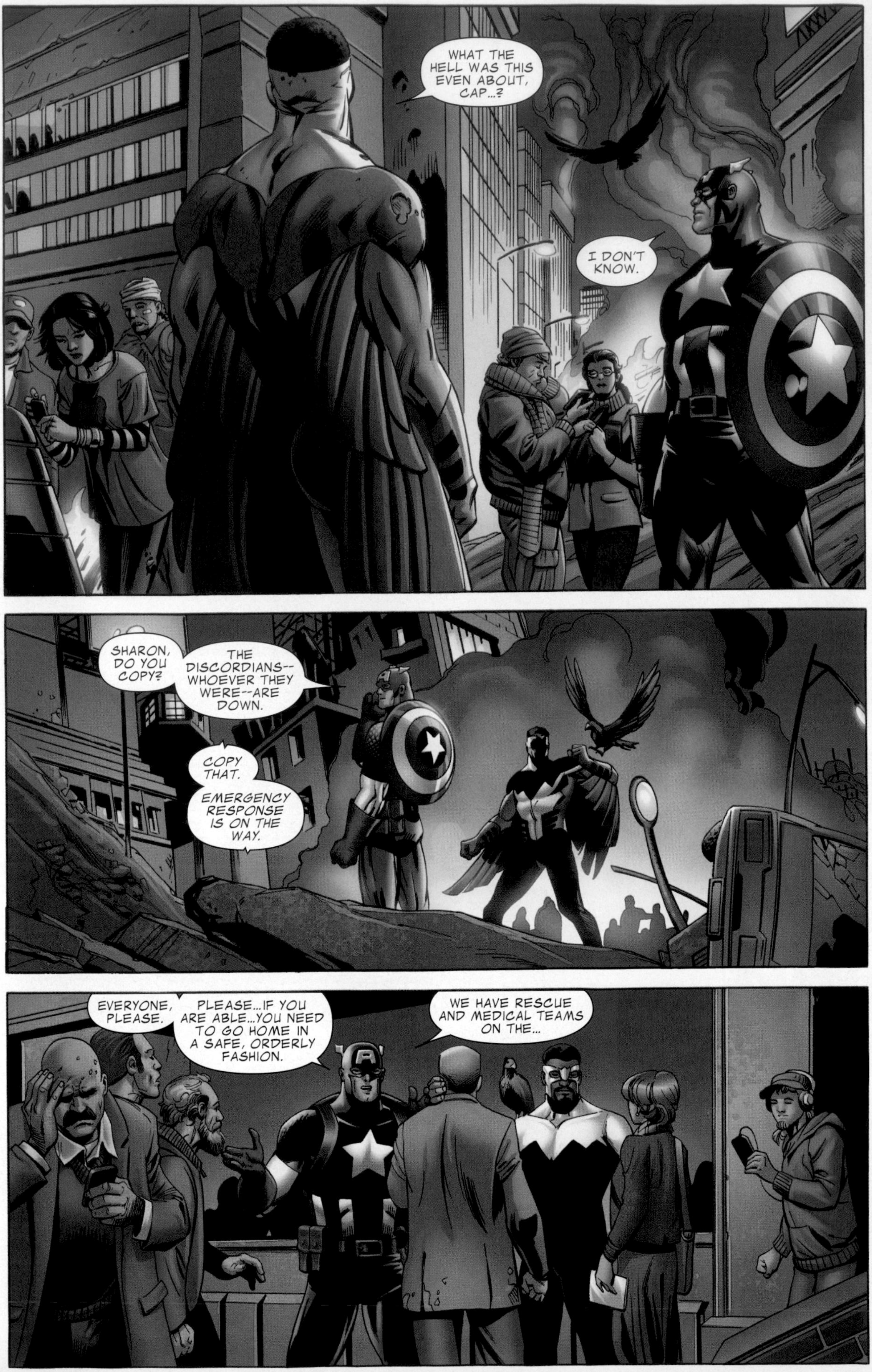
WHAT THE HELL WAS THIS EVEN ABOUT, CAP...?
I DON'T KNOW.
SHARON, DO YOU COPY?
THE DISCORDIANS-- WHOEVER THEY WERE--ARE DOWN.
COPY THAT.
EMERGENCY RESPONSE IS ON THE WAY.
EVERYONE, PLEASE.
PLEASE...IF YOU ARE ABLE...YOU NEED TO GO HOME IN A SAFE, ORDERLY FASHION.
WE HAVE RESCUE AND MEDICAL TEAMS ON THE...

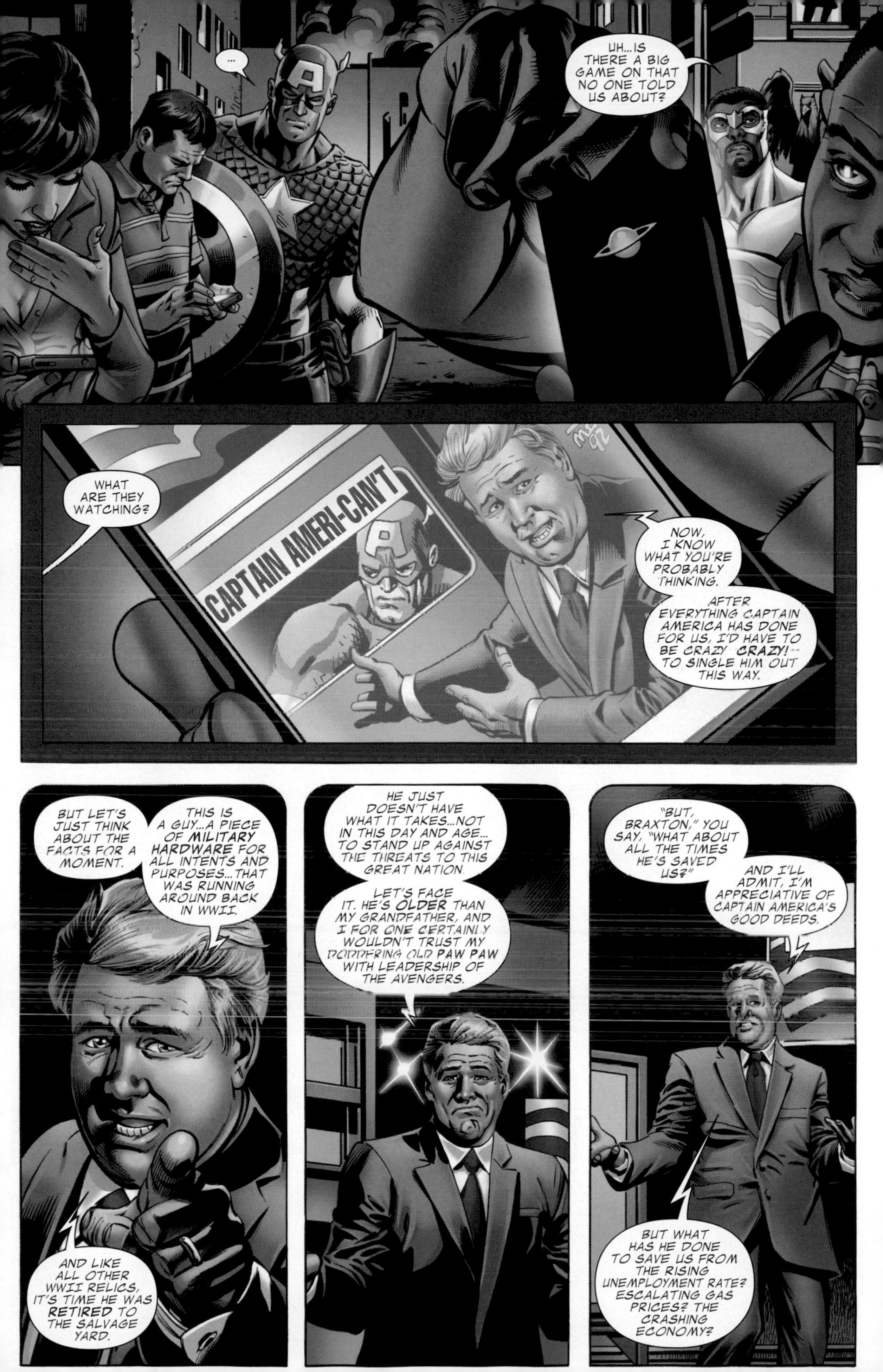
...
UH...IS THERE A BIG GAME ON THAT NO ONE TOLD US ABOUT?
WHAT ARE THEY WATCHING?
CAPTAIN AMERI-CAN'T
NOW, I KNOW WHAT YOU'RE PROBABLY THINKING.
AFTER EVERYTHING CAPTAIN AMERICA HAS DONE FOR US, I'D HAVE TO BE CRAZY --CRAZY!-- TO SINGLE HIM OUT THIS WAY.
BUT LET'S JUST THINK ABOUT THE FACTS FOR A MOMENT.
THIS IS A GUY...A PIECE OF MILITARY HARDWARE FOR ALL INTENTS AND PURPOSES...THAT WAS RUNNING AROUND BACK IN WWII.
AND LIKE ALL OTHER WWII RELICS, IT'S TIME HE WAS RETIRED TO THE SALVAGE YARD.
HE JUST DOESN'T HAVE WHAT IT TAKES...NOT IN THIS DAY AND AGE... TO STAND UP AGAINST THE THREATS TO THIS GREAT NATION.
LET'S FACE IT. HE'S OLDER THAN MY GRANDFATHER, AND I FOR ONE CERTAINLY WOULDN'T TRUST MY DODDERING OLD PAW PAW WITH LEADERSHIP OF THE AVENGERS.
"BUT, BRAXTON," YOU SAY, "WHAT ABOUT ALL THE TIMES HE'S SAVED US?"
AND I'LL ADMIT, I'M APPRECIATIVE OF CAPTAIN AMERICA'S GOOD DEEDS.
BUT WHAT HAS HE DONE TO SAVE US FROM THE RISING UNEMPLOYMENT RATE? ESCALATING GAS PRICES? THE CRASHING ECONOMY?

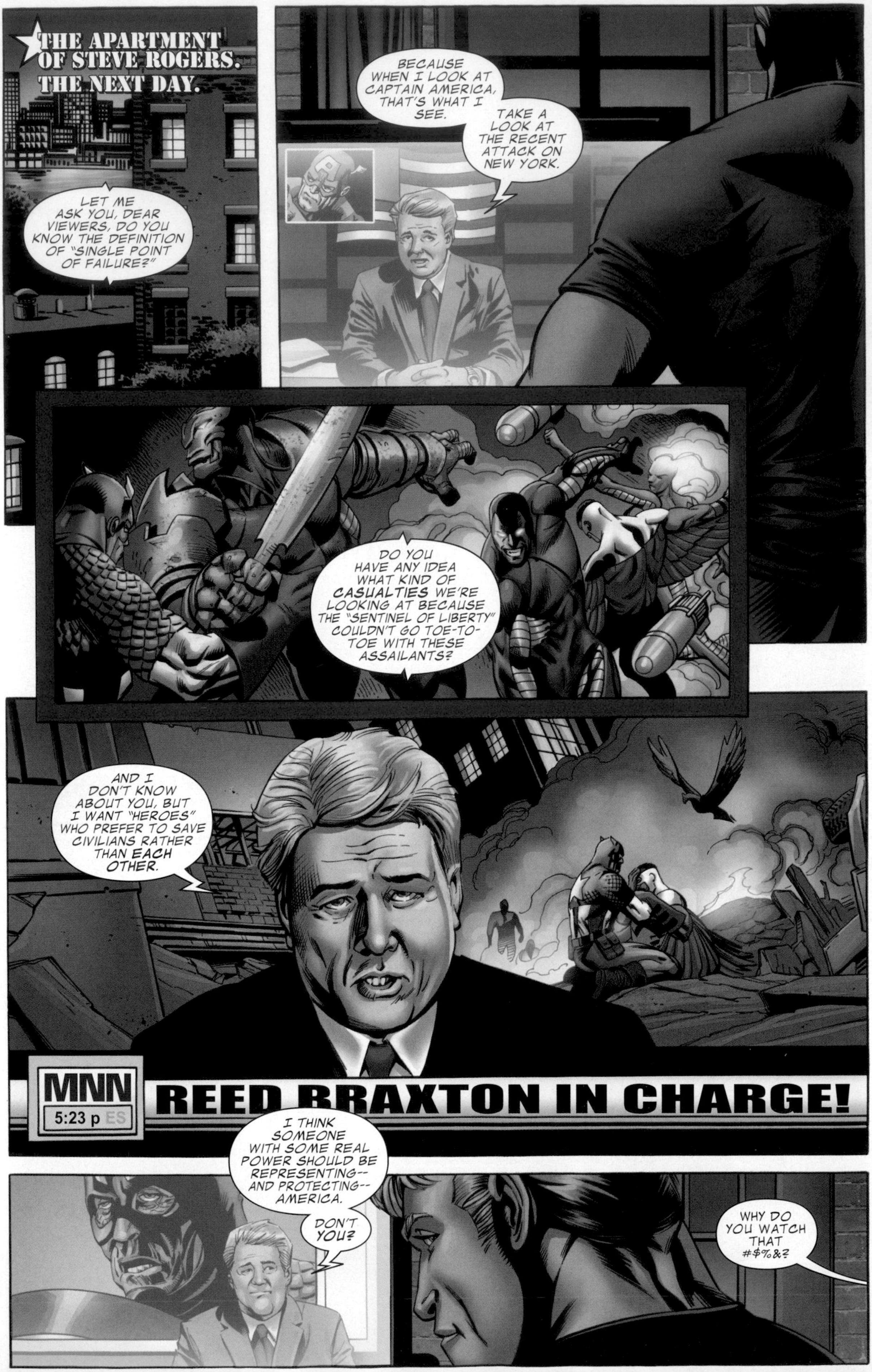
THE APARTMENT OF STEVE ROGERS. THE NEXT DAY.
LET ME ASK YOU, DEAR VIEWERS, DO YOU KNOW THE DEFINITION OF "SINGLE POINT OF FAILURE?"
BECAUSE WHEN I LOOK AT CAPTAIN AMERICA, THAT'S WHAT I SEE.
TAKE A LOOK AT THE RECENT ATTACK ON NEW YORK.
DO YOU HAVE ANY IDEA WHAT KIND OF CASUALTIES WE'RE LOOKING AT BECAUSE THE "SENTINEL OF LIBERTY" COULDN'T GO TOE-TO-TOE WITH THESE ASSAILANTS?
AND I DON'T KNOW ABOUT YOU, BUT I WANT "HEROES" WHO PREFER TO SAVE CIVILIANS RATHER THAN EACH OTHER.
MNN
5:23 p ES
REED BRAXTON IN CHARGE!
I THINK SOMEONE WITH SOME REAL POWER SHOULD BE REPRESENTING-- AND PROTECTING-- AMERICA.
DON'T YOU?
WHY DO YOU WATCH THAT #$%&?

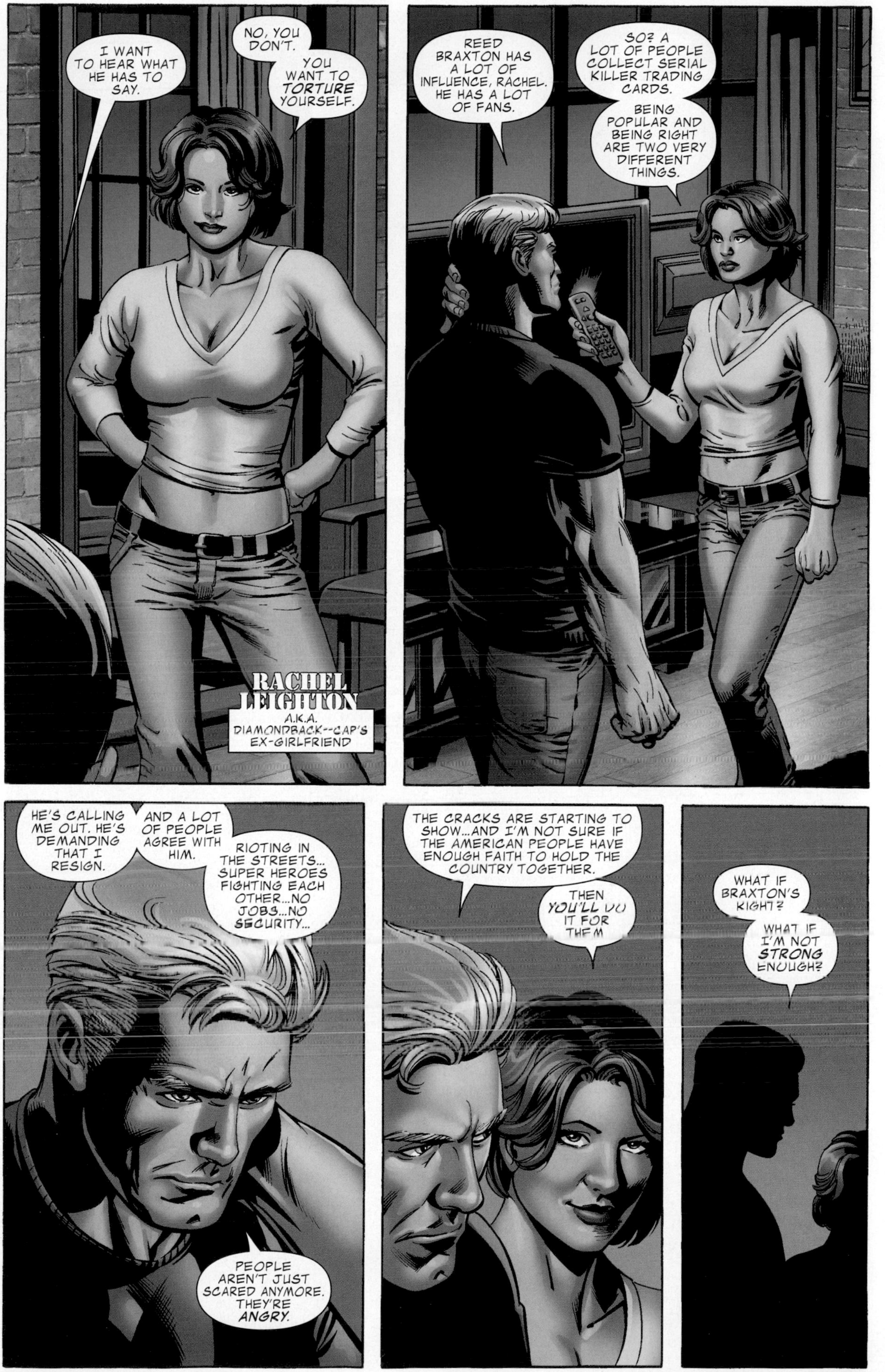
I WANT TO HEAR WHAT HE HAS TO SAY.
NO, YOU DON'T.
YOU WANT TO TORTURE YOURSELF.
RACHEL LEIGHTON
A.K.A. DIAMONDBACK--CAP'S EX-GIRLFRIEND
REED BRAXTON HAS A LOT OF INFLUENCE, RACHEL. HE HAS A LOT OF FANS.
SO? A LOT OF PEOPLE COLLECT SERIAL KILLER TRADING CARDS.
BEING POPULAR AND BEING RIGHT ARE TWO VERY DIFFERENT THINGS.
HE'S CALLING ME OUT. HE'S DEMANDING THAT I RESIGN.
AND A LOT OF PEOPLE AGREE WITH HIM.
RIOTING IN THE STREETS... SUPER HEROES FIGHTING EACH OTHER...NO JOBS...NO SECURITY...
PEOPLE AREN'T JUST SCARED ANYMORE. THEY'RE ANGRY.
THE CRACKS ARE STARTING TO SHOW...AND I'M NOT SURE IF THE AMERICAN PEOPLE HAVE ENOUGH FAITH TO HOLD THE COUNTRY TOGETHER.
THEN YOU'LL DO IT FOR THEM.
WHAT IF BRAXTON'S RIGHT?
WHAT IF I'M NOT STRONG ENOUGH?

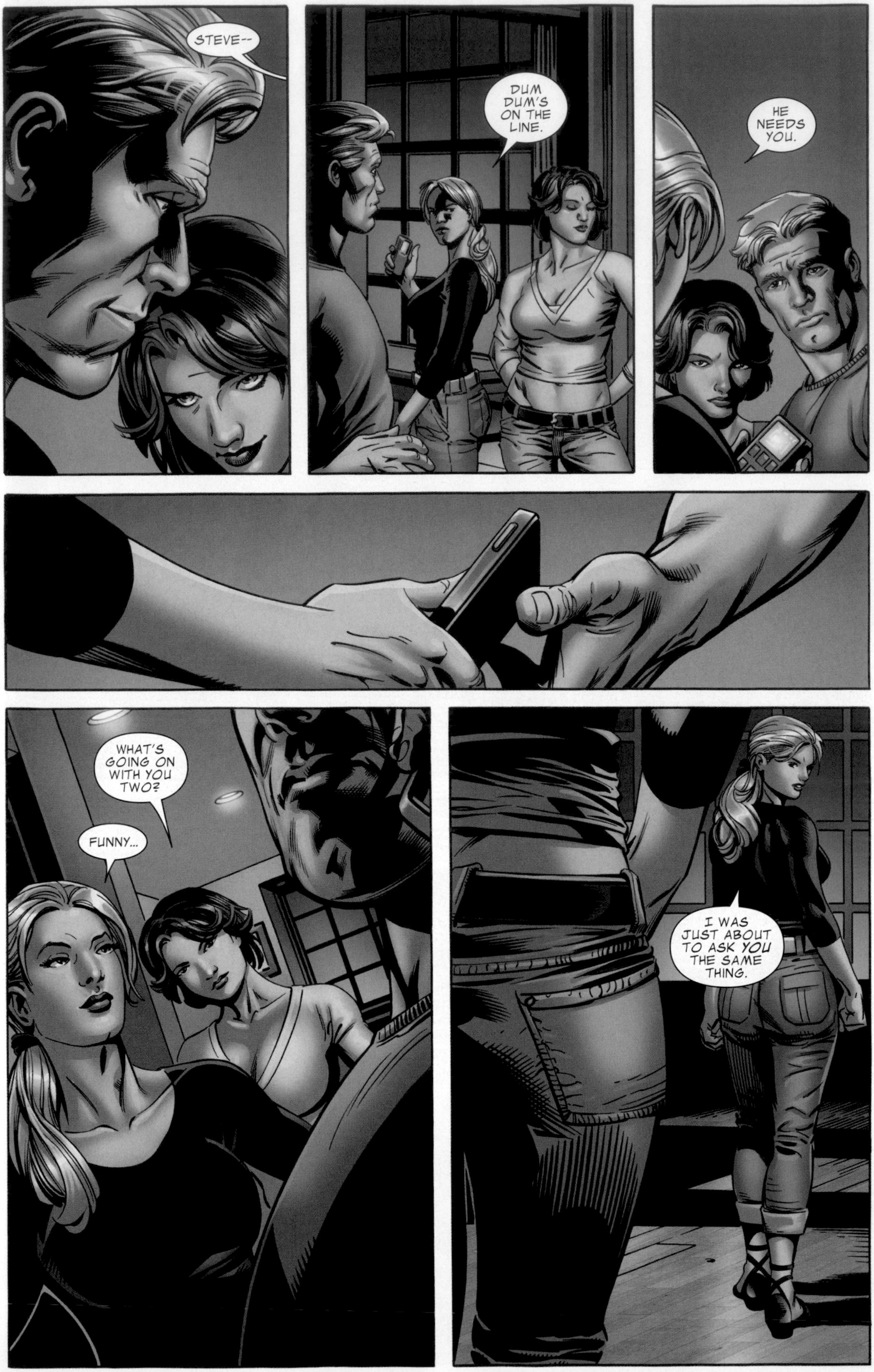
STEVE--
DUM DUM'S ON THE LINE.
HE NEEDS YOU.
WHAT'S GOING ON WITH YOU TWO?
FUNNY...
I WAS JUST ABOUT TO ASK *YOU* THE SAME THING.

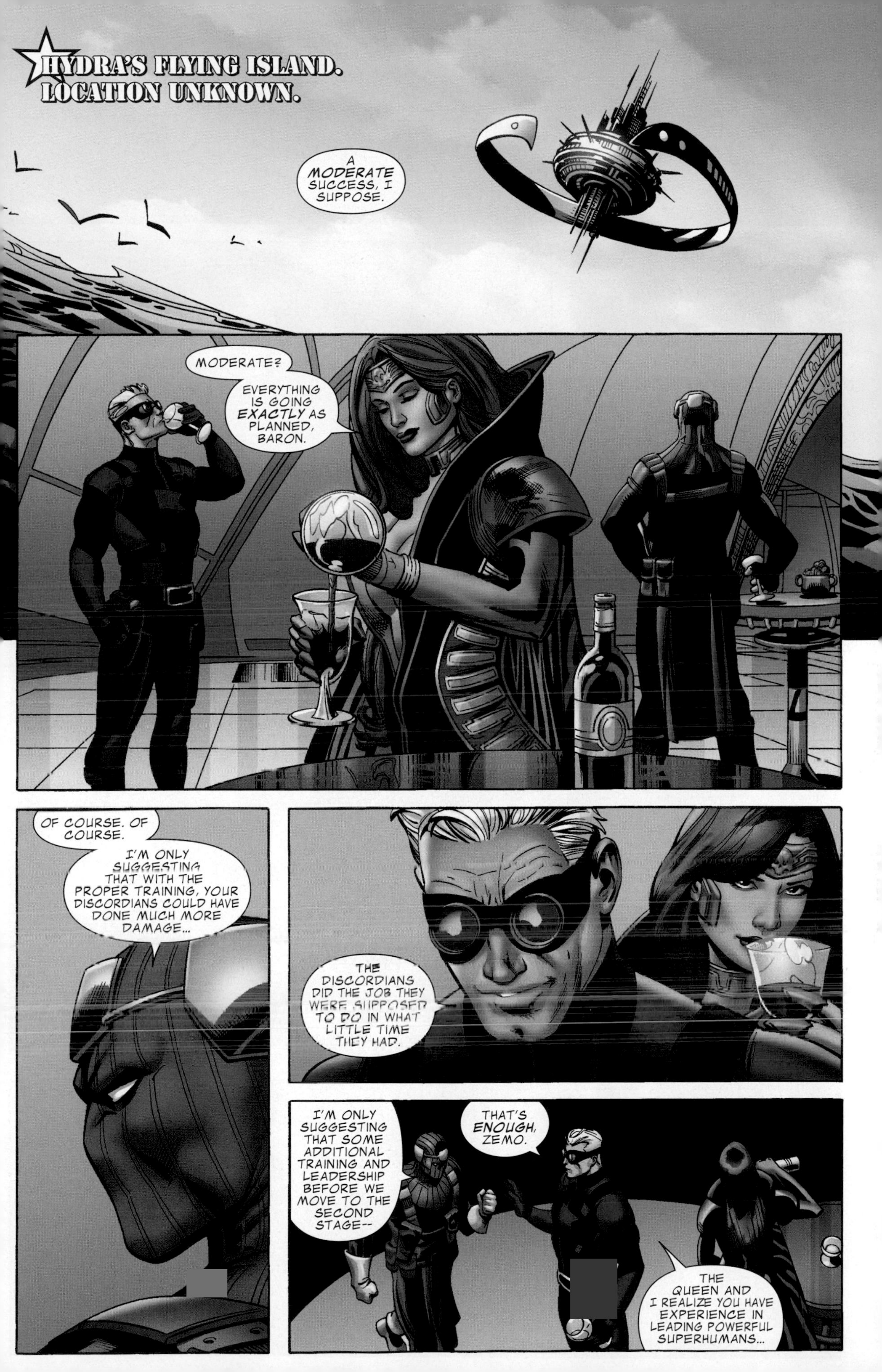
HYDRA'S FLYING ISLAND. LOCATION UNKNOWN.
A MODERATE SUCCESS, I SUPPOSE.
MODERATE?
EVERYTHING IS GOING EXACTLY AS PLANNED, BARON.
OF COURSE. OF COURSE.
I'M ONLY SUGGESTING THAT WITH THE PROPER TRAINING, YOUR DISCORDIANS COULD HAVE DONE MUCH MORE DAMAGE...
THE DISCORDIANS DID THE JOB THEY WERE SUPPOSED TO DO IN WHAT LITTLE TIME THEY HAD.
I'M ONLY SUGGESTING THAT SOME ADDITIONAL TRAINING AND LEADERSHIP BEFORE WE MOVE TO THE SECOND STAGE--
THAT'S ENOUGH, ZEMO.
THE QUEEN AND I REALIZE YOU HAVE EXPERIENCE IN LEADING POWERFUL SUPERHUMANS...

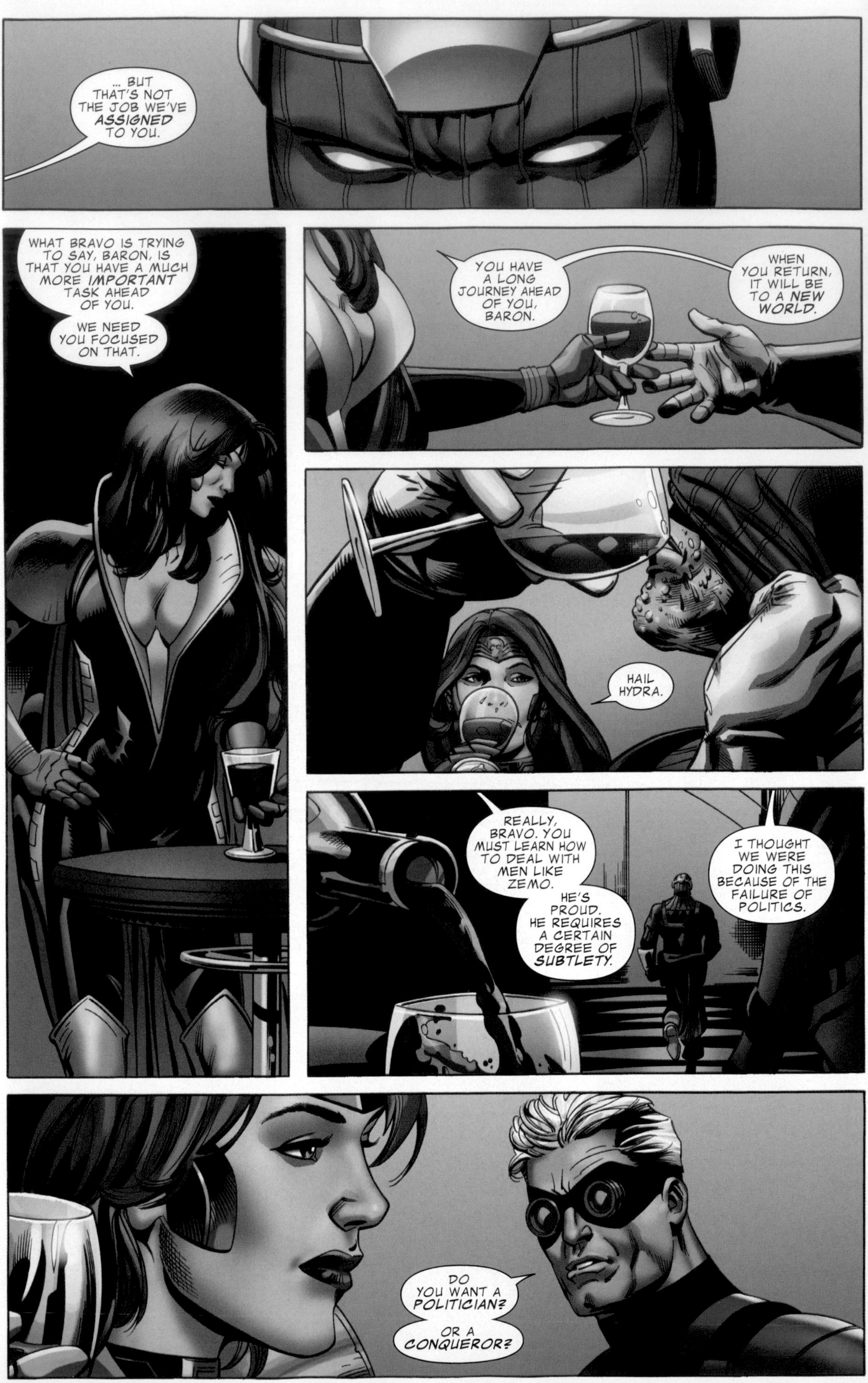
... BUT THAT'S NOT THE JOB WE'VE ASSIGNED TO YOU.
WHAT BRAVO IS TRYING TO SAY, BARON, IS THAT YOU HAVE A MUCH MORE IMPORTANT TASK AHEAD OF YOU.
WE NEED YOU FOCUSED ON THAT.
YOU HAVE A LONG JOURNEY AHEAD OF YOU, BARON.
WHEN YOU RETURN, IT WILL BE TO A NEW WORLD.
HAIL HYDRA.
REALLY, BRAVO. YOU MUST LEARN HOW TO DEAL WITH MEN LIKE ZEMO.
HE'S PROUD. HE REQUIRES A CERTAIN DEGREE OF SUBTLETY.
I THOUGHT WE WERE DOING THIS BECAUSE OF THE FAILURE OF POLITICS.
DO YOU WANT A POLITICIAN?
OR A CONQUEROR?

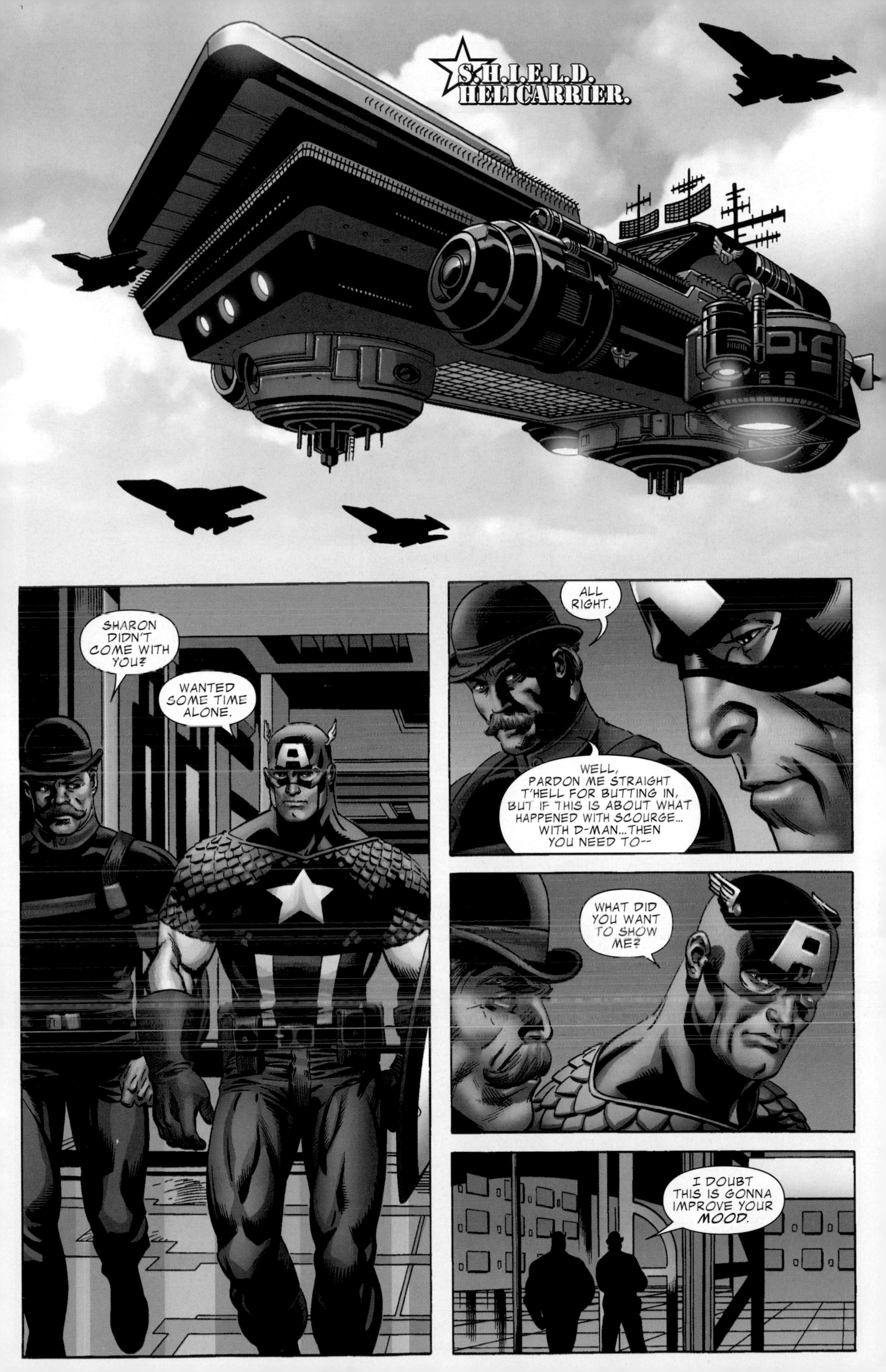
S.H.I.E.L.D. HELICARRIER.
SHARON DIDN'T COME WITH YOU?
WANTED SOME TIME ALONE.
ALL RIGHT.
WELL, PARDON ME STRAIGHT T'HELL FOR BUTTING IN, BUT IF THIS IS ABOUT WHAT HAPPENED WITH SCOURGE... WITH D-MAN...THEN YOU NEED TO--
WHAT DID YOU WANT TO SHOW ME?
I DOUBT THIS IS GONNA IMPROVE YOUR MOOD.

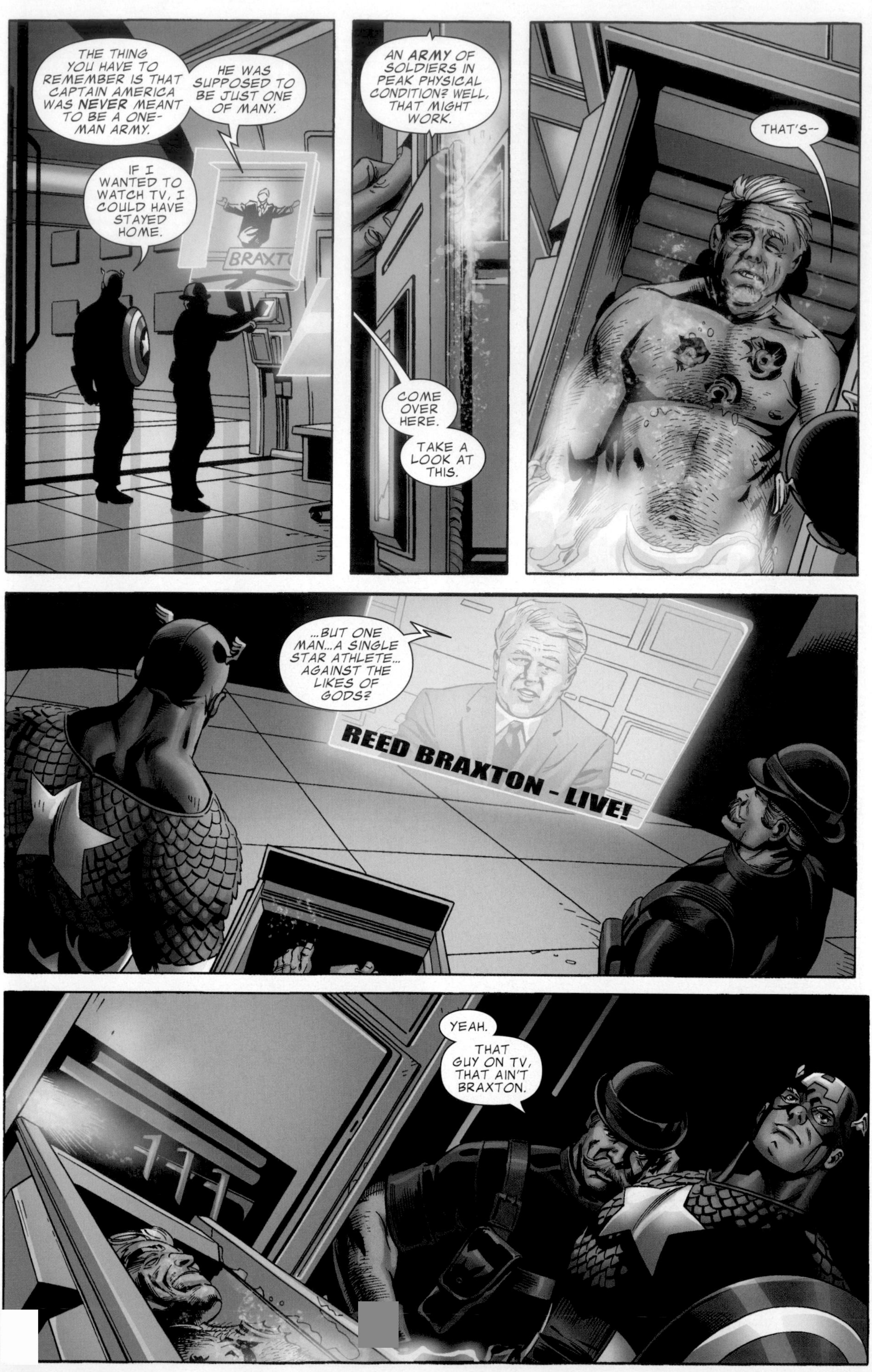

THE THING YOU HAVE TO REMEMBER IS THAT CAPTAIN AMERICA WAS NEVER MEANT TO BE A ONE-MAN ARMY.
HE WAS SUPPOSED TO BE JUST ONE OF MANY.
BRAXTO
IF I WANTED TO WATCH TV, I COULD HAVE STAYED HOME.
AN ARMY OF SOLDIERS IN PEAK PHYSICAL CONDITION? WELL, THAT MIGHT WORK.
COME OVER HERE.
TAKE A LOOK AT THIS.
THAT'S--
...BUT ONE MAN...A SINGLE STAR ATHLETE... AGAINST THE LIKES OF GODS?
REED BRAXTON - LIVE!
YEAH.
THAT GUY ON TV, THAT AIN'T BRAXTON.

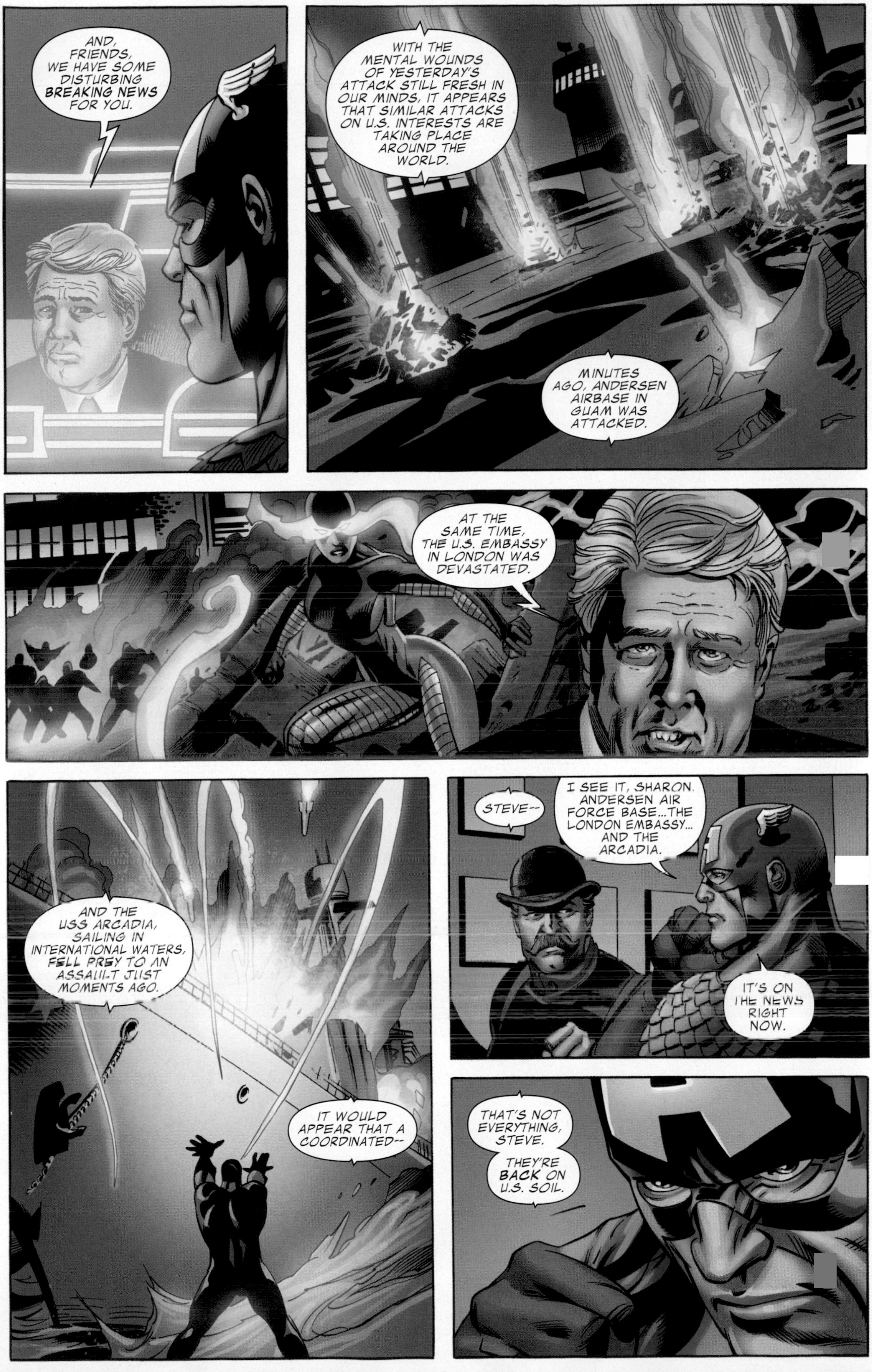
AND, FRIENDS, WE HAVE SOME DISTURBING BREAKING NEWS FOR YOU.
WITH THE MENTAL WOUNDS OF YESTERDAY'S ATTACK STILL FRESH IN OUR MINDS, IT APPEARS THAT SIMILAR ATTACKS ON U.S. INTERESTS ARE TAKING PLACE AROUND THE WORLD.
MINUTES AGO, ANDERSEN AIRBASE IN GUAM WAS ATTACKED.
AT THE SAME TIME, THE U.S. EMBASSY IN LONDON WAS DEVASTATED.
AND THE USS ARCADIA, SAILING IN INTERNATIONAL WATERS, FELL PREY TO AN ASSAULT JUST MOMENTS AGO.
IT WOULD APPEAR THAT A COORDINATED--
STEVE--
I SEE IT, SHARON. ANDERSEN AIR FORCE BASE...THE LONDON EMBASSY... AND THE ARCADIA.
IT'S ON THE NEWS RIGHT NOW.
THAT'S NOT EVERYTHING, STEVE.
THEY'RE BACK ON U.S. SOIL.

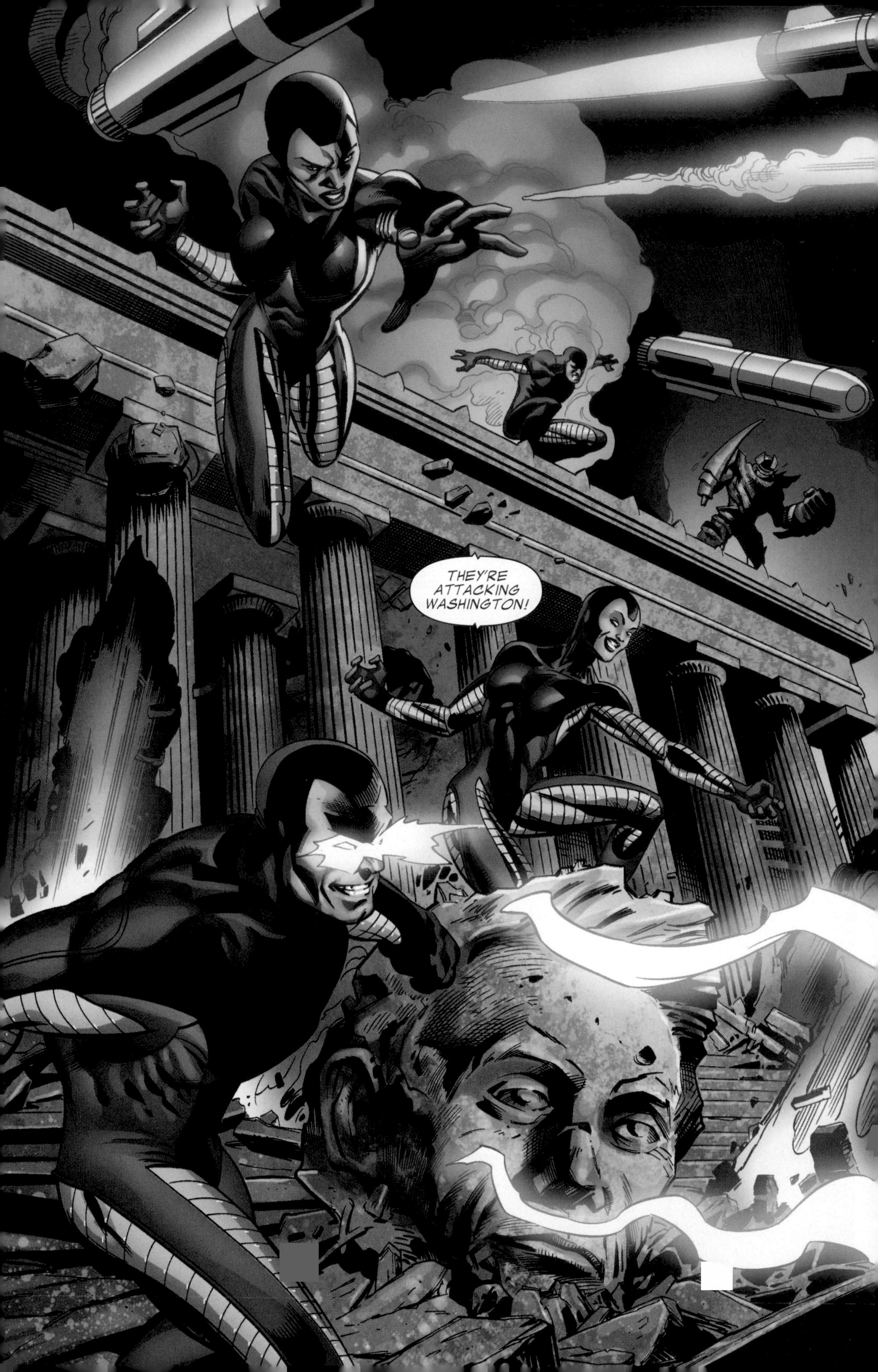
THEY'RE ATTACKING WASHINGTON!

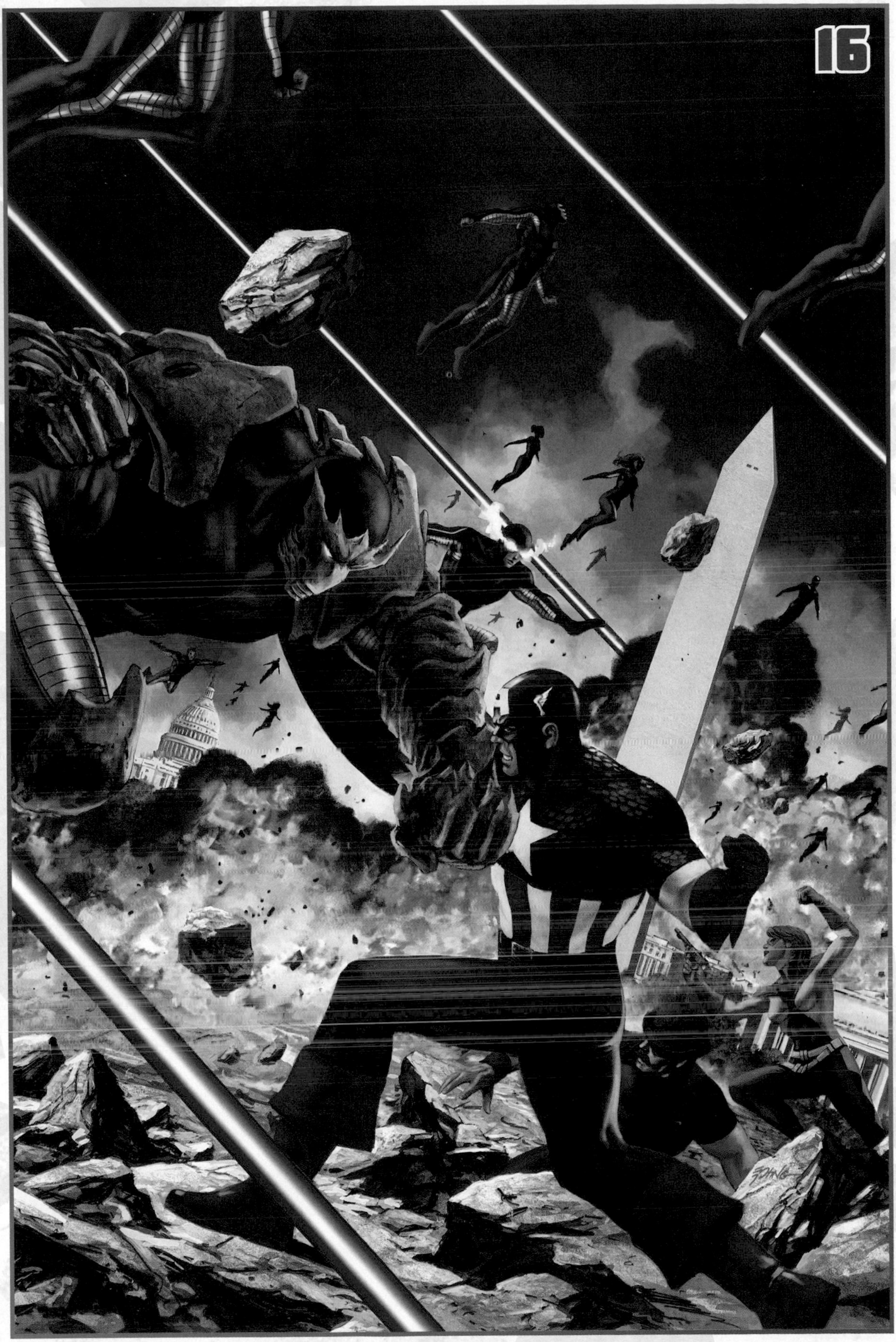
16

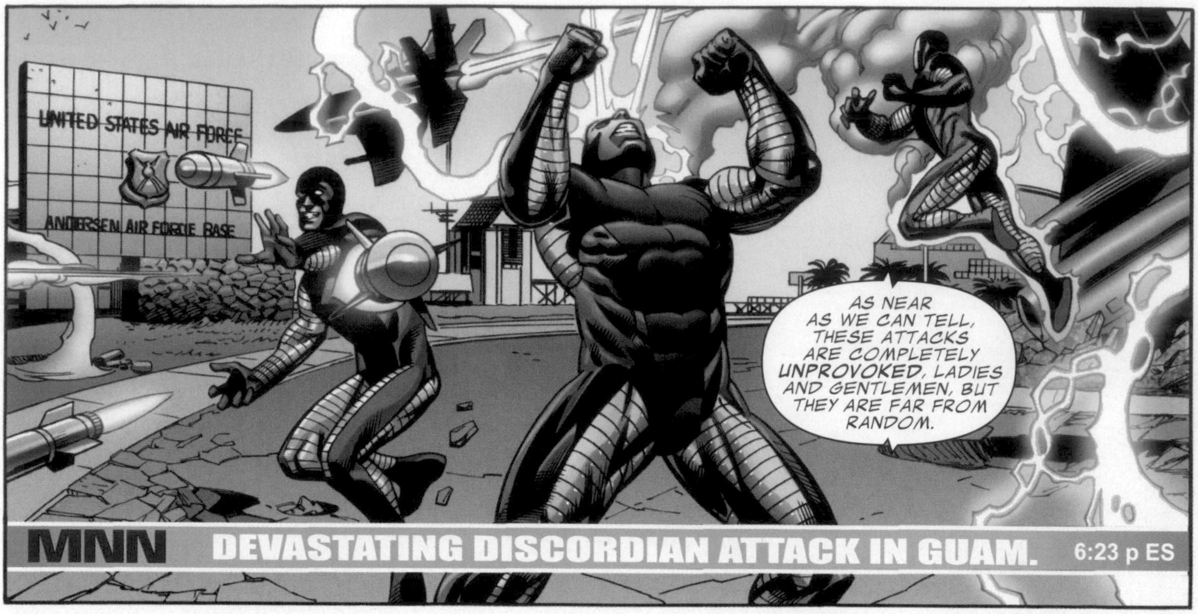
UNITED STATES AIR FORCE
ANDERSEN AIR FORCE BASE
AS NEAR AS WE CAN TELL, THESE ATTACKS ARE COMPLETELY UNPROVOKED, LADIES AND GENTLEMEN, BUT THEY ARE FAR FROM RANDOM.
MNN
DEVASTATING DISCORDIAN ATTACK IN GUAM.
6:23 p ES

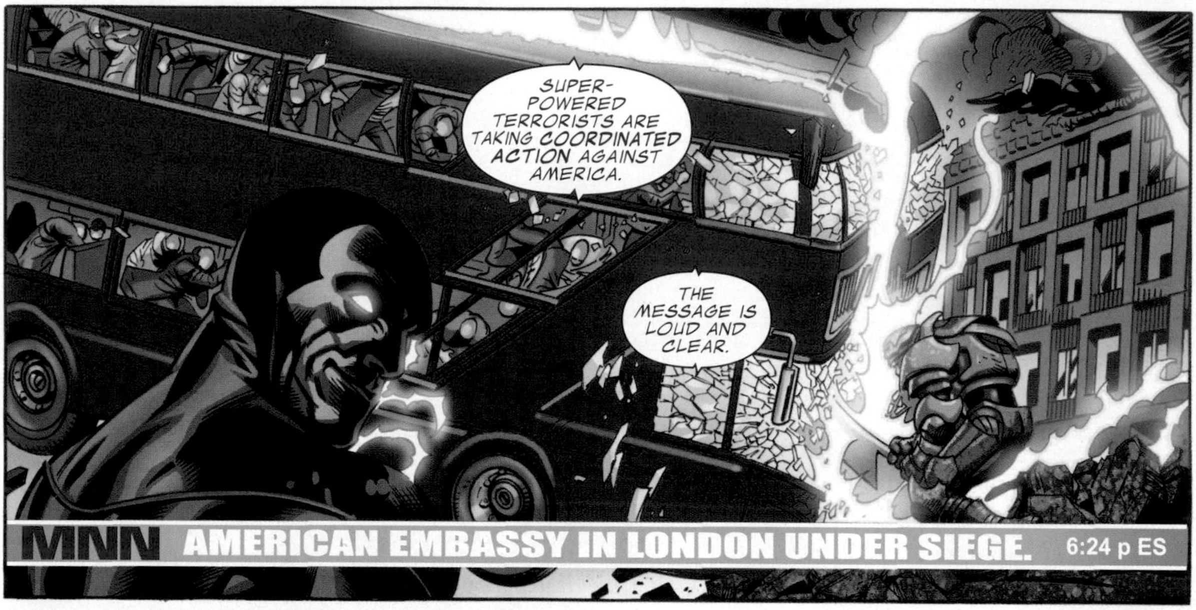
SUPER-POWERED TERRORISTS ARE TAKING COORDINATED ACTION AGAINST AMERICA.
THE MESSAGE IS LOUD AND CLEAR.
MNN
AMERICAN EMBASSY IN LONDON UNDER SIEGE.
6:24 p ES

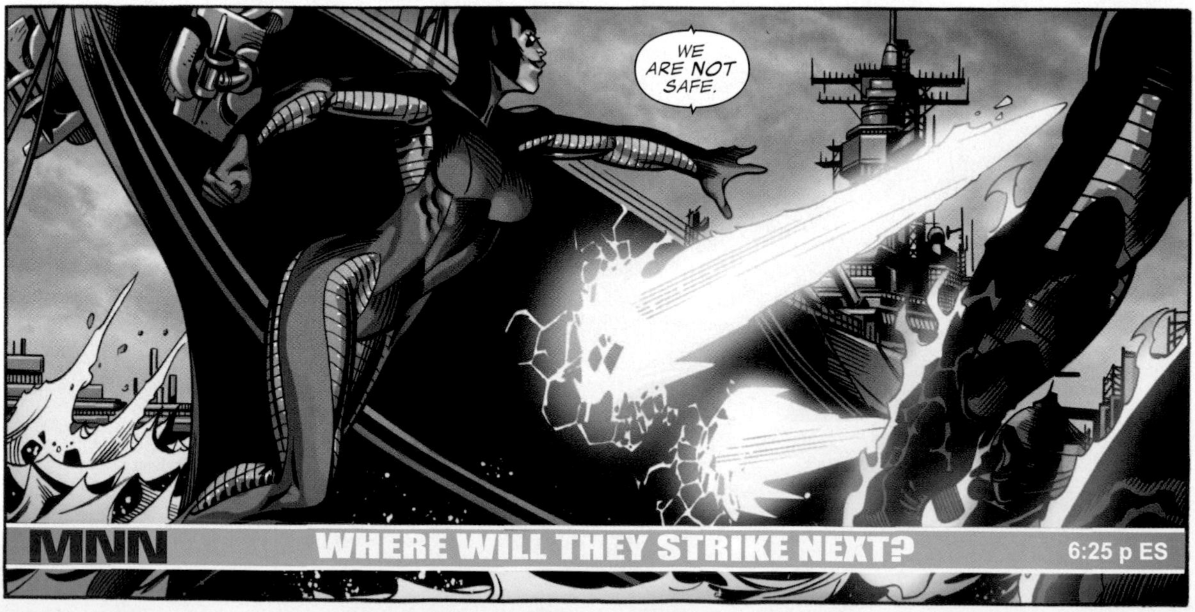
WE ARE NOT SAFE.
MNN
WHERE WILL THEY STRIKE NEXT?
6:25 p ES

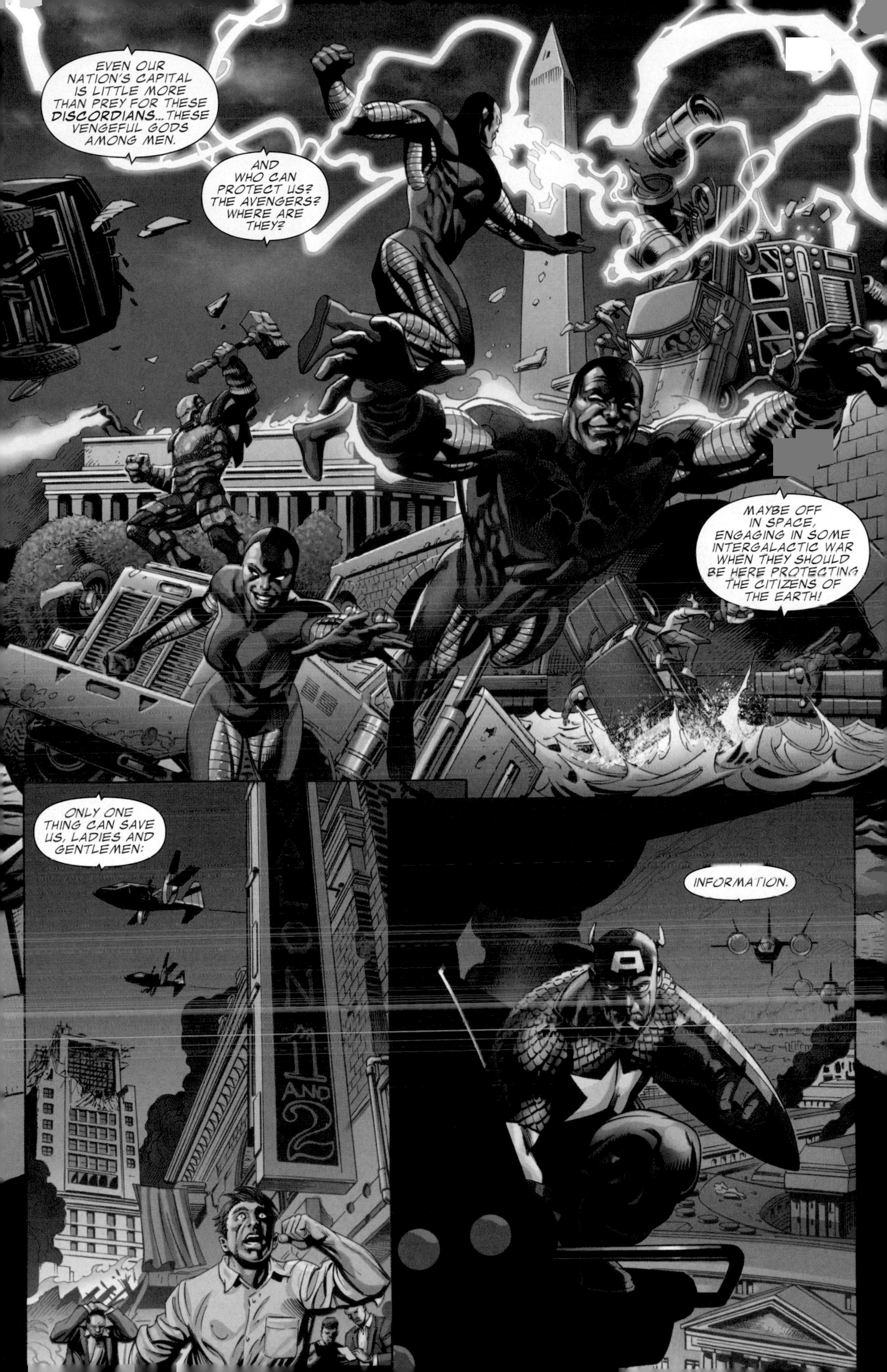
EVEN OUR NATION'S CAPITAL IS LITTLE MORE THAN PREY FOR THESE DISCORDIANS... THESE VENGEFUL GODS AMONG MEN.
AND WHO CAN PROTECT US? THE AVENGERS? WHERE ARE THEY?
MAYBE OFF IN SPACE, ENGAGING IN SOME INTERGALACTIC WAR WHEN THEY SHOULD BE HERE PROTECTING THE CITIZENS OF THE EARTH!
ONLY ONE THING CAN SAVE US, LADIES AND GENTLEMEN:
INFORMATION.

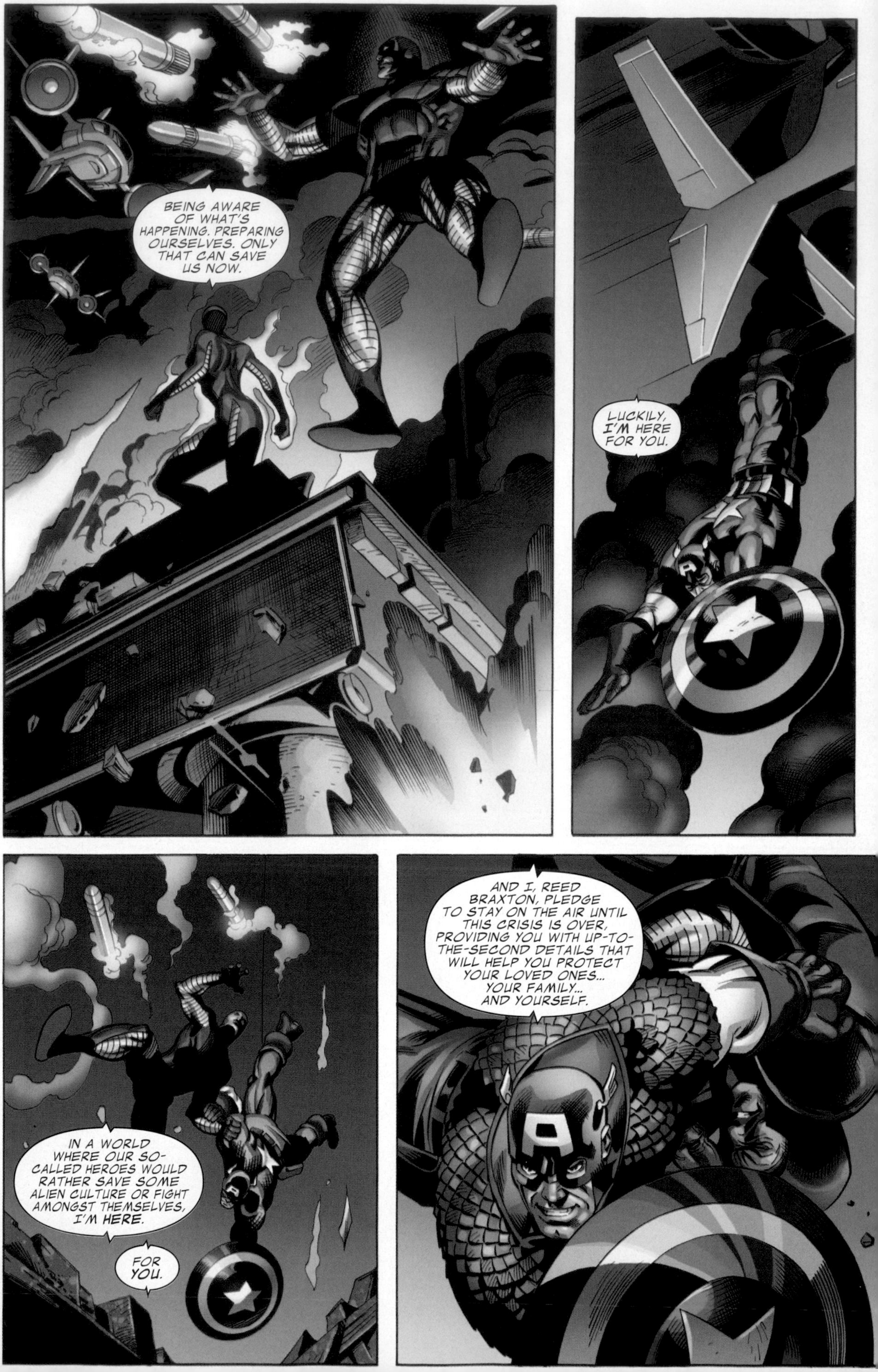
BEING AWARE OF WHAT'S HAPPENING. PREPARING OURSELVES. ONLY THAT CAN SAVE US NOW.
LUCKILY, I'M HERE FOR YOU.
IN A WORLD WHERE OUR SO-CALLED HEROES WOULD RATHER SAVE SOME ALIEN CULTURE OR FIGHT AMONGST THEMSELVES, I'M HERE.
FOR YOU.
AND I, REED BRAXTON, PLEDGE TO STAY ON THE AIR UNTIL THIS CRISIS IS OVER, PROVIDING YOU WITH UP-TO-THE-SECOND DETAILS THAT WILL HELP YOU PROTECT YOUR LOVED ONES... YOUR FAMILY... AND YOURSELF.

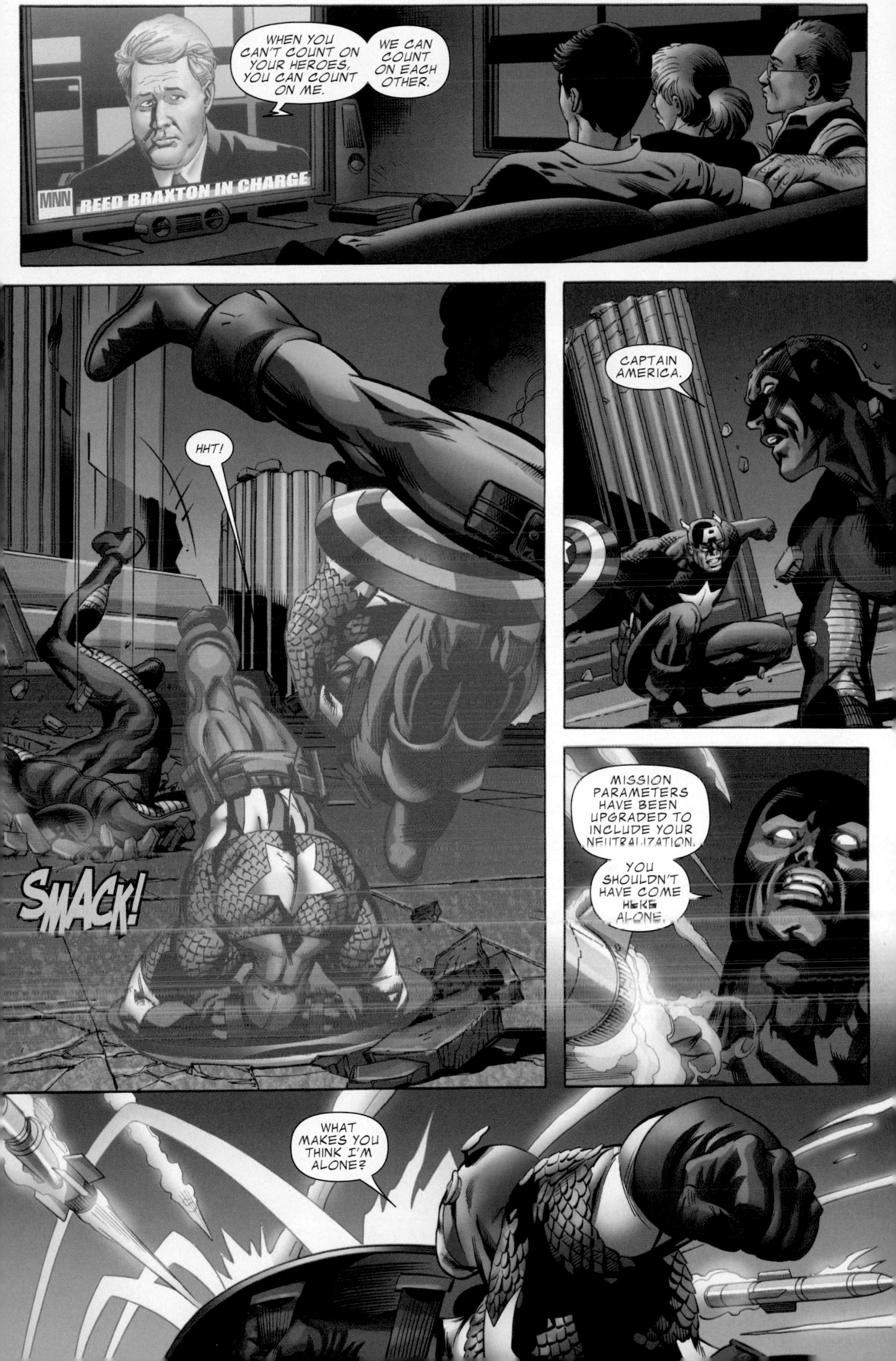
WHEN YOU CAN'T COUNT ON YOUR HEROES, YOU CAN COUNT ON ME.
WE CAN COUNT ON EACH OTHER.
MNN REED BRAXTON IN CHARGE
HHT!
SMACK!
CAPTAIN AMERICA.
MISSION PARAMETERS HAVE BEEN UPGRADED TO INCLUDE YOUR NEUTRALIZATION.
YOU SHOULDN'T HAVE COME HERE ALONE.
WHAT MAKES YOU THINK I'M ALONE?

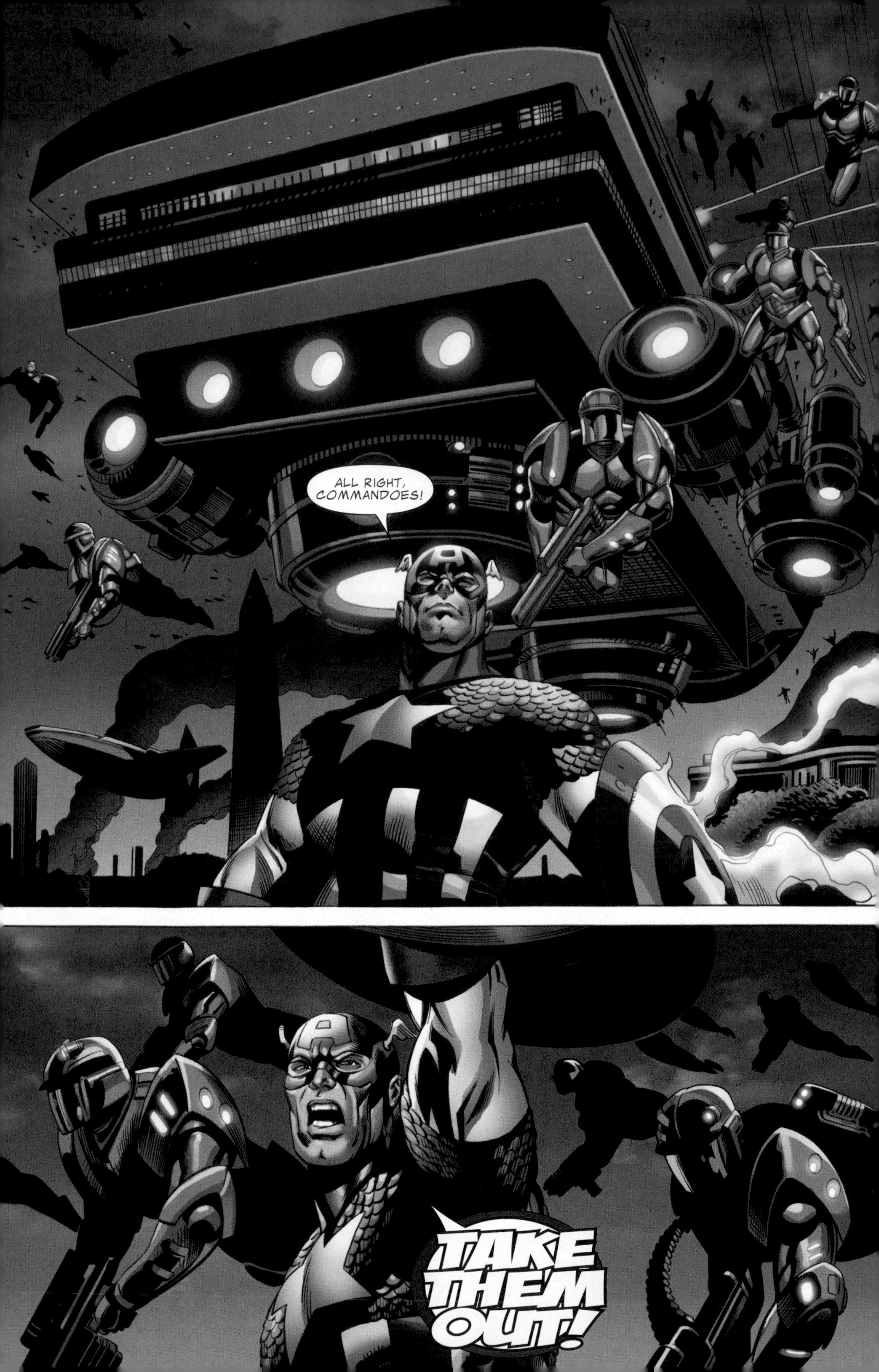
ALL RIGHT, COMMANDOES!
TAKE THEM OUT!

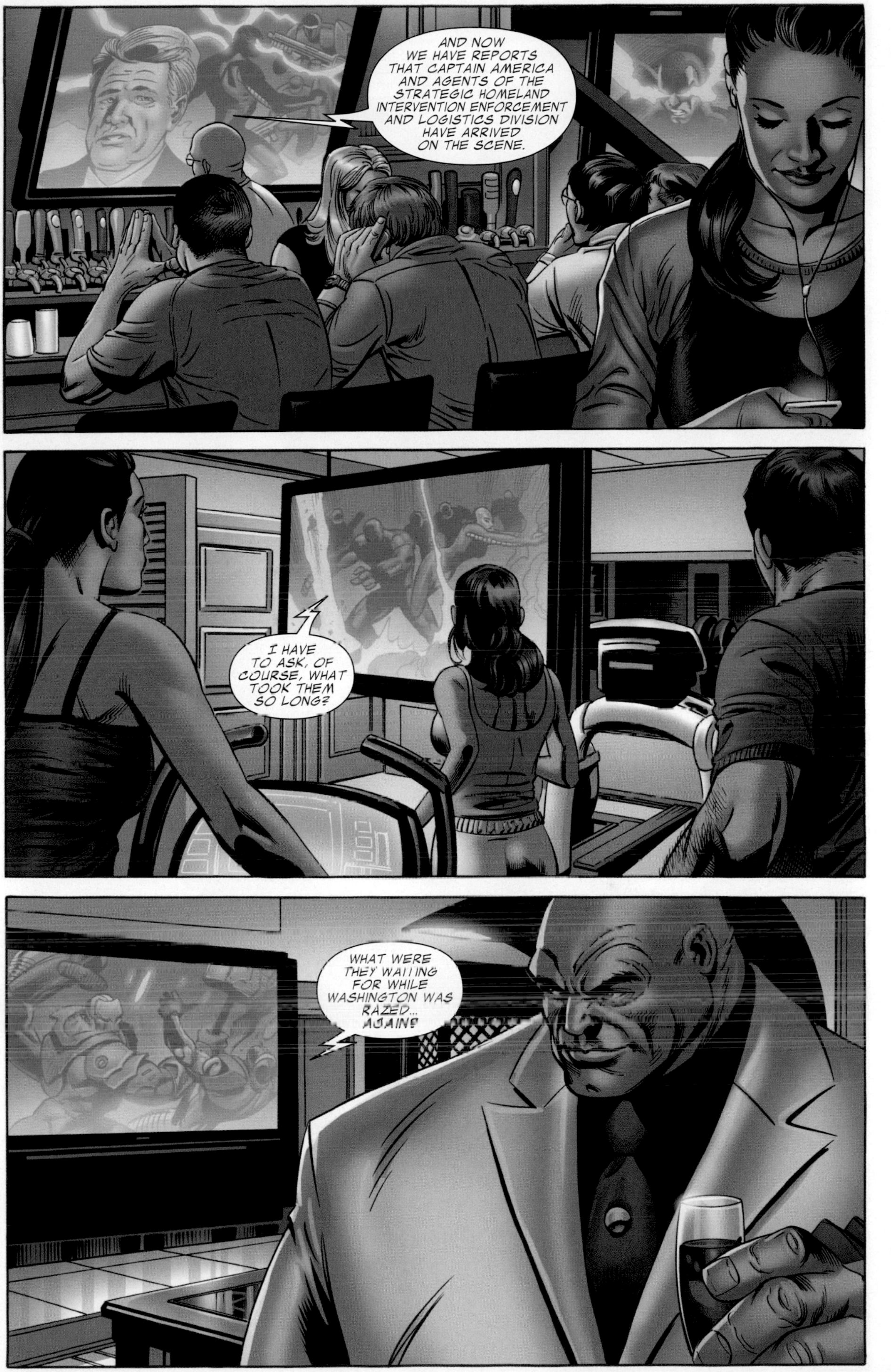
AND NOW WE HAVE REPORTS THAT CAPTAIN AMERICA AND AGENTS OF THE STRATEGIC HOMELAND INTERVENTION ENFORCEMENT AND LOGISTICS DIVISION HAVE ARRIVED ON THE SCENE.
I HAVE TO ASK, OF COURSE, WHAT TOOK THEM SO LONG?
WHAT WERE THEY WAITING FOR WHILE WASHINGTON WAS RAZED... AGAIN?

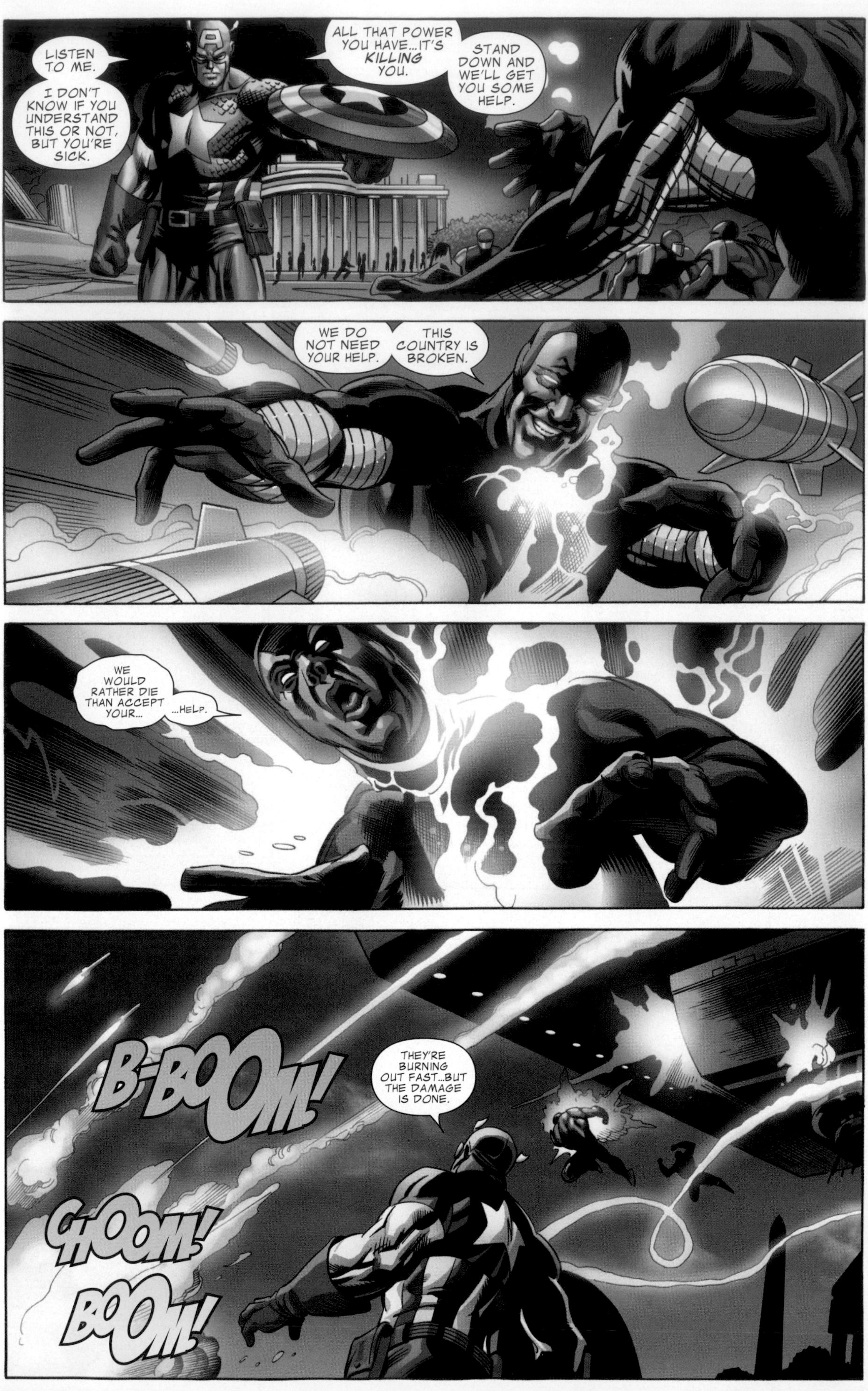

LISTEN TO ME.
I DON'T KNOW IF YOU UNDERSTAND THIS OR NOT, BUT YOU'RE SICK.
ALL THAT POWER YOU HAVE...IT'S KILLING YOU.
STAND DOWN AND WE'LL GET YOU SOME HELP.
WE DO NOT NEED YOUR HELP.
THIS COUNTRY IS BROKEN.
WE WOULD RATHER DIE THAN ACCEPT YOUR...
...HELP.
B-BOOM!
THEY'RE BURNING OUT FAST...BUT THE DAMAGE IS DONE.
CHOOM!
BOOM!

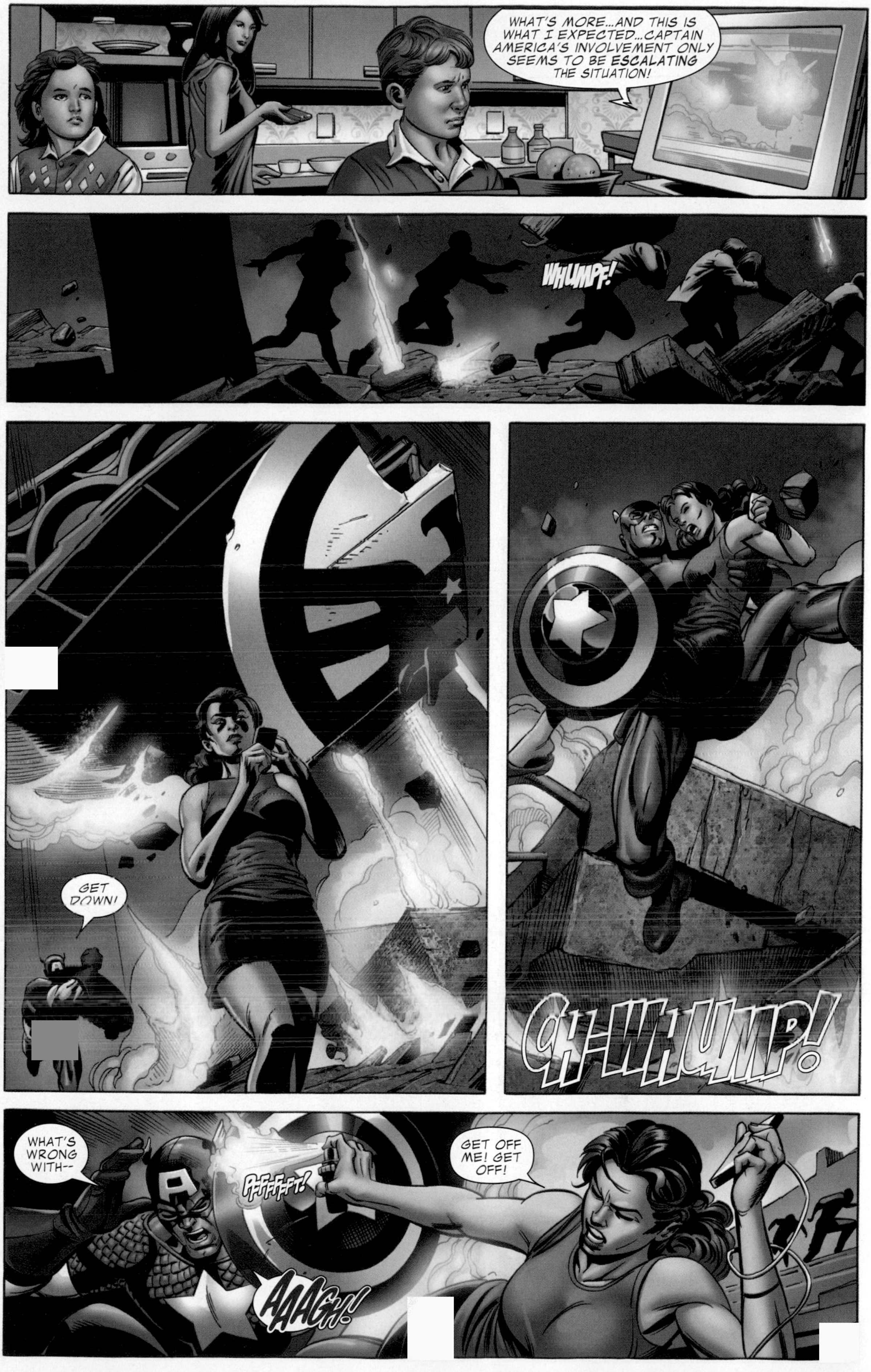
WHAT'S MORE...AND THIS IS WHAT I EXPECTED...CAPTAIN AMERICA'S INVOLVEMENT ONLY SEEMS TO BE ESCALATING THE SITUATION!
WHUMPF!
GET DOWN!
CH-WHUMP!
WHAT'S WRONG WITH--
PFFFFFT!
GET OFF ME! GET OFF!
AAAGH!

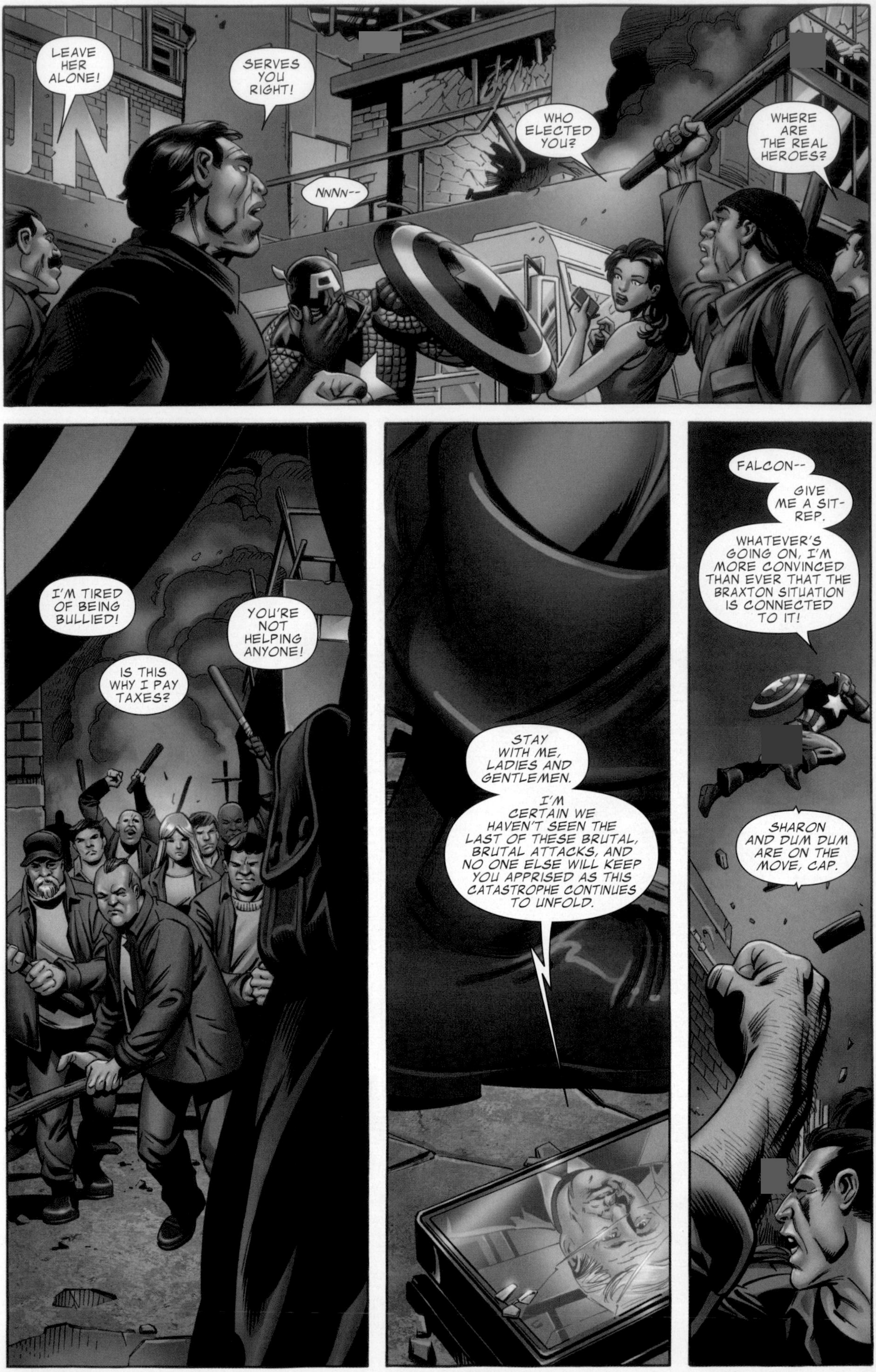
LEAVE HER ALONE!
SERVES YOU RIGHT!
NNNN--
WHO ELECTED YOU?
WHERE ARE THE REAL HEROES?
I'M TIRED OF BEING BULLIED!
IS THIS WHY I PAY TAXES?
YOU'RE NOT HELPING ANYONE!
STAY WITH ME, LADIES AND GENTLEMEN.
I'M CERTAIN WE HAVEN'T SEEN THE LAST OF THESE BRUTAL, BRUTAL ATTACKS, AND NO ONE ELSE WILL KEEP YOU APPRISED AS THIS CATASTROPHE CONTINUES TO UNFOLD.
FALCON--
GIVE ME A SIT-REP.
WHATEVER'S GOING ON, I'M MORE CONVINCED THAN EVER THAT THE BRAXTON SITUATION IS CONNECTED TO IT!
SHARON AND DUM DUM ARE ON THE MOVE, CAP.

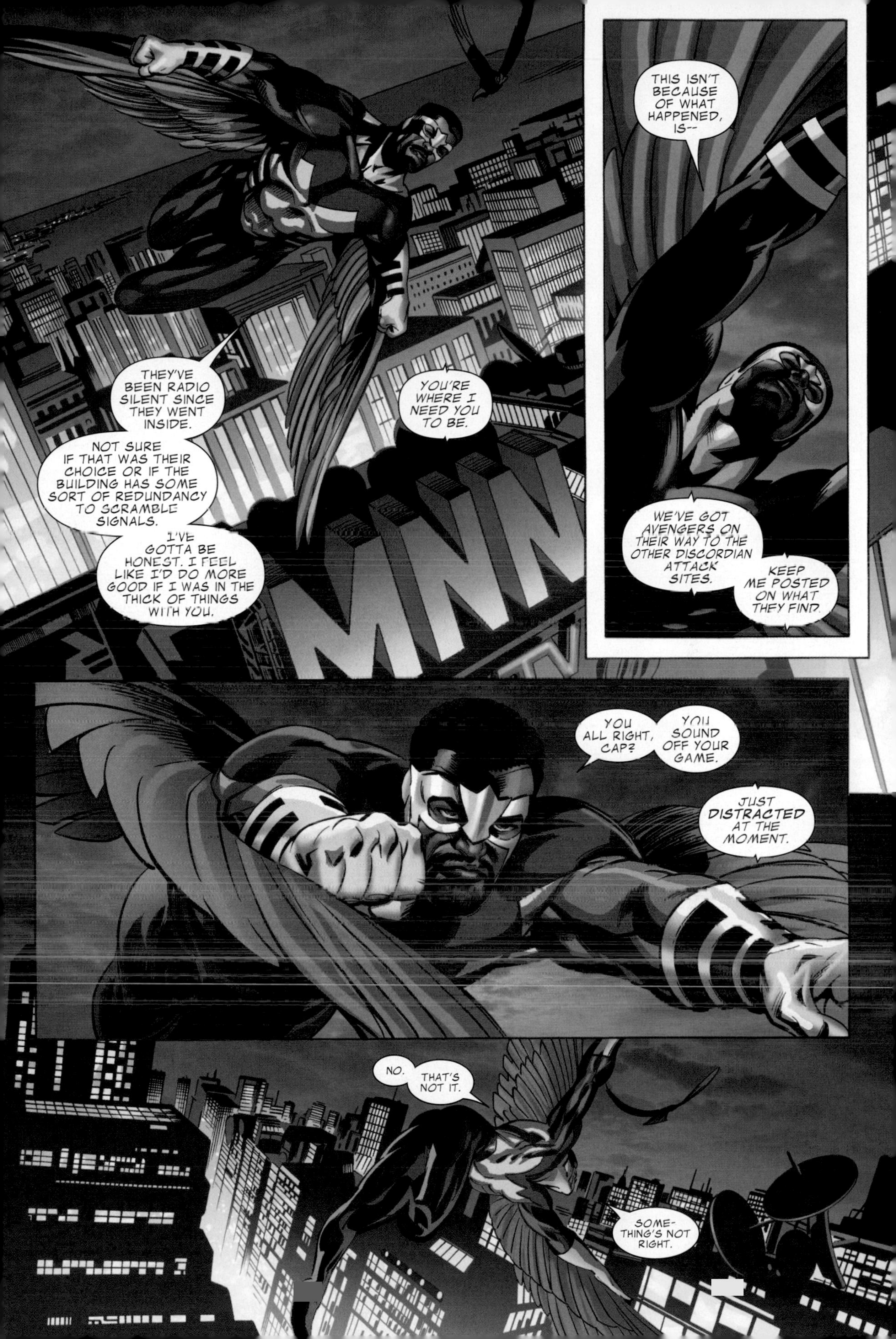
THEY'VE BEEN RADIO SILENT SINCE THEY WENT INSIDE.
NOT SURE IF THAT WAS THEIR CHOICE OR IF THE BUILDING HAS SOME SORT OF REDUNDANCY TO SCRAMBLE SIGNALS.
I'VE GOTTA BE HONEST. I FEEL LIKE I'D DO MORE GOOD IF I WAS IN THE THICK OF THINGS WITH YOU.
YOU'RE WHERE I NEED YOU TO BE.
THIS ISN'T BECAUSE OF WHAT HAPPENED, IS--
WE'VE GOT AVENGERS ON THEIR WAY TO THE OTHER DISCORDIAN ATTACK SITES.
KEEP ME POSTED ON WHAT THEY FIND.
MNN
YOU ALL RIGHT, CAP?
YOU SOUND OFF YOUR GAME.
JUST DISTRACTED AT THE MOMENT.
NO.
THAT'S NOT IT.
SOME-THING'S NOT RIGHT.

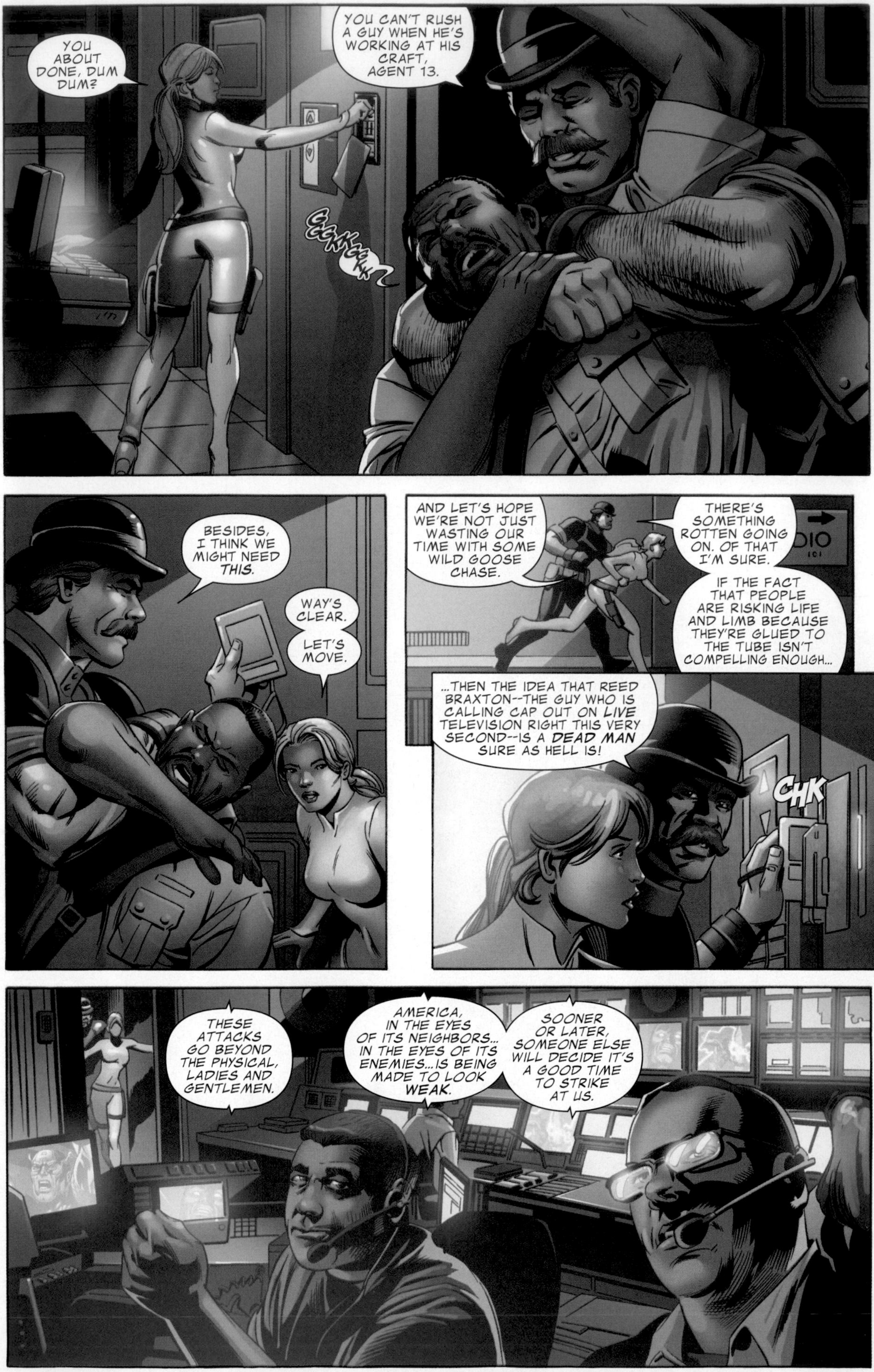
YOU ABOUT DONE, DUM DUM?
YOU CAN'T RUSH A GUY WHEN HE'S WORKING AT HIS CRAFT, AGENT 13.
GGKKGGKK
BESIDES, I THINK WE MIGHT NEED THIS.
WAY'S CLEAR.
LET'S MOVE.
AND LET'S HOPE WE'RE NOT JUST WASTING OUR TIME WITH SOME WILD GOOSE CHASE.
THERE'S SOMETHING ROTTEN GOING ON. OF THAT I'M SURE.
IF THE FACT THAT PEOPLE ARE RISKING LIFE AND LIMB BECAUSE THEY'RE GLUED TO THE TUBE ISN'T COMPELLING ENOUGH...
...THEN THE IDEA THAT REED BRAXTON--THE GUY WHO IS CALLING CAP OUT ON LIVE TELEVISION RIGHT THIS VERY SECOND--IS A DEAD MAN SURE AS HELL IS!
CHK
THESE ATTACKS GO BEYOND THE PHYSICAL, LADIES AND GENTLEMEN.
AMERICA, IN THE EYES OF ITS NEIGHBORS... IN THE EYES OF ITS ENEMIES... IS BEING MADE TO LOOK WEAK.
SOONER OR LATER, SOMEONE ELSE WILL DECIDE IT'S A GOOD TIME TO STRIKE AT US.

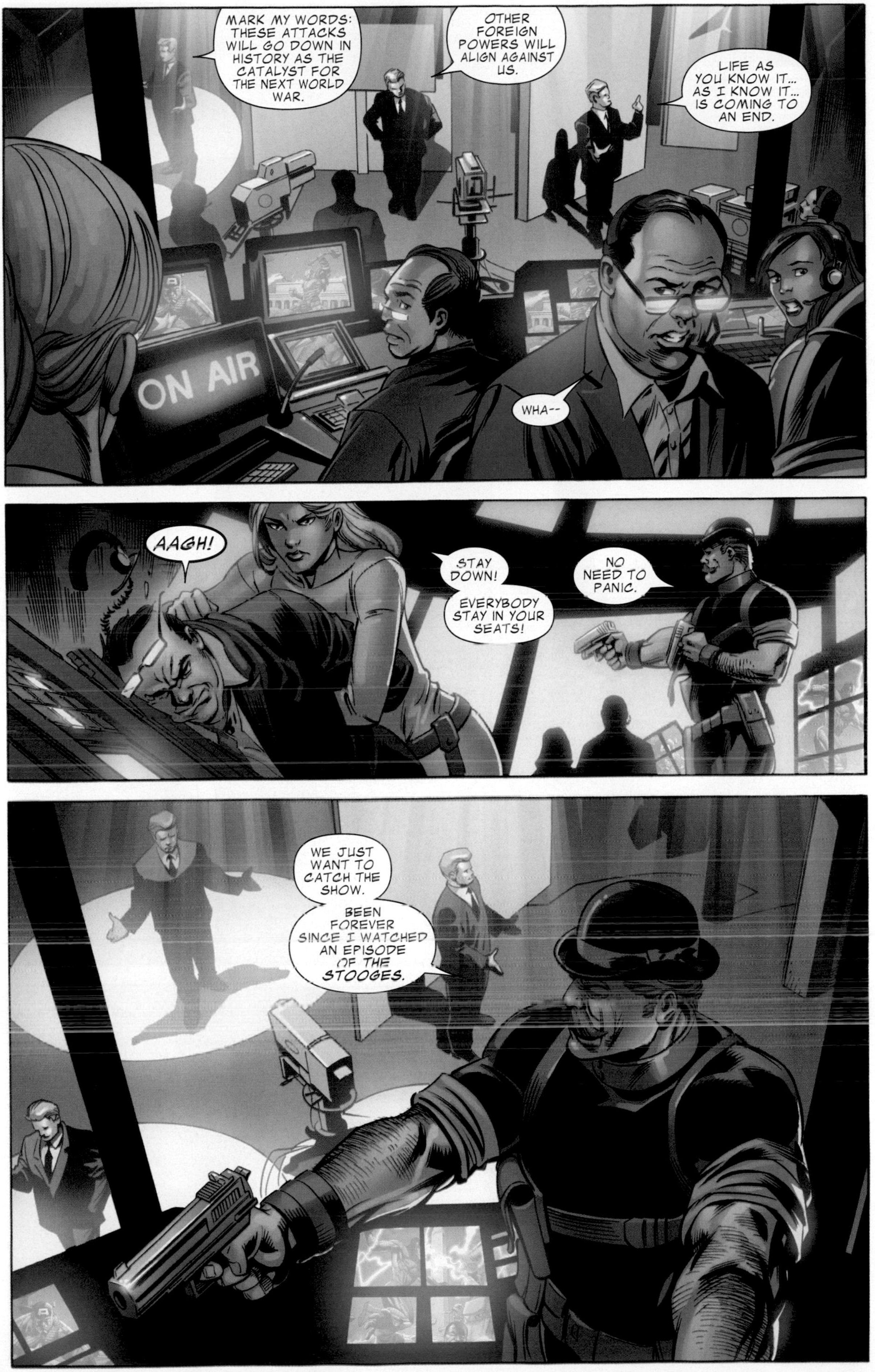
MARK MY WORDS: THESE ATTACKS WILL GO DOWN IN HISTORY AS THE CATALYST FOR THE NEXT WORLD WAR.
OTHER FOREIGN POWERS WILL ALIGN AGAINST US.
LIFE AS YOU KNOW IT... AS I KNOW IT... IS COMING TO AN END.
ON AIR
WHA--
AAGH!
STAY DOWN!
EVERYBODY STAY IN YOUR SEATS!
NO NEED TO PANIC.
WE JUST WANT TO CATCH THE SHOW.
BEEN FOREVER SINCE I WATCHED AN EPISODE OF THE STOOGES.

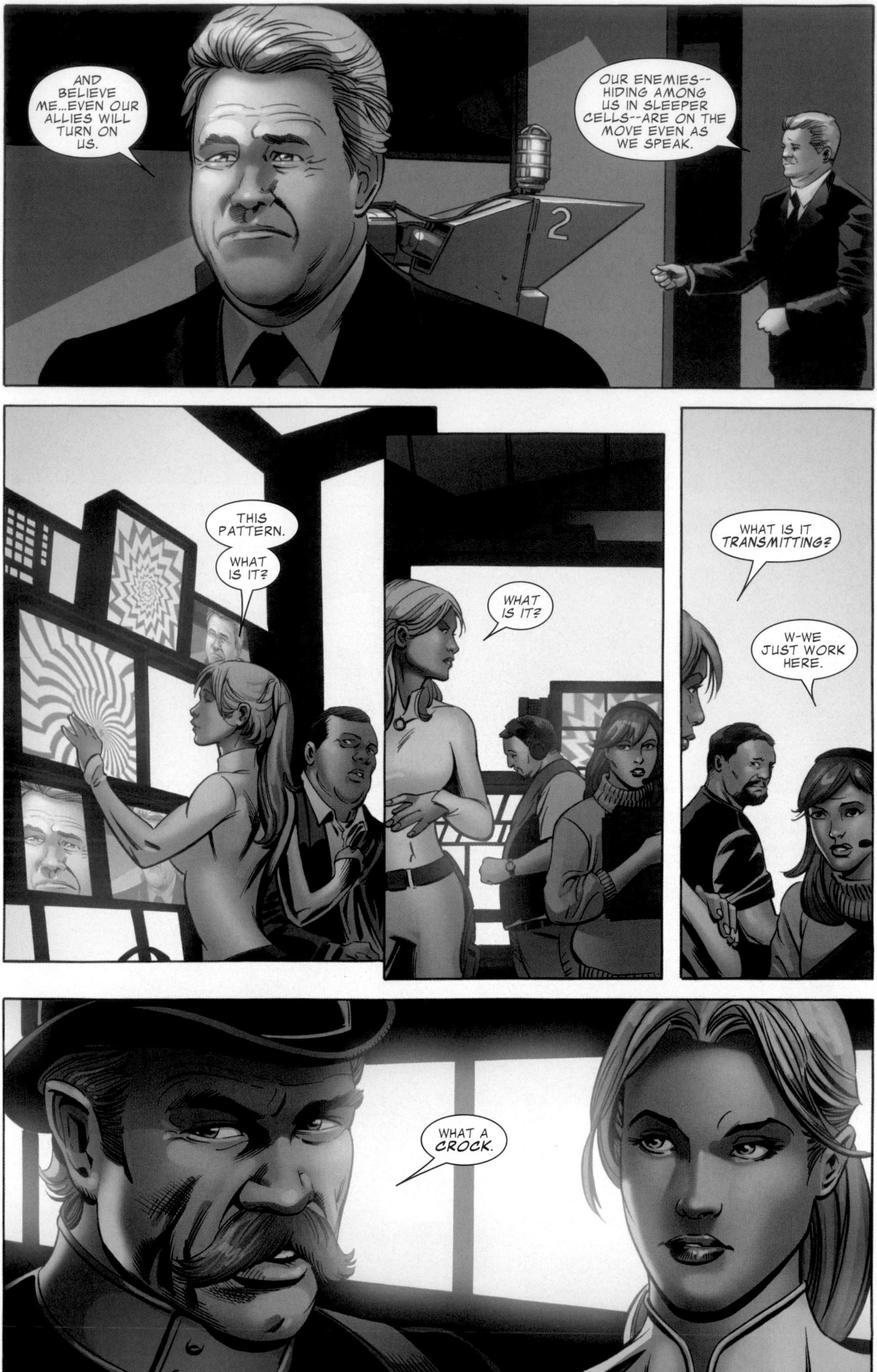
AND BELIEVE ME...EVEN OUR ALLIES WILL TURN ON US.
OUR ENEMIES--HIDING AMONG US IN SLEEPER CELLS--ARE ON THE MOVE EVEN AS WE SPEAK.
THIS PATTERN.
WHAT IS IT?
WHAT IS IT?
WHAT IS IT TRANSMITTING?
W-WE JUST WORK HERE.
WHAT A CROCK.

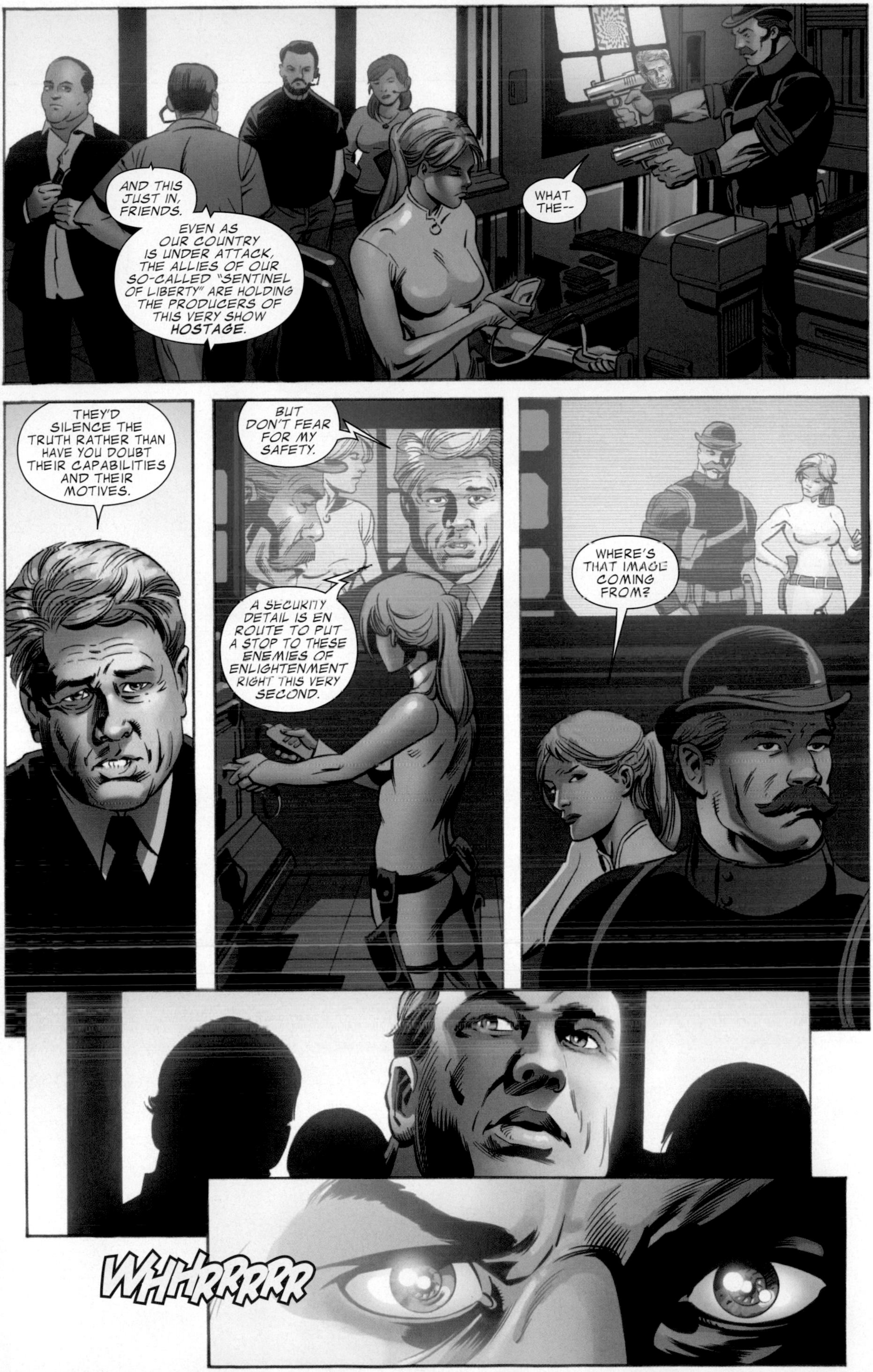
AND THIS JUST IN, FRIENDS.
EVEN AS OUR COUNTRY IS UNDER ATTACK, THE ALLIES OF OUR SO-CALLED "SENTINEL OF LIBERTY" ARE HOLDING THE PRODUCERS OF THIS VERY SHOW HOSTAGE.
WHAT THE--
THEY'D SILENCE THE TRUTH RATHER THAN HAVE YOU DOUBT THEIR CAPABILITIES AND THEIR MOTIVES.
BUT DON'T FEAR FOR MY SAFETY.
A SECURITY DETAIL IS EN ROUTE TO PUT A STOP TO THESE ENEMIES OF ENLIGHTENMENT RIGHT THIS VERY SECOND.
WHERE'S THAT IMAGE COMING FROM?
WHHRRRRR

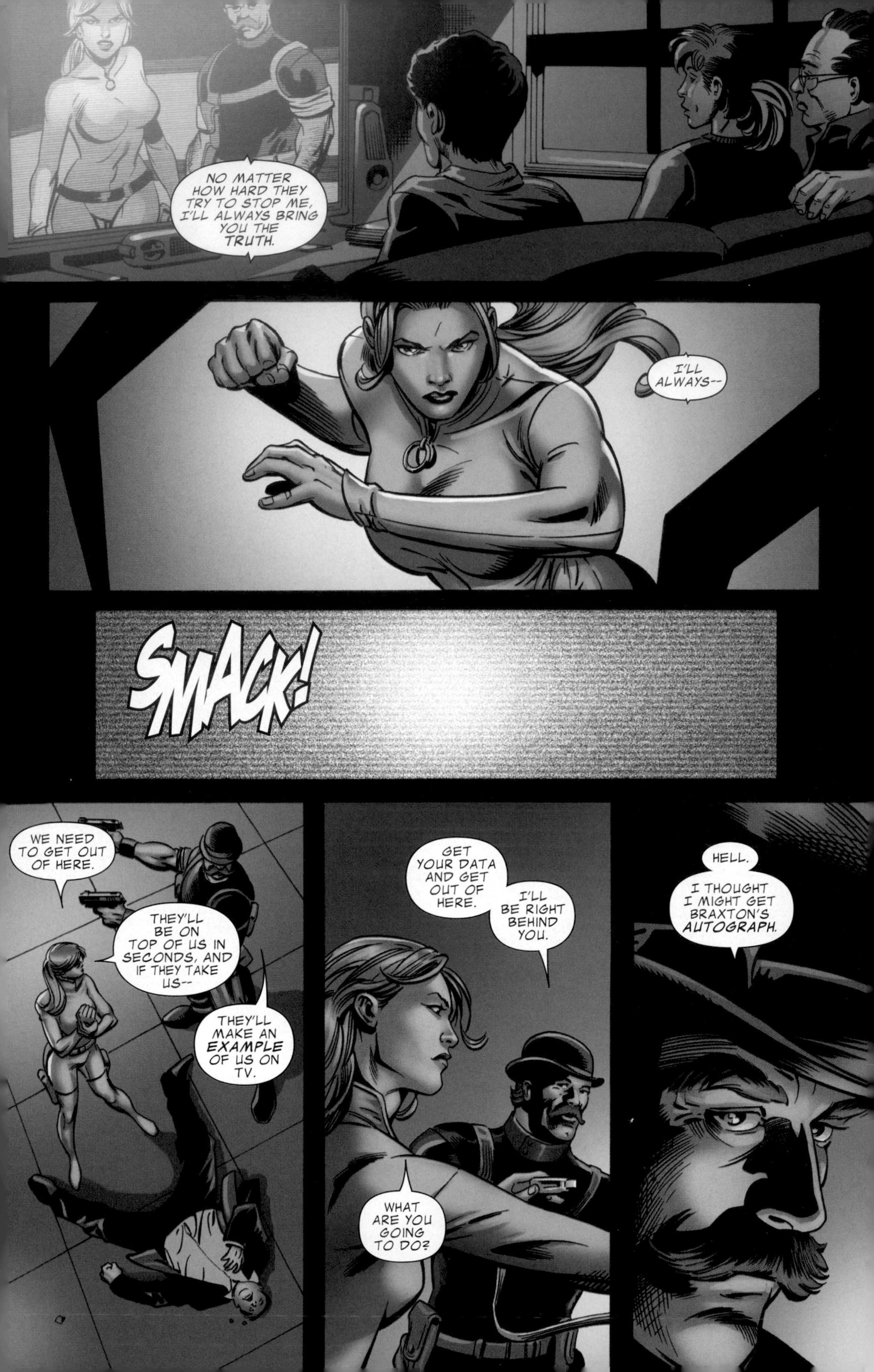
NO MATTER HOW HARD THEY TRY TO STOP ME, I'LL ALWAYS BRING YOU THE TRUTH.
I'LL ALWAYS--
SMACK!
WE NEED TO GET OUT OF HERE.
THEY'LL BE ON TOP OF US IN SECONDS, AND IF THEY TAKE US--
THEY'LL MAKE AN EXAMPLE OF US ON TV.
GET YOUR DATA AND GET OUT OF HERE.
I'LL BE RIGHT BEHIND YOU.
WHAT ARE YOU GOING TO DO?
HELL.
I THOUGHT I MIGHT GET BRAXTON'S AUTOGRAPH.

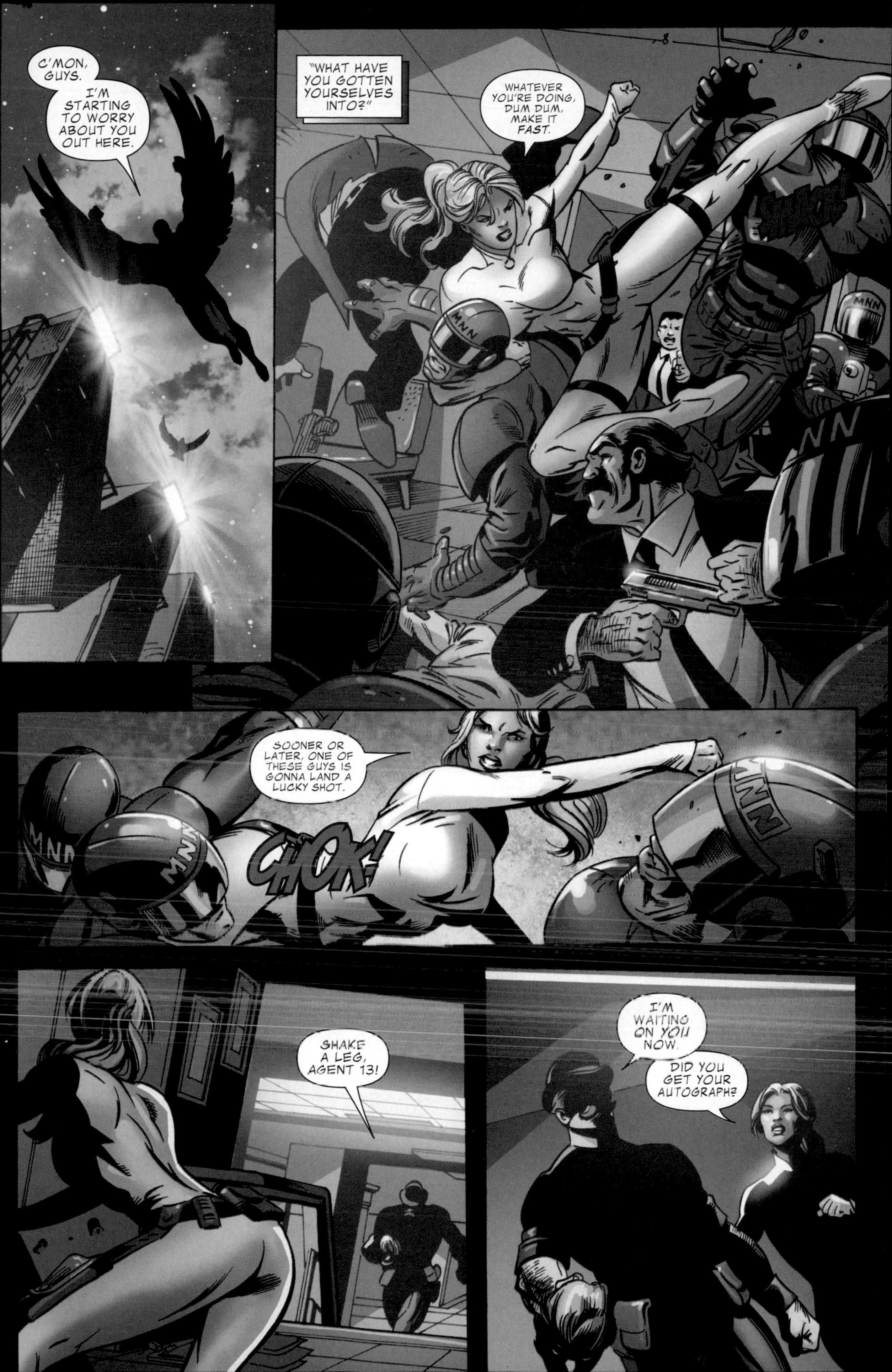

C'MON, GUYS.
I'M STARTING TO WORRY ABOUT YOU OUT HERE.
"WHAT HAVE YOU GOTTEN YOURSELVES INTO?"
WHATEVER YOU'RE DOING, DUM DUM, MAKE IT FAST.
SOONER OR LATER, ONE OF THESE GUYS IS GONNA LAND A LUCKY SHOT.
CHOK!
SHAKE A LEG, AGENT 13!
I'M WAITING ON YOU NOW.
DID YOU GET YOUR AUTOGRAPH?

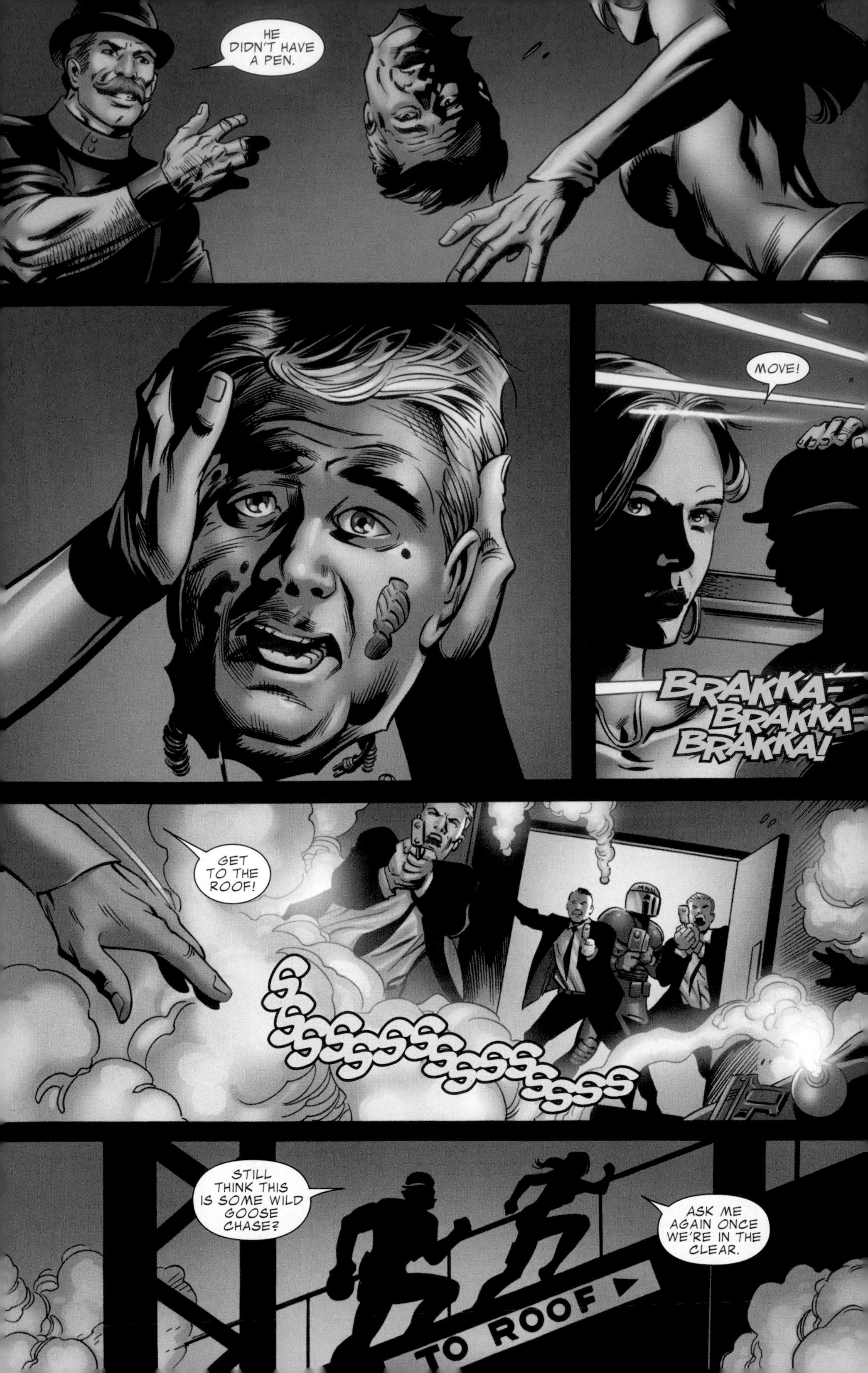
HE DIDN'T HAVE A PEN.
MOVE!
BRAKKA-BRAKKA-BRAKKA!
GET TO THE ROOF!
SSSSSSSSSSSSSSSS
STILL THINK THIS IS SOME WILD GOOSE CHASE?
ASK ME AGAIN ONCE WE'RE IN THE CLEAR.
TO ROOF

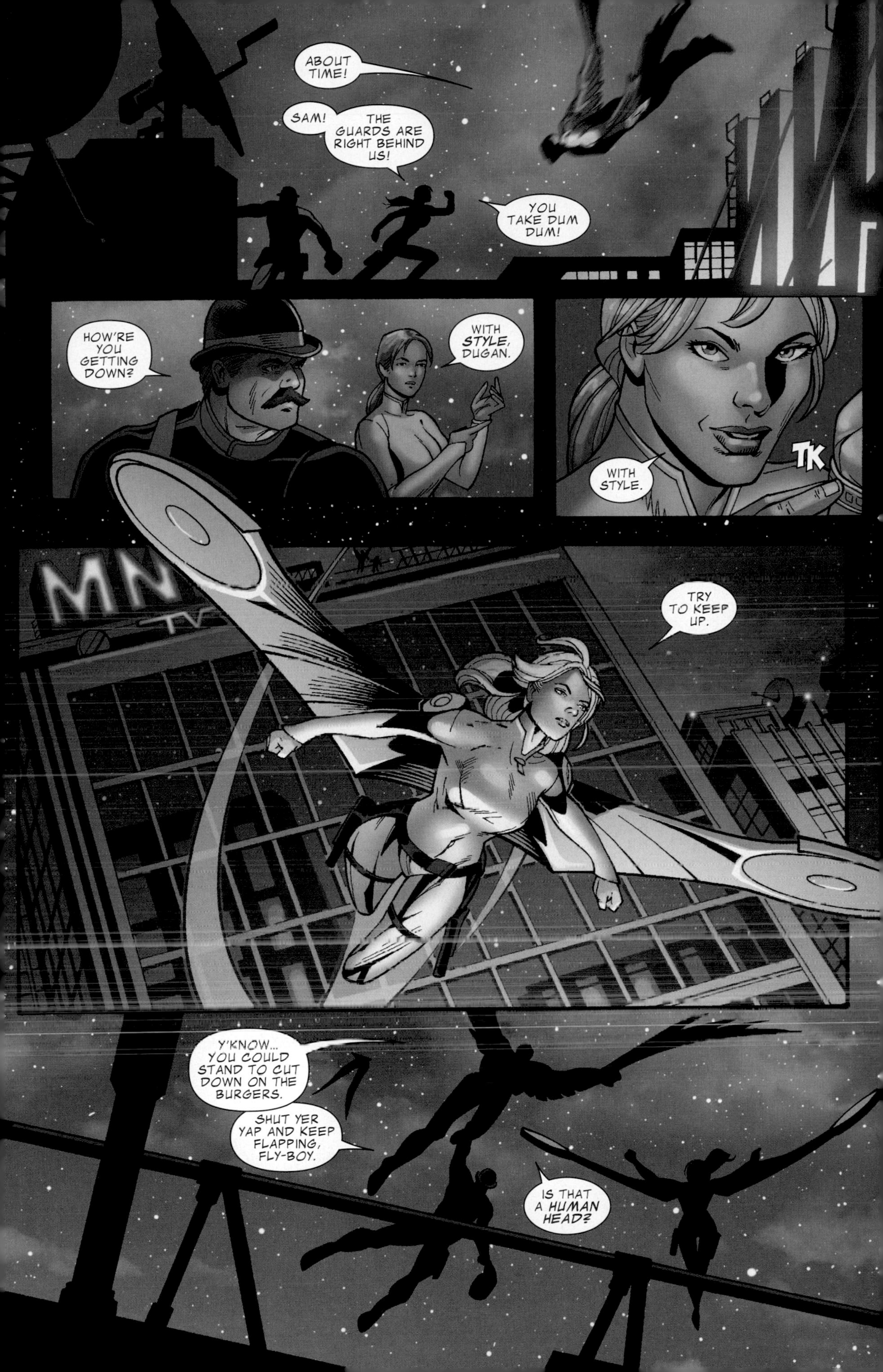
ABOUT TIME!
SAM!
THE GUARDS ARE RIGHT BEHIND US!
YOU TAKE DUM DUM!
HOW'RE YOU GETTING DOWN?
WITH STYLE, DUGAN.
WITH STYLE.
TK
MN
TV
TRY TO KEEP UP.
Y'KNOW... YOU COULD STAND TO CUT DOWN ON THE BURGERS.
SHUT YER YAP AND KEEP FLAPPING, FLY-BOY.
IS THAT A HUMAN HEAD?

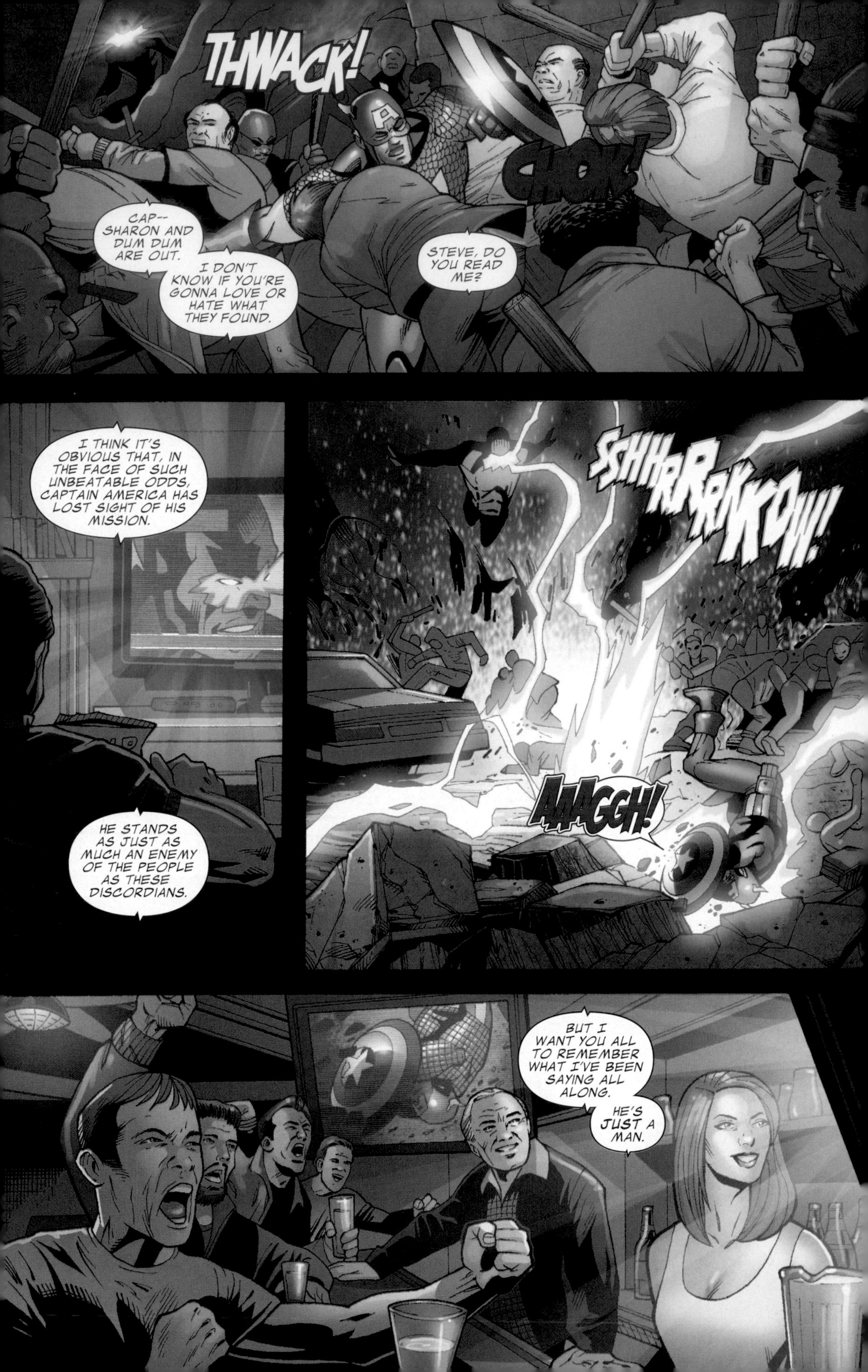
THWACK!
CHOK!
CAP-- SHARON AND DUM DUM ARE OUT.
I DON'T KNOW IF YOU'RE GONNA LOVE OR HATE WHAT THEY FOUND.
STEVE, DO YOU READ ME?
I THINK IT'S OBVIOUS THAT, IN THE FACE OF SUCH UNBEATABLE ODDS, CAPTAIN AMERICA HAS LOST SIGHT OF HIS MISSION.
HE STANDS AS JUST AS MUCH AN ENEMY OF THE PEOPLE AS THESE DISCORDIANS.
SCHHRRRKKOW!!
AAAGGH!
BUT I WANT YOU ALL TO REMEMBER WHAT I'VE BEEN SAYING ALL ALONG.
HE'S JUST A MAN.

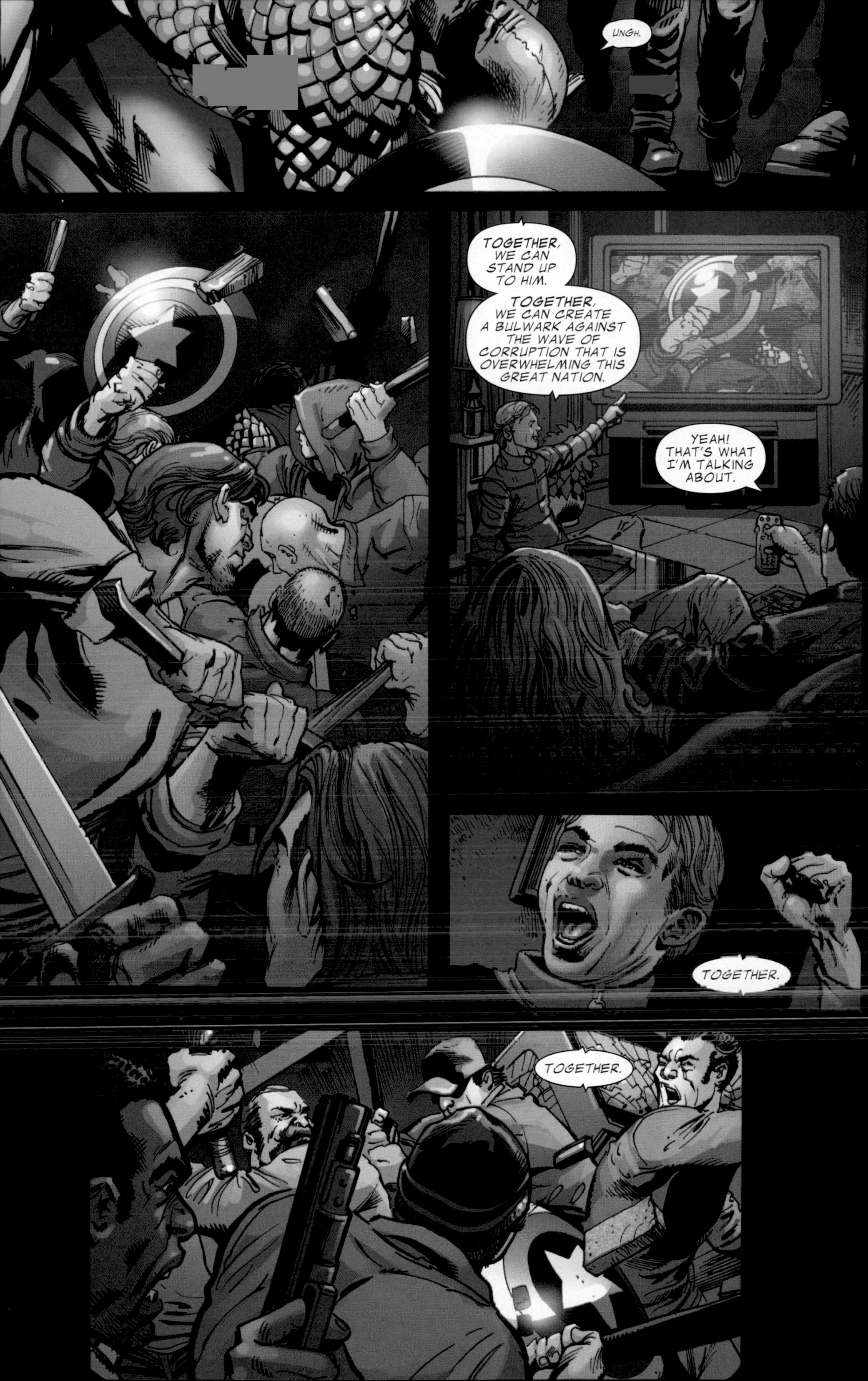
UNGH.
TOGETHER, WE CAN STAND UP TO HIM.
TOGETHER, WE CAN CREATE A BULWARK AGAINST THE WAVE OF CORRUPTION THAT IS OVERWHELMING THIS GREAT NATION.
YEAH! THAT'S WHAT I'M TALKING ABOUT.
TOGETHER.
TOGETHER.

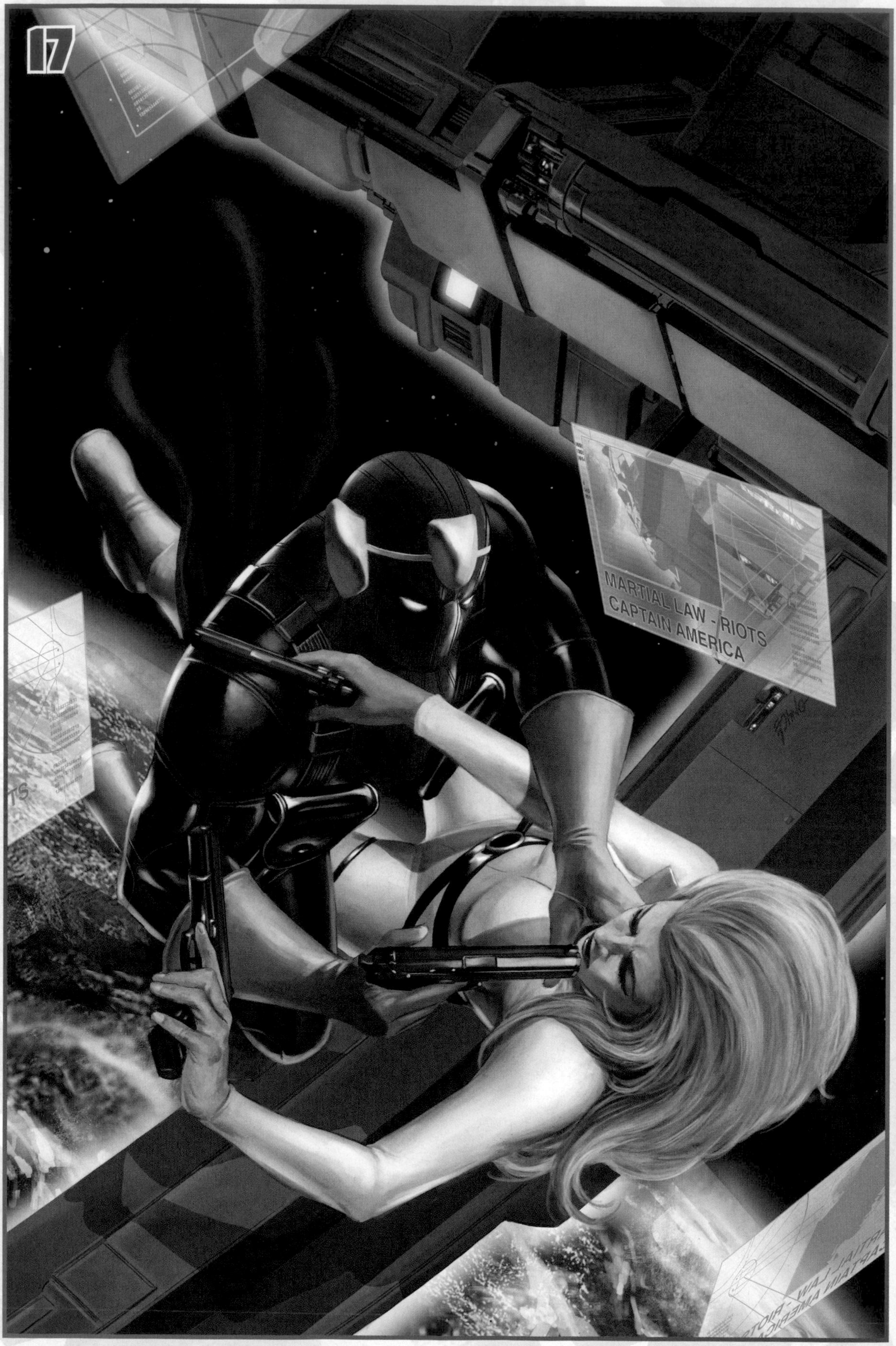
17
MARTIAL LAW - RIOTS
CAPTAIN AMERICA

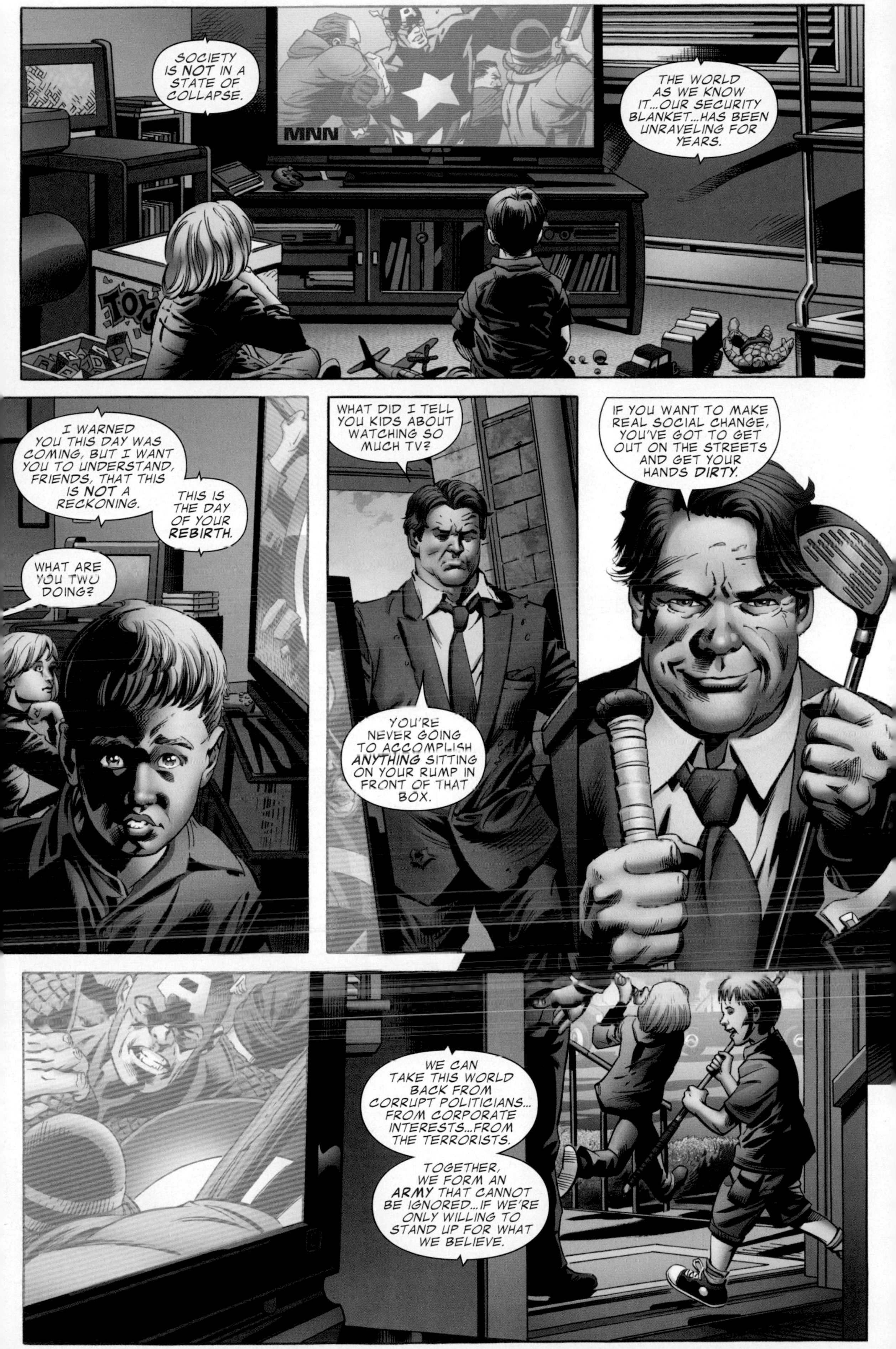
SOCIETY IS NOT IN A STATE OF COLLAPSE.
MNN
THE WORLD AS WE KNOW IT...OUR SECURITY BLANKET...HAS BEEN UNRAVELING FOR YEARS.
I WARNED YOU THIS DAY WAS COMING, BUT I WANT YOU TO UNDERSTAND, FRIENDS, THAT THIS IS NOT A RECKONING.
THIS IS THE DAY OF YOUR REBIRTH.
WHAT ARE YOU TWO DOING?
WHAT DID I TELL YOU KIDS ABOUT WATCHING SO MUCH TV?
YOU'RE NEVER GOING TO ACCOMPLISH ANYTHING SITTING ON YOUR RUMP IN FRONT OF THAT BOX.
IF YOU WANT TO MAKE REAL SOCIAL CHANGE, YOU'VE GOT TO GET OUT ON THE STREETS AND GET YOUR HANDS DIRTY.
WE CAN TAKE THIS WORLD BACK FROM CORRUPT POLITICIANS... FROM CORPORATE INTERESTS...FROM THE TERRORISTS.
TOGETHER, WE FORM AN ARMY THAT CANNOT BE IGNORED...IF WE'RE ONLY WILLING TO STAND UP FOR WHAT WE BELIEVE.

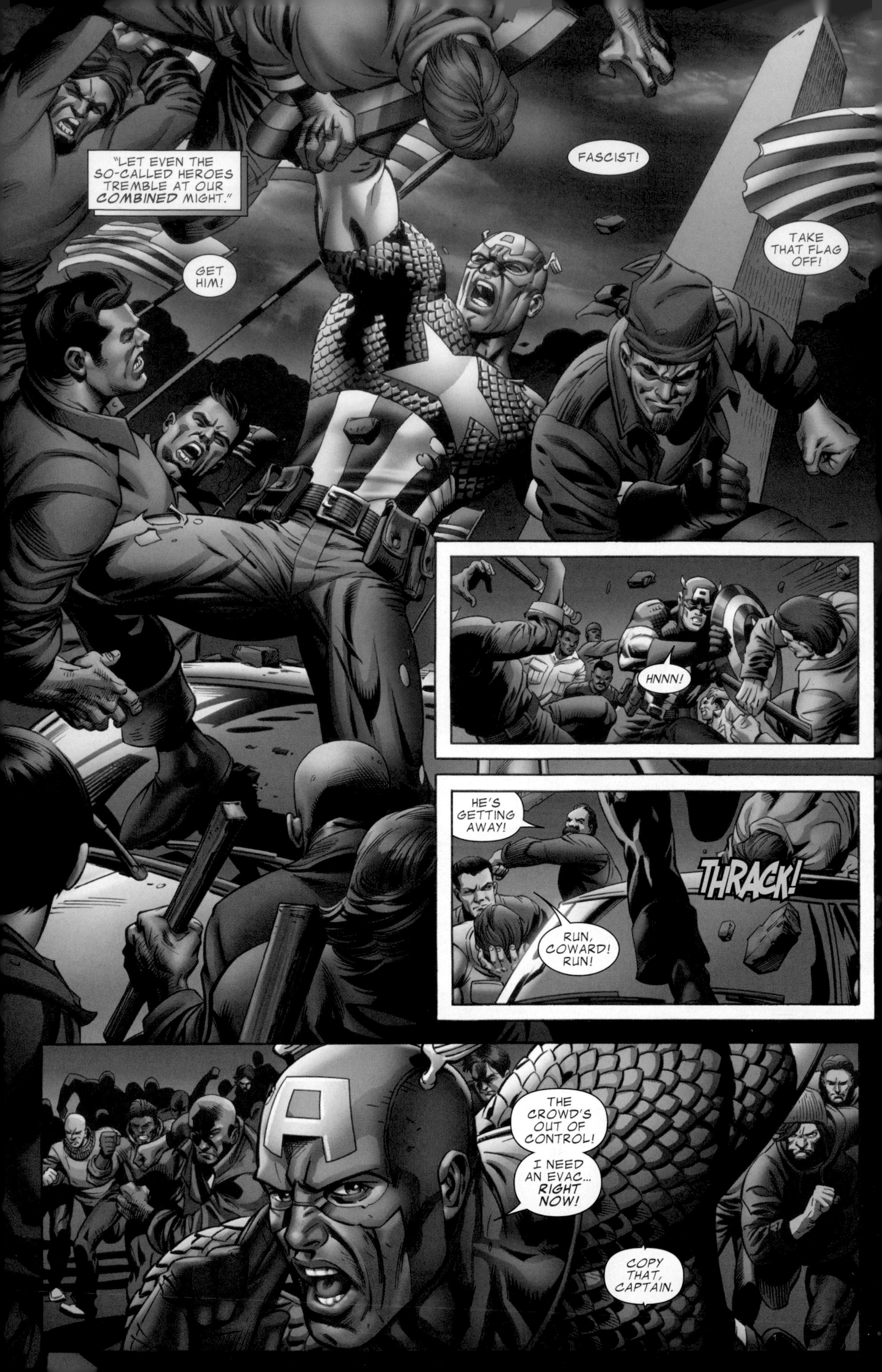
"LET EVEN THE SO-CALLED HEROES TREMBLE AT OUR COMBINED MIGHT."
FASCIST!
GET HIM!
TAKE THAT FLAG OFF!
HNNN!
HE'S GETTING AWAY!
THRACK!
RUN, COWARD! RUN!
THE CROWD'S OUT OF CONTROL!
I NEED AN EVAC... RIGHT NOW!
COPY THAT, CAPTAIN.

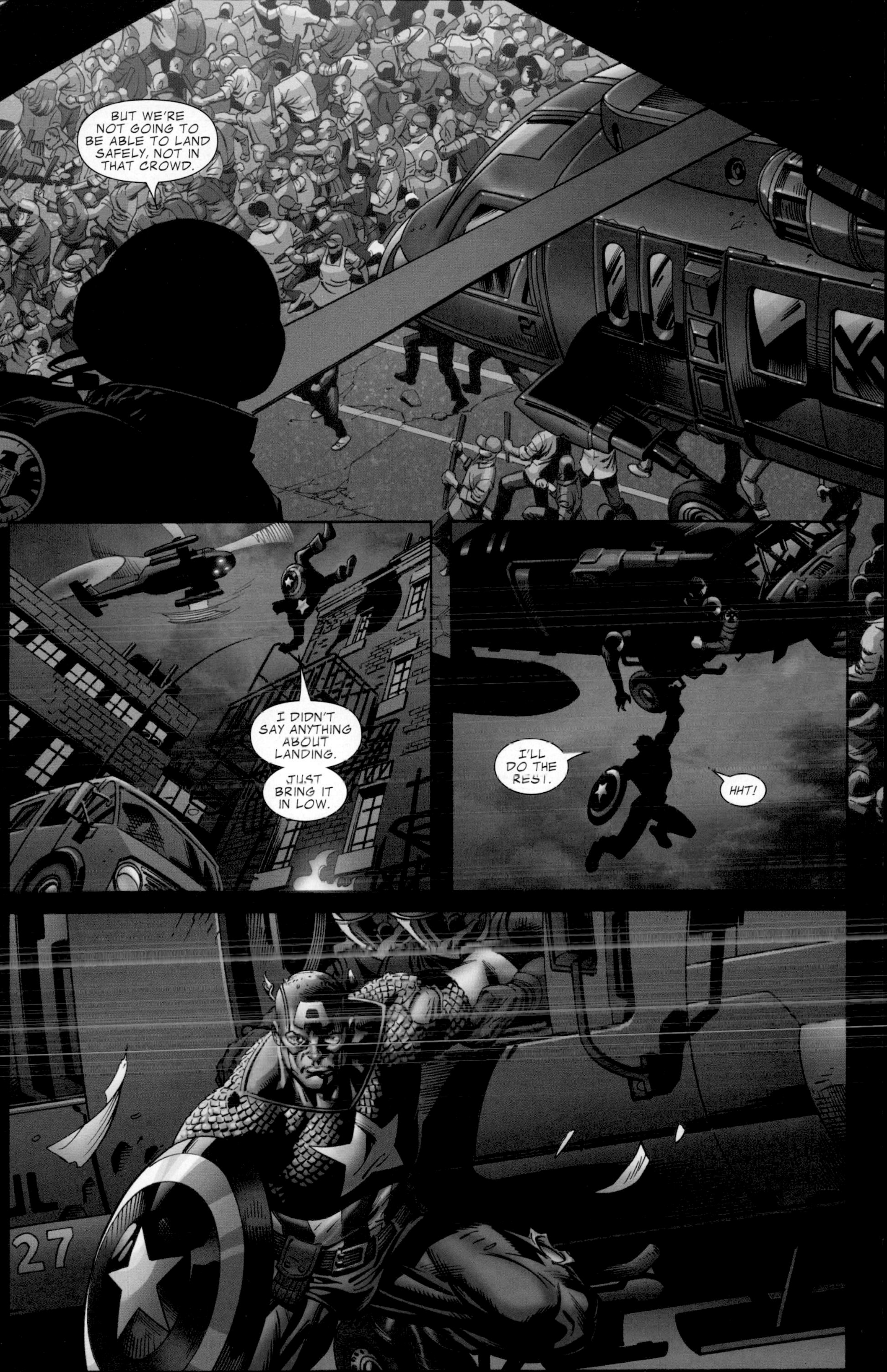
BUT WE'RE NOT GOING TO BE ABLE TO LAND SAFELY, NOT IN THAT CROWD.
I DIDN'T SAY ANYTHING ABOUT LANDING.
JUST BRING IT IN LOW.
I'LL DO THE REST.
HHT!

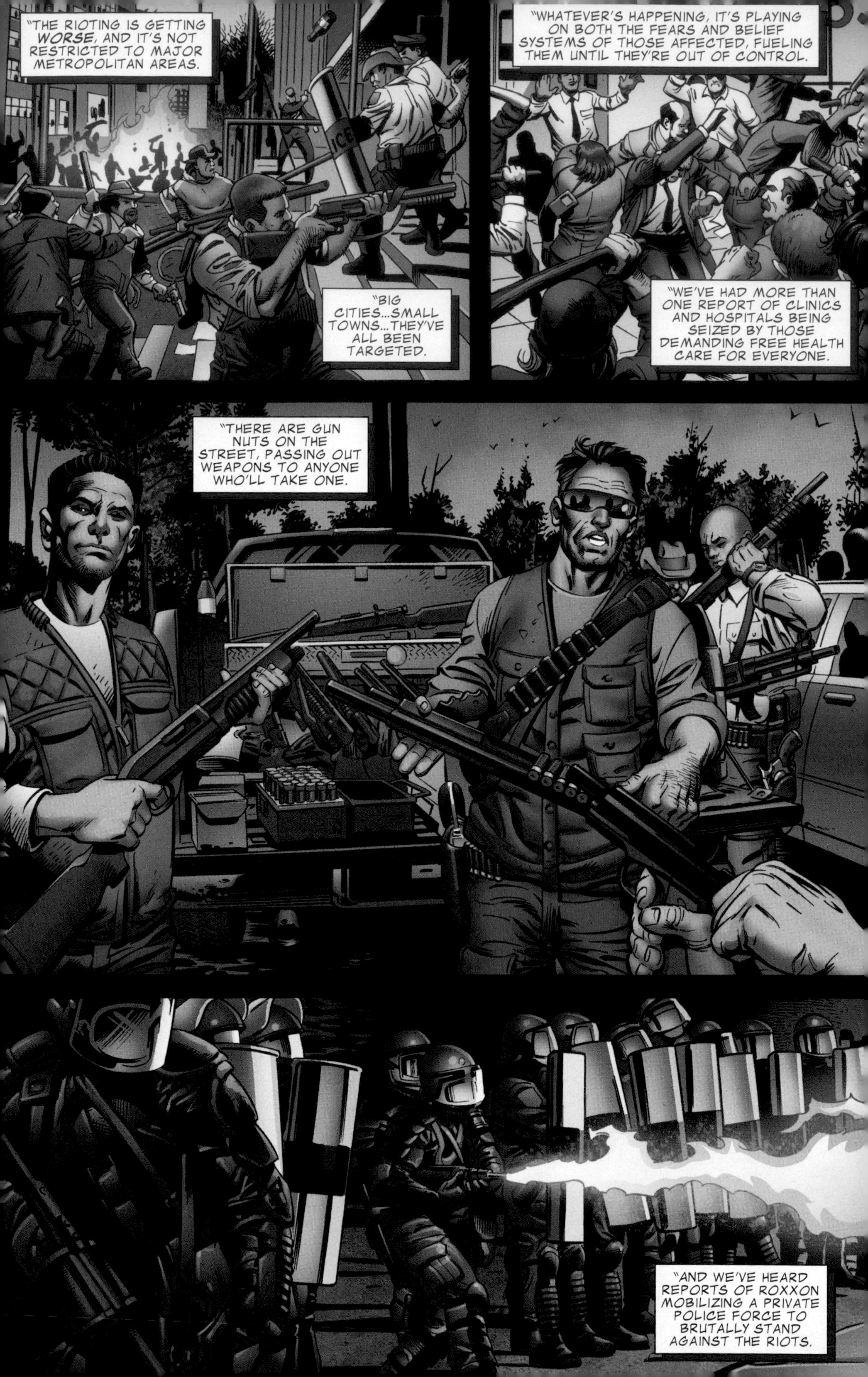
"THE RIOTING IS GETTING *WORSE*, AND IT'S NOT RESTRICTED TO MAJOR METROPOLITAN AREAS.
"BIG CITIES...SMALL TOWNS...THEY'VE ALL BEEN TARGETED.
"WHATEVER'S HAPPENING, IT'S PLAYING ON BOTH THE FEARS AND BELIEF SYSTEMS OF THOSE AFFECTED, FUELING THEM UNTIL THEY'RE OUT OF CONTROL.
"WE'VE HAD MORE THAN ONE REPORT OF CLINICS AND HOSPITALS BEING SEIZED BY THOSE DEMANDING FREE HEALTH CARE FOR EVERYONE.
"THERE ARE GUN NUTS ON THE STREET, PASSING OUT WEAPONS TO ANYONE WHO'LL TAKE ONE.
"AND WE'VE HEARD REPORTS OF ROXXON MOBILIZING A PRIVATE POLICE FORCE TO BRUTALLY STAND AGAINST THE RIOTS.

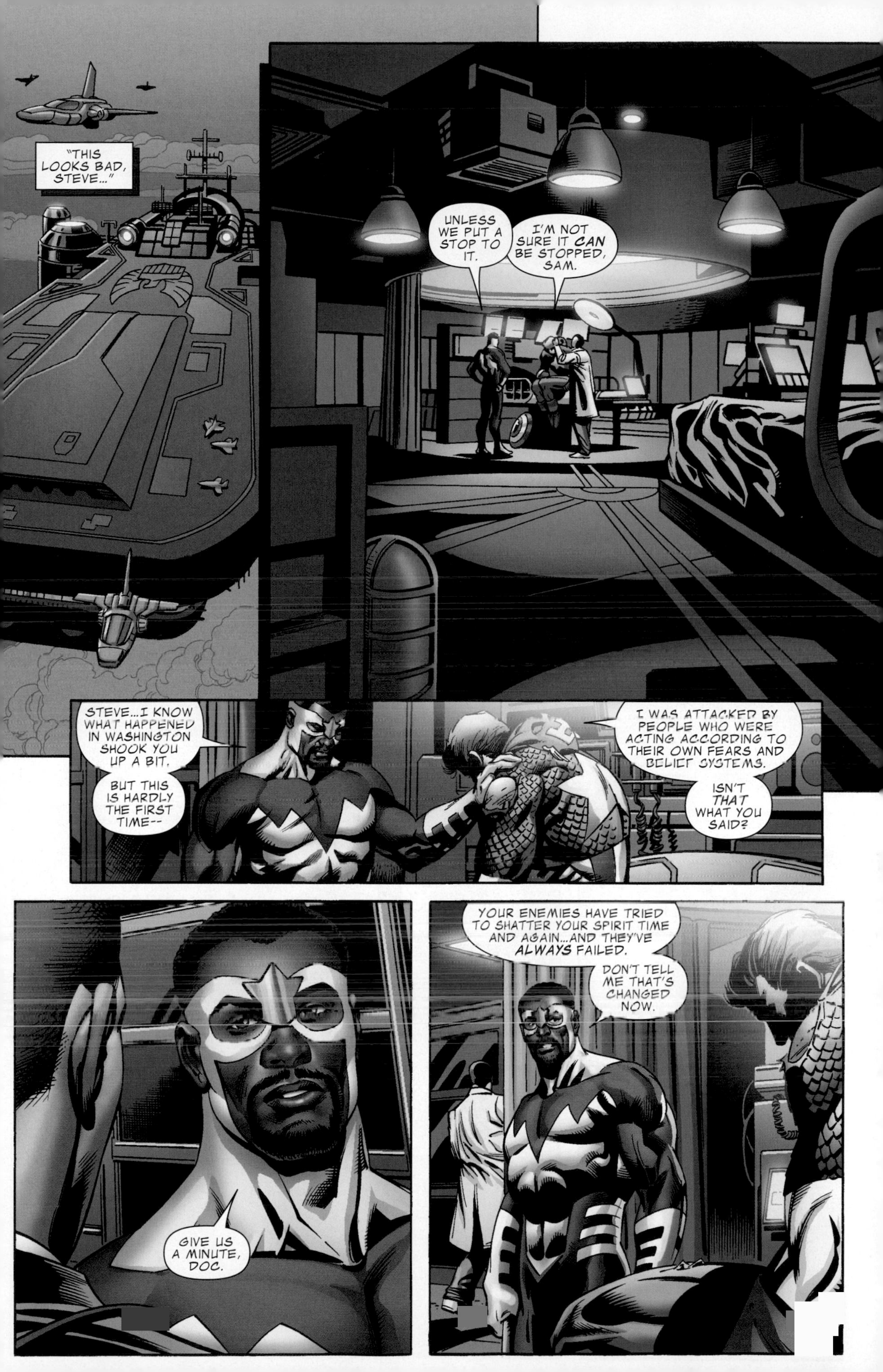
"THIS LOOKS BAD, STEVE..."
UNLESS WE PUT A STOP TO IT.
I'M NOT SURE IT CAN BE STOPPED, SAM.
STEVE...I KNOW WHAT HAPPENED IN WASHINGTON SHOOK YOU UP A BIT.
BUT THIS IS HARDLY THE FIRST TIME--
I WAS ATTACKED BY PEOPLE WHO WERE ACTING ACCORDING TO THEIR OWN FEARS AND BELIEF SYSTEMS.
ISN'T THAT WHAT YOU SAID?
GIVE US A MINUTE, DOC.
YOUR ENEMIES HAVE TRIED TO SHATTER YOUR SPIRIT TIME AND AGAIN...AND THEY'VE ALWAYS FAILED.
DON'T TELL ME THAT'S CHANGED NOW.

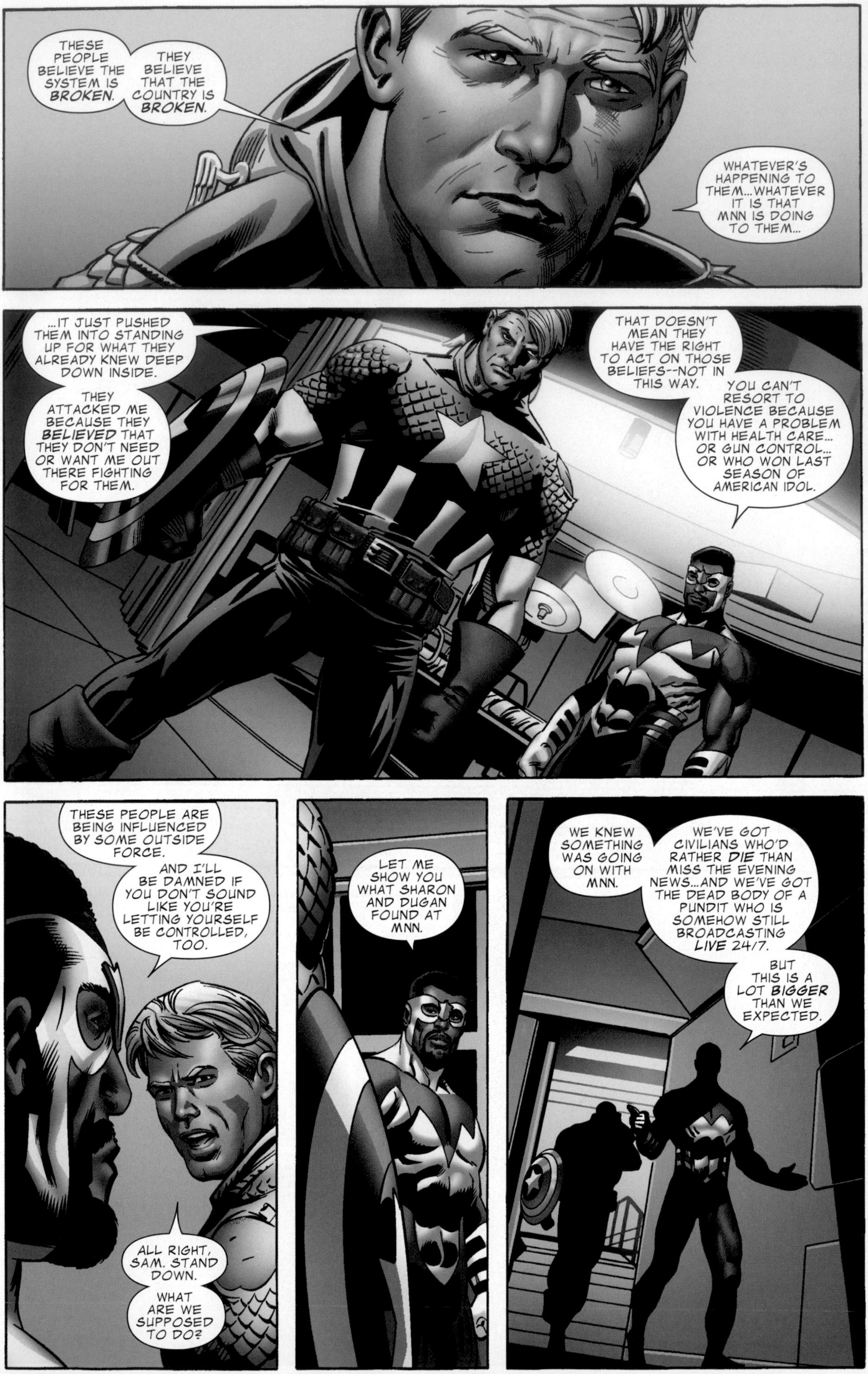
THESE PEOPLE BELIEVE THE SYSTEM IS BROKEN.
THEY BELIEVE THAT THE COUNTRY IS BROKEN.
WHATEVER'S HAPPENING TO THEM...WHATEVER IT IS THAT MNN IS DOING TO THEM...
...IT JUST PUSHED THEM INTO STANDING UP FOR WHAT THEY ALREADY KNEW DEEP DOWN INSIDE.
THEY ATTACKED ME BECAUSE THEY BELIEVED THAT THEY DON'T NEED OR WANT ME OUT THERE FIGHTING FOR THEM.
THAT DOESN'T MEAN THEY HAVE THE RIGHT TO ACT ON THOSE BELIEFS--NOT IN THIS WAY.
YOU CAN'T RESORT TO VIOLENCE BECAUSE YOU HAVE A PROBLEM WITH HEALTH CARE... OR GUN CONTROL... OR WHO WON LAST SEASON OF AMERICAN IDOL.
THESE PEOPLE ARE BEING INFLUENCED BY SOME OUTSIDE FORCE.
AND I'LL BE DAMNED IF YOU DON'T SOUND LIKE YOU'RE LETTING YOURSELF BE CONTROLLED, TOO.
ALL RIGHT, SAM. STAND DOWN.
WHAT ARE WE SUPPOSED TO DO?
LET ME SHOW YOU WHAT SHARON AND DUGAN FOUND AT MNN.
WE KNEW SOMETHING WAS GOING ON WITH MNN.
WE'VE GOT CIVILIANS WHO'D RATHER DIE THAN MISS THE EVENING NEWS...AND WE'VE GOT THE DEAD BODY OF A PUNDIT WHO IS SOMEHOW STILL BROADCASTING LIVE 24/7.
BUT THIS IS A LOT BIGGER THAN WE EXPECTED.

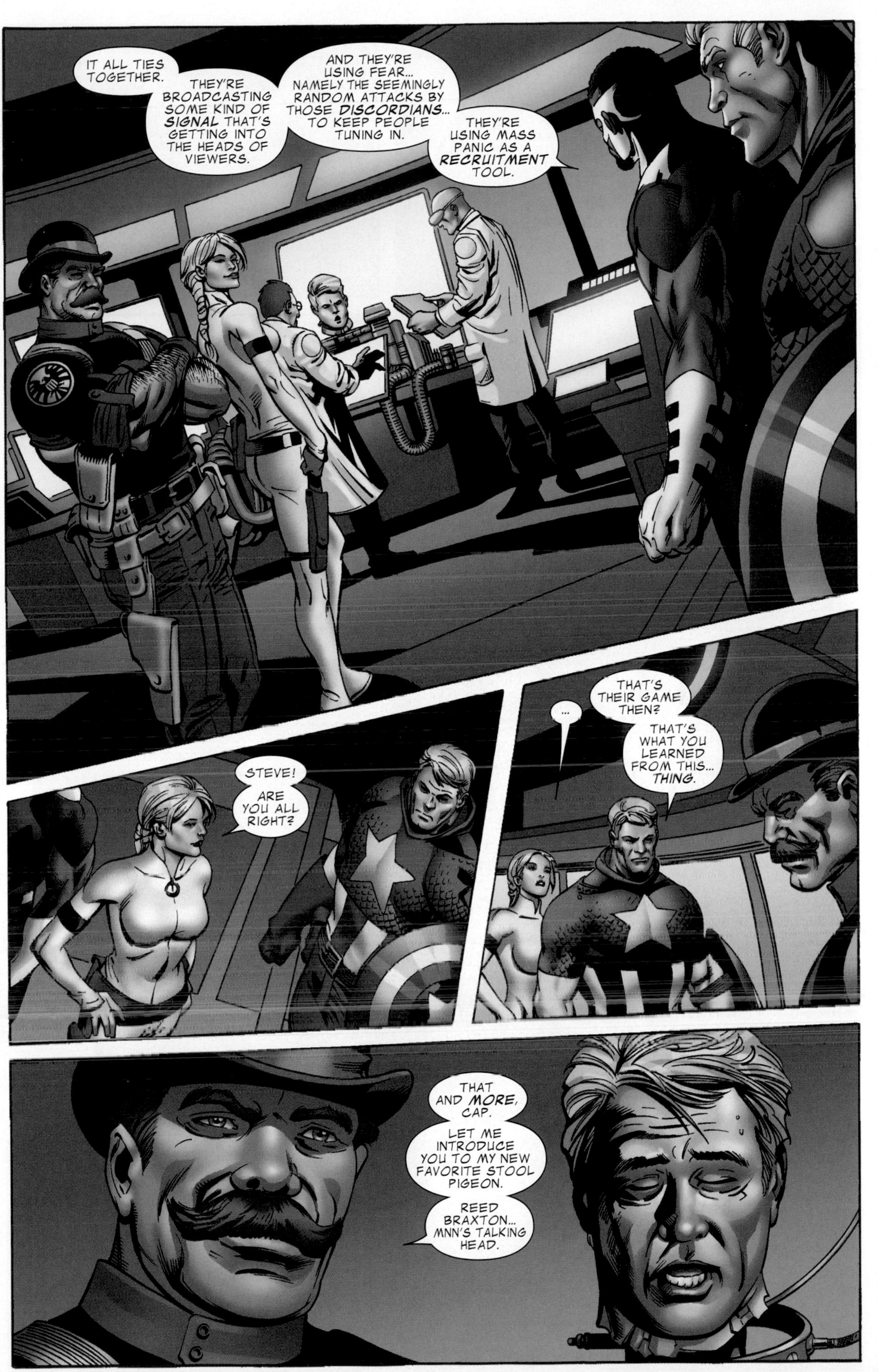
IT ALL TIES TOGETHER.
THEY'RE BROADCASTING SOME KIND OF SIGNAL THAT'S GETTING INTO THE HEADS OF VIEWERS.
AND THEY'RE USING FEAR... NAMELY THE SEEMINGLY RANDOM ATTACKS BY THOSE DISCORDIANS... TO KEEP PEOPLE TUNING IN.
THEY'RE USING MASS PANIC AS A RECRUITMENT TOOL.
STEVE!
ARE YOU ALL RIGHT?
...
THAT'S THEIR GAME THEN?
THAT'S WHAT YOU LEARNED FROM THIS... THING.
THAT AND MORE, CAP.
LET ME INTRODUCE YOU TO MY NEW FAVORITE STOOL PIGEON.
REED BRAXTON... MNN'S TALKING HEAD.

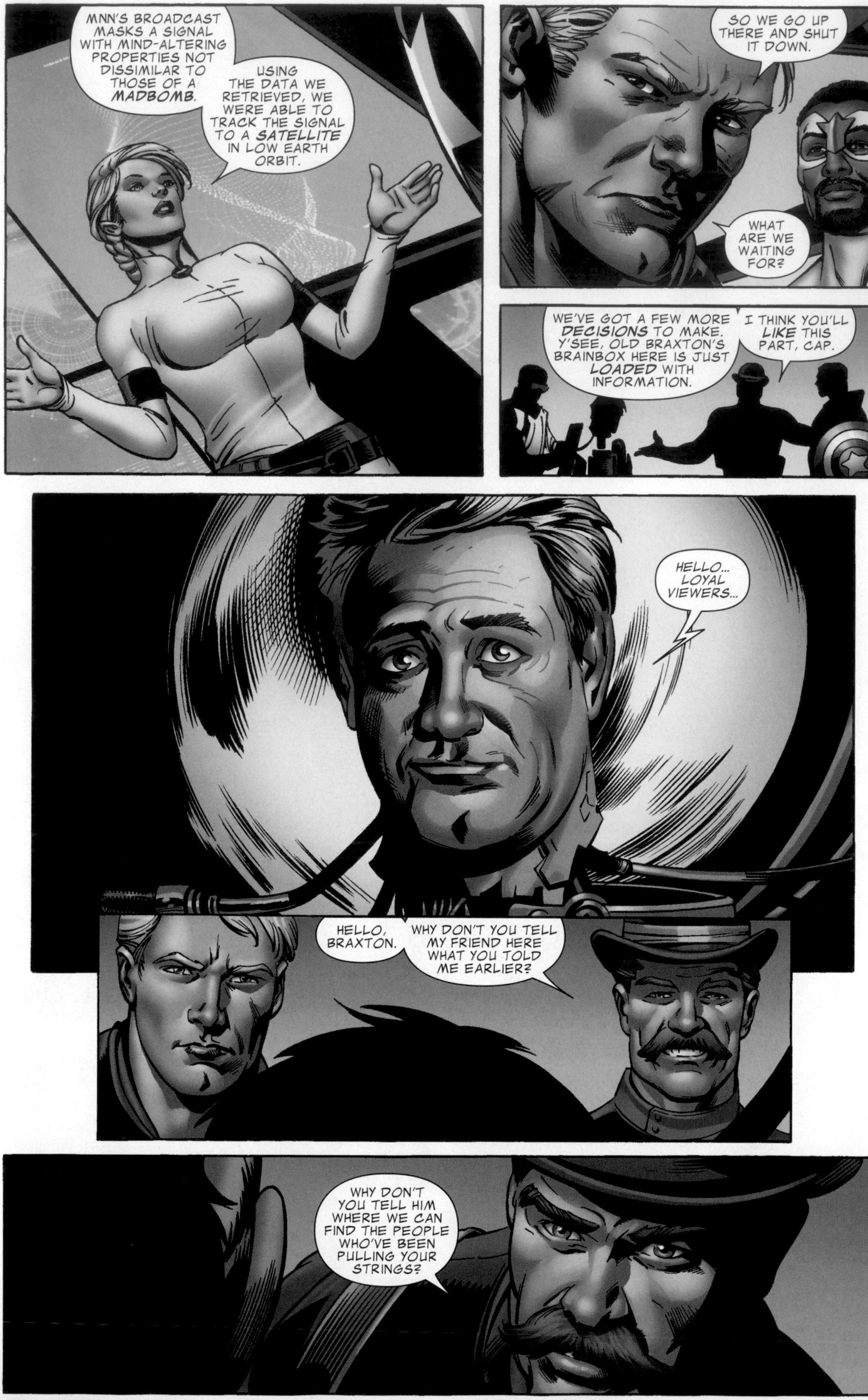
MNN'S BROADCAST MASKS A SIGNAL WITH MIND-ALTERING PROPERTIES NOT DISSIMILAR TO THOSE OF A MADBOMB.
USING THE DATA WE RETRIEVED, WE WERE ABLE TO TRACK THE SIGNAL TO A SATELLITE IN LOW EARTH ORBIT.
SO WE GO UP THERE AND SHUT IT DOWN.
WHAT ARE WE WAITING FOR?
WE'VE GOT A FEW MORE DECISIONS TO MAKE. Y'SEE, OLD BRAXTON'S BRAINBOX HERE IS JUST LOADED WITH INFORMATION.
I THINK YOU'LL LIKE THIS PART, CAP.
HELLO... LOYAL VIEWERS...
HELLO, BRAXTON.
WHY DON'T YOU TELL MY FRIEND HERE WHAT YOU TOLD ME EARLIER?
WHY DON'T YOU TELL HIM WHERE WE CAN FIND THE PEOPLE WHO'VE BEEN PULLING YOUR STRINGS?

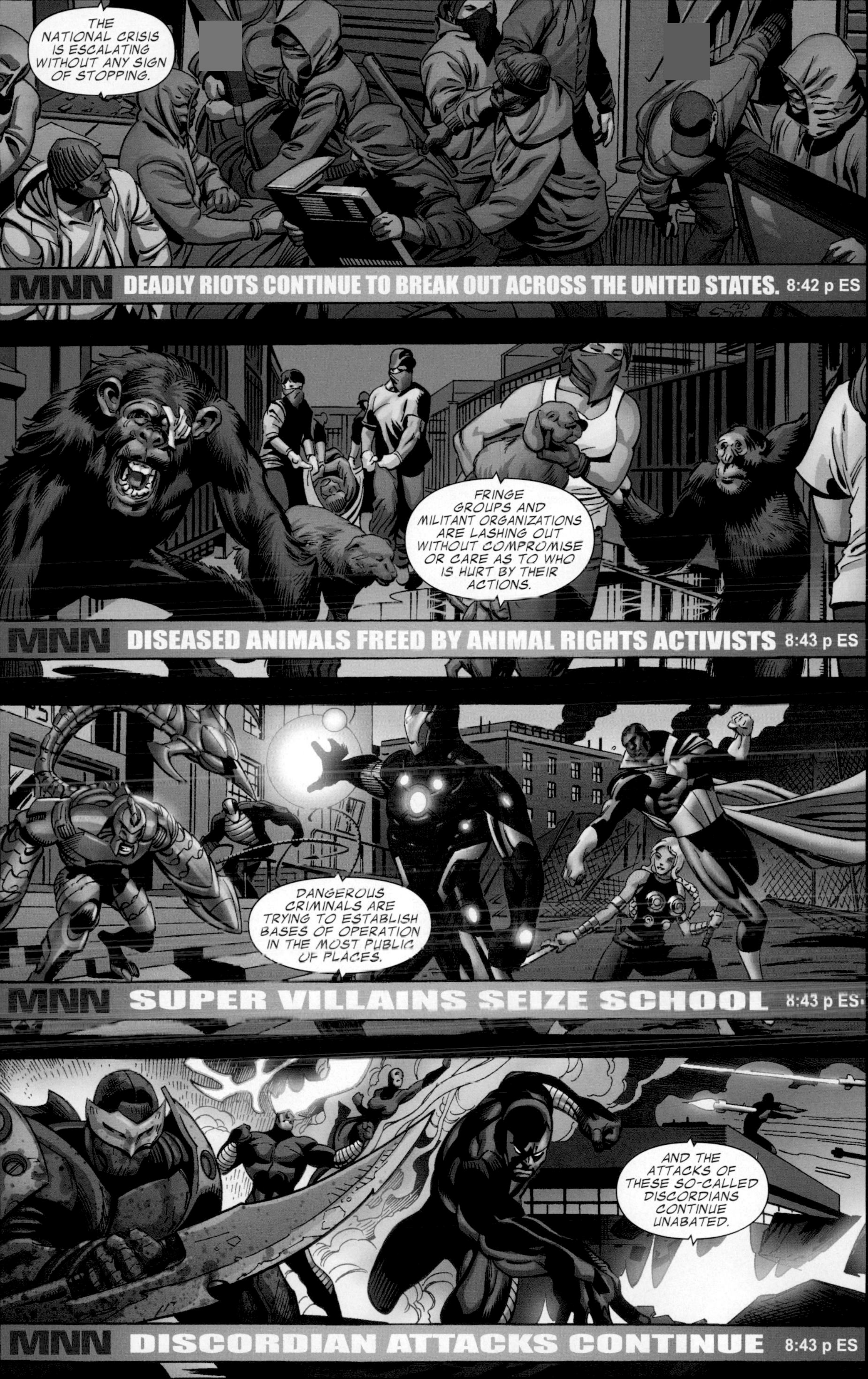
THE NATIONAL CRISIS IS ESCALATING WITHOUT ANY SIGN OF STOPPING.
MNN DEADLY RIOTS CONTINUE TO BREAK OUT ACROSS THE UNITED STATES. 8:42 p ES
FRINGE GROUPS AND MILITANT ORGANIZATIONS ARE LASHING OUT WITHOUT COMPROMISE OR CARE AS TO WHO IS HURT BY THEIR ACTIONS.
MNN DISEASED ANIMALS FREED BY ANIMAL RIGHTS ACTIVISTS 8:43 p ES
DANGEROUS CRIMINALS ARE TRYING TO ESTABLISH BASES OF OPERATION IN THE MOST PUBLIC OF PLACES.
MNN SUPER VILLAINS SEIZE SCHOOL 8:43 p ES
AND THE ATTACKS OF THESE SO-CALLED DISCORDIANS CONTINUE UNABATED.
MNN DISCORDIAN ATTACKS CONTINUE 8:43 p ES

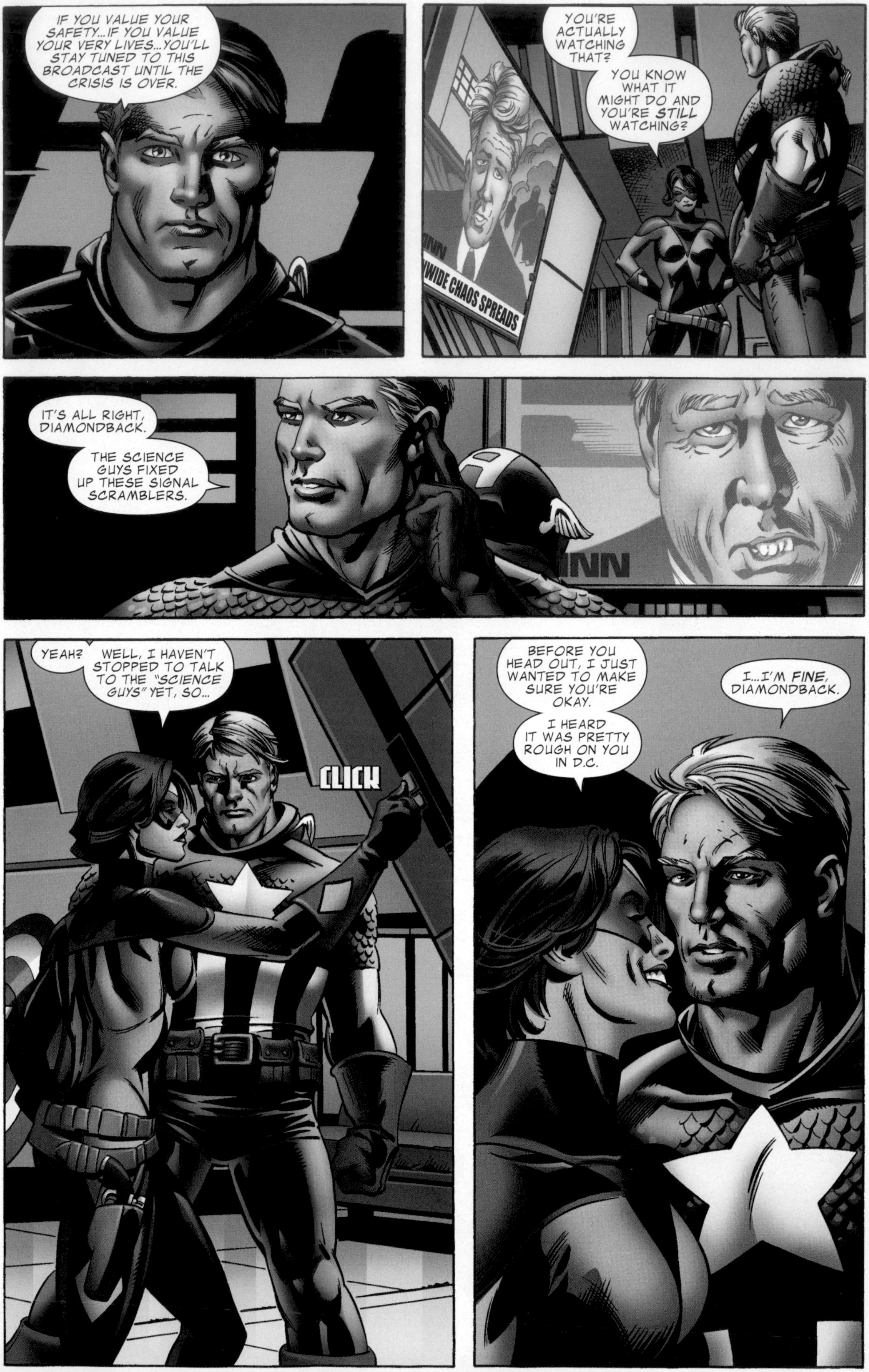
IF YOU VALUE YOUR SAFETY...IF YOU VALUE YOUR VERY LIVES...YOU'LL STAY TUNED TO THIS BROADCAST UNTIL THE CRISIS IS OVER.
YOU'RE ACTUALLY WATCHING THAT?
YOU KNOW WHAT IT MIGHT DO AND YOU'RE STILL WATCHING?
WIDE CHAOS SPREADS
IT'S ALL RIGHT, DIAMONDBACK.
THE SCIENCE GUYS FIXED UP THESE SIGNAL SCRAMBLERS.
YEAH?
WELL, I HAVEN'T STOPPED TO TALK TO THE "SCIENCE GUYS" YET, SO...
CLICK
BEFORE YOU HEAD OUT, I JUST WANTED TO MAKE SURE YOU'RE OKAY.
I HEARD IT WAS PRETTY ROUGH ON YOU IN D.C.
I...I'M FINE, DIAMONDBACK.

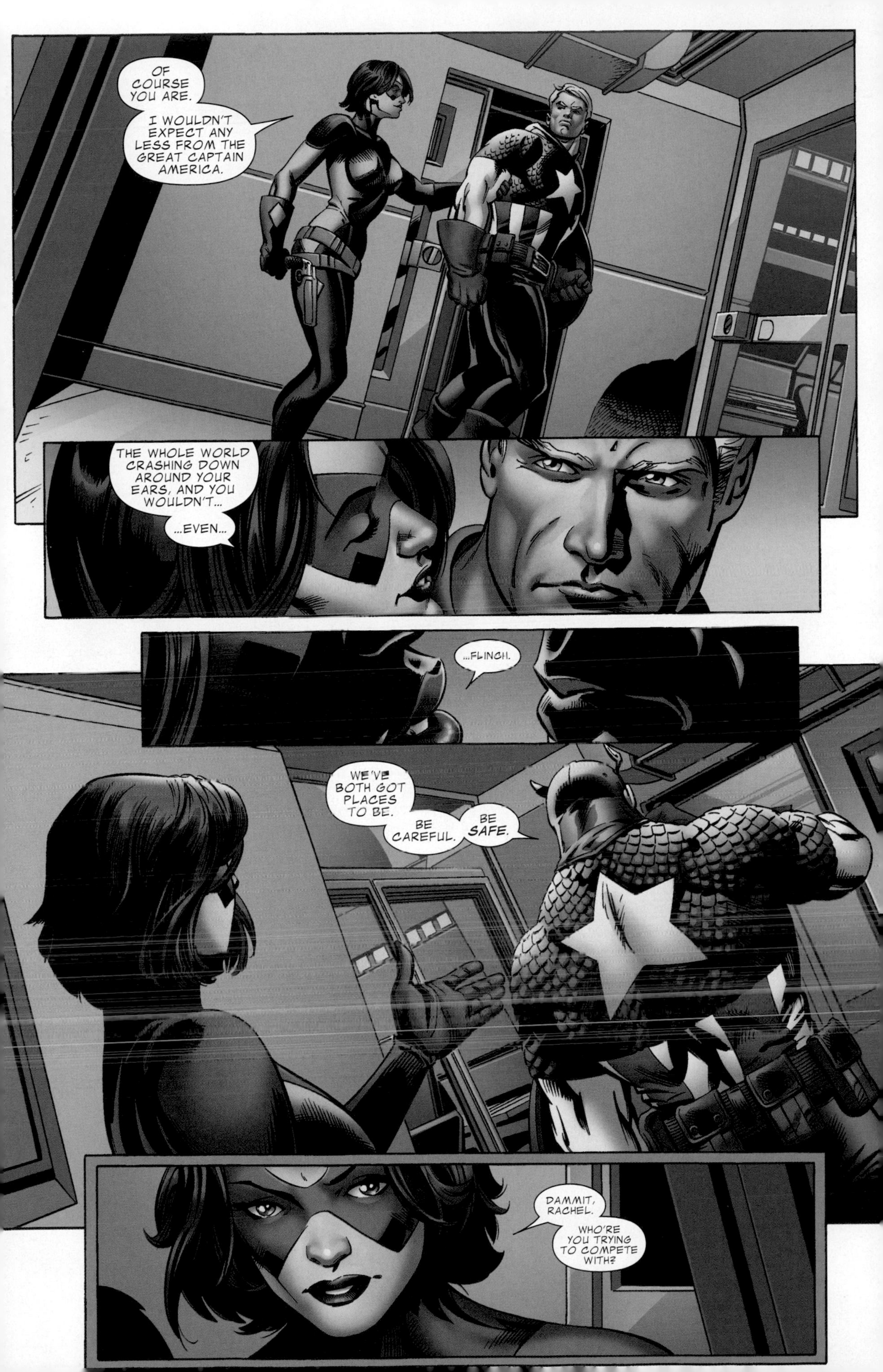
OF COURSE YOU ARE.
I WOULDN'T EXPECT ANY LESS FROM THE GREAT CAPTAIN AMERICA.
THE WHOLE WORLD CRASHING DOWN AROUND YOUR EARS, AND YOU WOULDN'T...
...EVEN...
...FLINCH.
WE'VE BOTH GOT PLACES TO BE.
BE CAREFUL.
BE SAFE.
DAMMIT, RACHEL.
WHO'RE YOU TRYING TO COMPETE WITH?

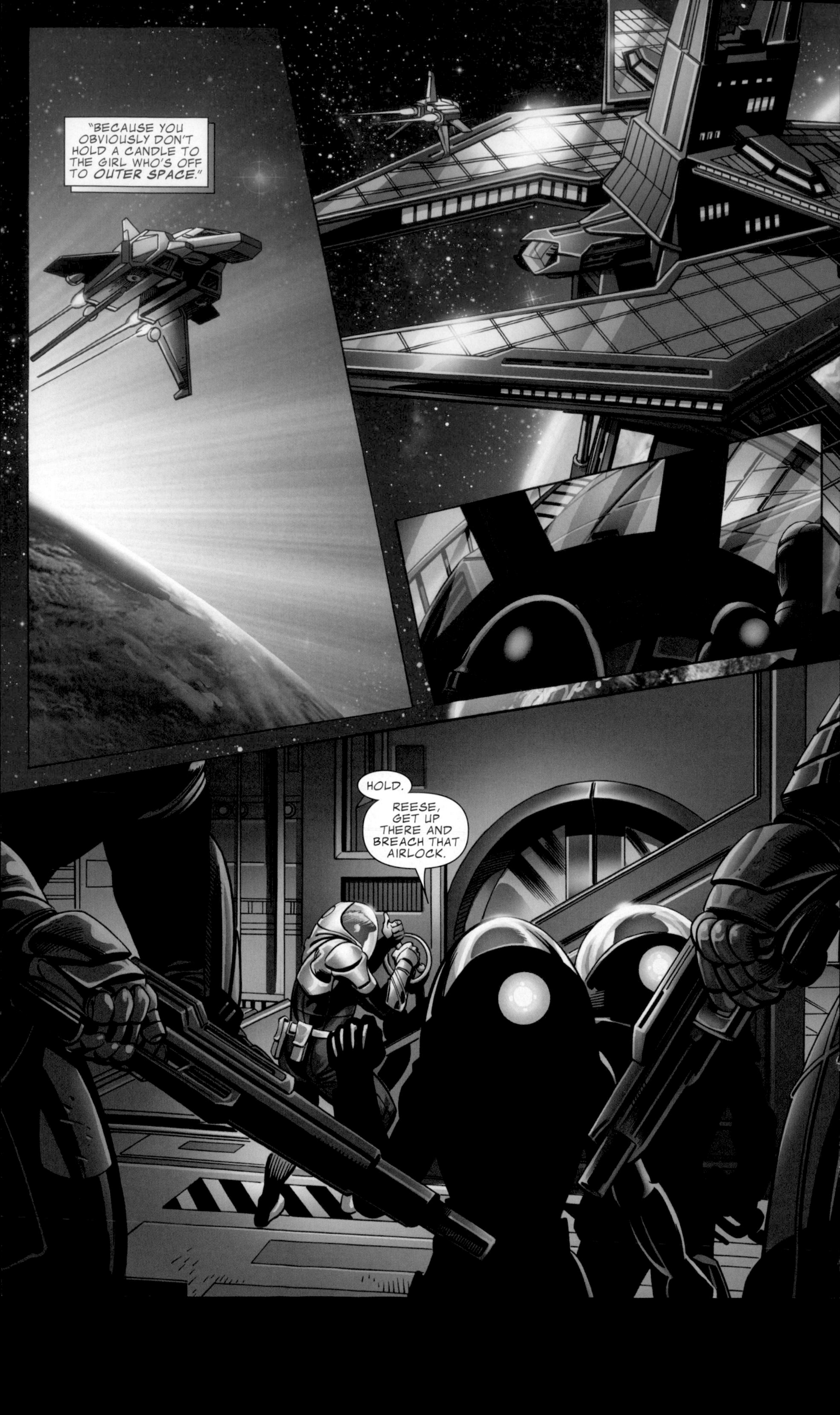
"BECAUSE YOU OBVIOUSLY DON'T HOLD A CANDLE TO THE GIRL WHO'S OFF TO OUTER SPACE."
HOLD.
REESE, GET UP THERE AND BREACH THAT AIRLOCK.

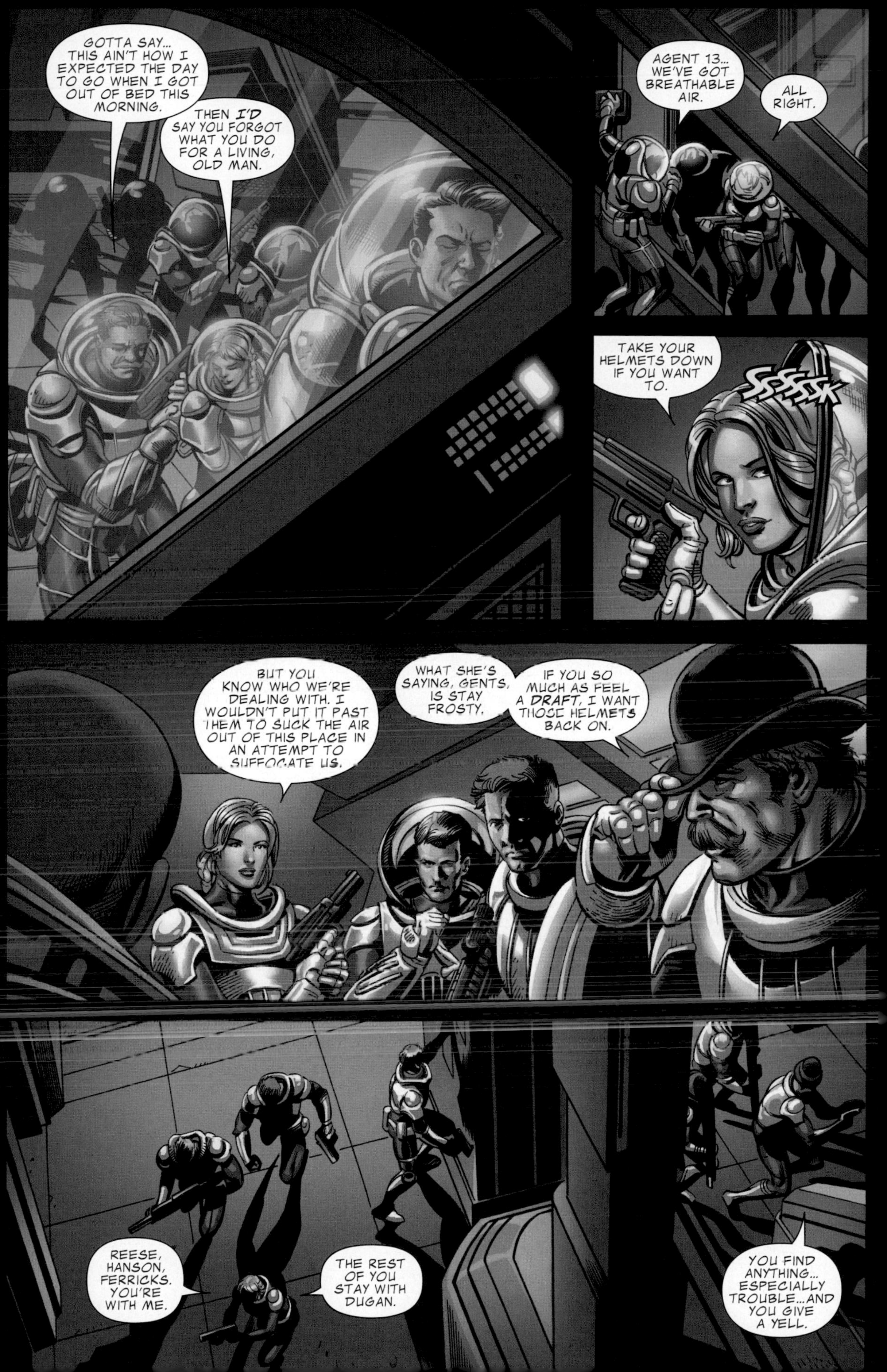
GOTTA SAY... THIS AIN'T HOW I EXPECTED THE DAY TO GO WHEN I GOT OUT OF BED THIS MORNING.
THEN I'D SAY YOU FORGOT WHAT YOU DO FOR A LIVING, OLD MAN.
AGENT 13... WE'VE GOT BREATHABLE AIR.
ALL RIGHT.
TAKE YOUR HELMETS DOWN IF YOU WANT TO.
SSSSSK
BUT YOU KNOW WHO WE'RE DEALING WITH. I WOULDN'T PUT IT PAST THEM TO SUCK THE AIR OUT OF THIS PLACE IN AN ATTEMPT TO SUFFOCATE US.
WHAT SHE'S SAYING, GENTS, IS STAY FROSTY.
IF YOU SO MUCH AS FEEL A DRAFT, I WANT THOSE HELMETS BACK ON.
REESE, HANSON, FERRICKS. YOU'RE WITH ME.
THE REST OF YOU STAY WITH DUGAN.
YOU FIND ANYTHING... ESPECIALLY TROUBLE... AND YOU GIVE A YELL.

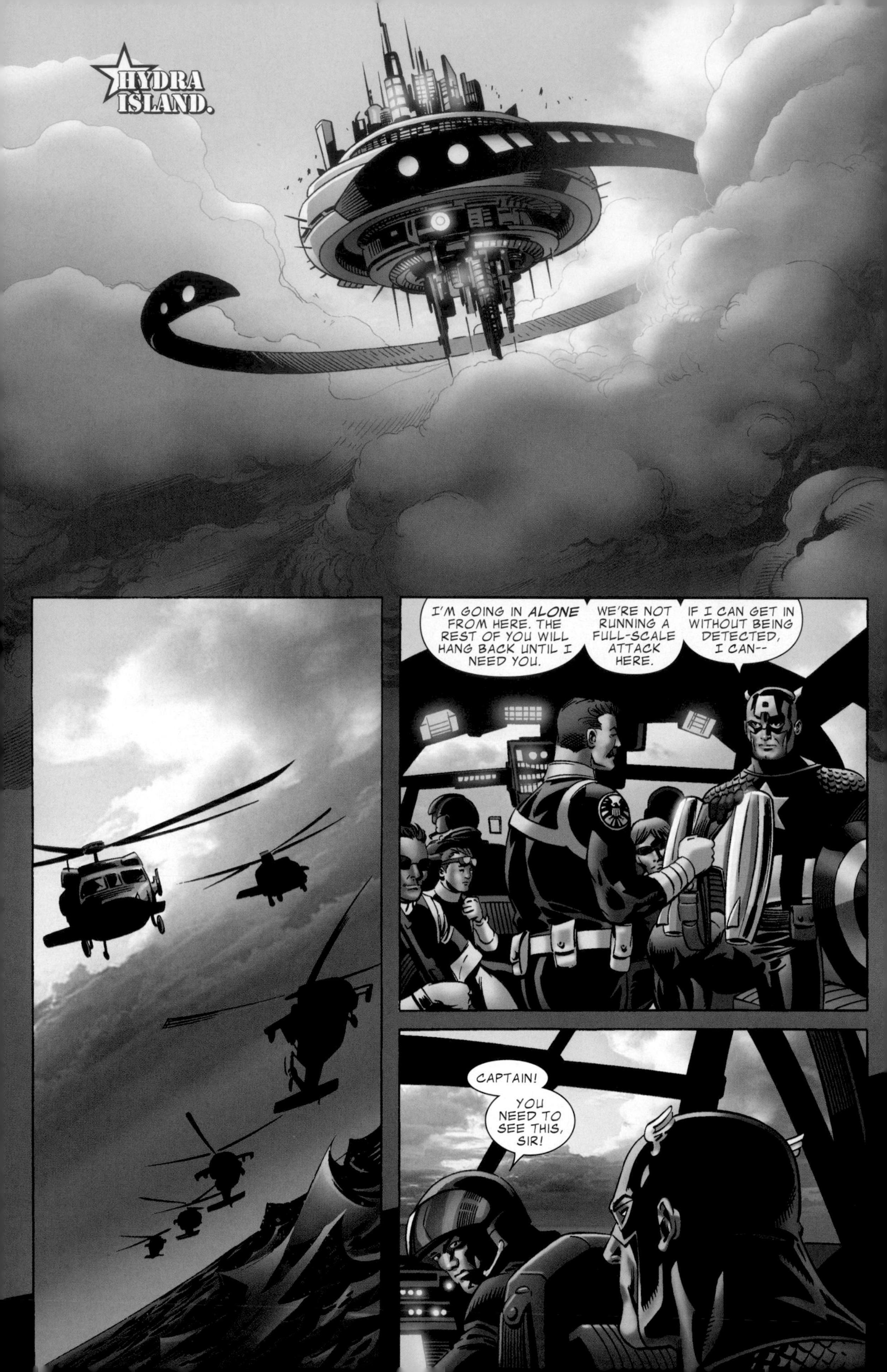
HYDRA ISLAND.
I'M GOING IN ALONE FROM HERE. THE REST OF YOU WILL HANG BACK UNTIL I NEED YOU.
WE'RE NOT RUNNING A FULL-SCALE ATTACK HERE.
IF I CAN GET IN WITHOUT BEING DETECTED, I CAN--
CAPTAIN!
YOU NEED TO SEE THIS, SIR!

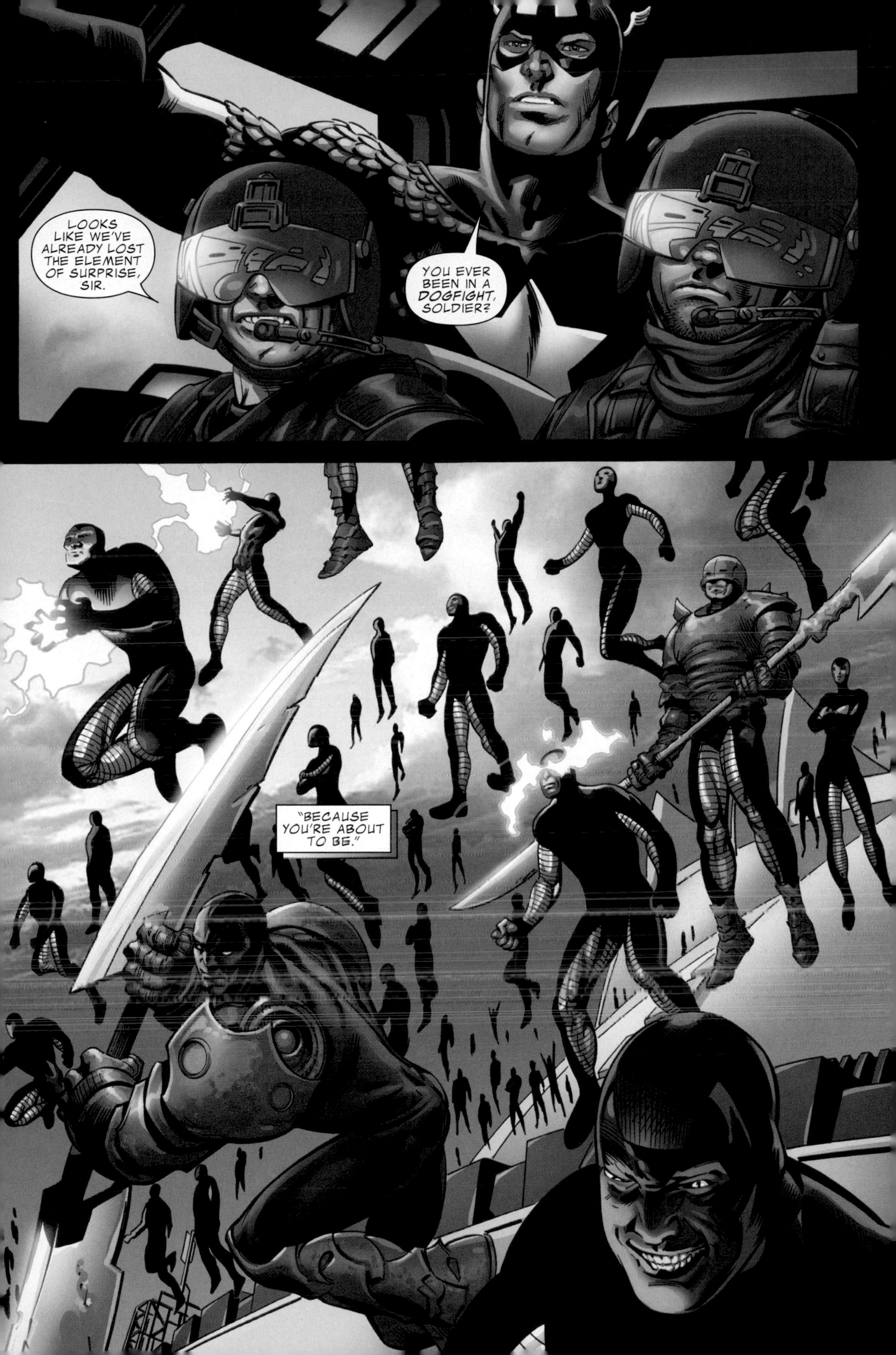
LOOKS LIKE WE'VE ALREADY LOST THE ELEMENT OF SURPRISE, SIR.
YOU EVER BEEN IN A DOGFIGHT, SOLDIER?
"BECAUSE YOU'RE ABOUT TO BE."

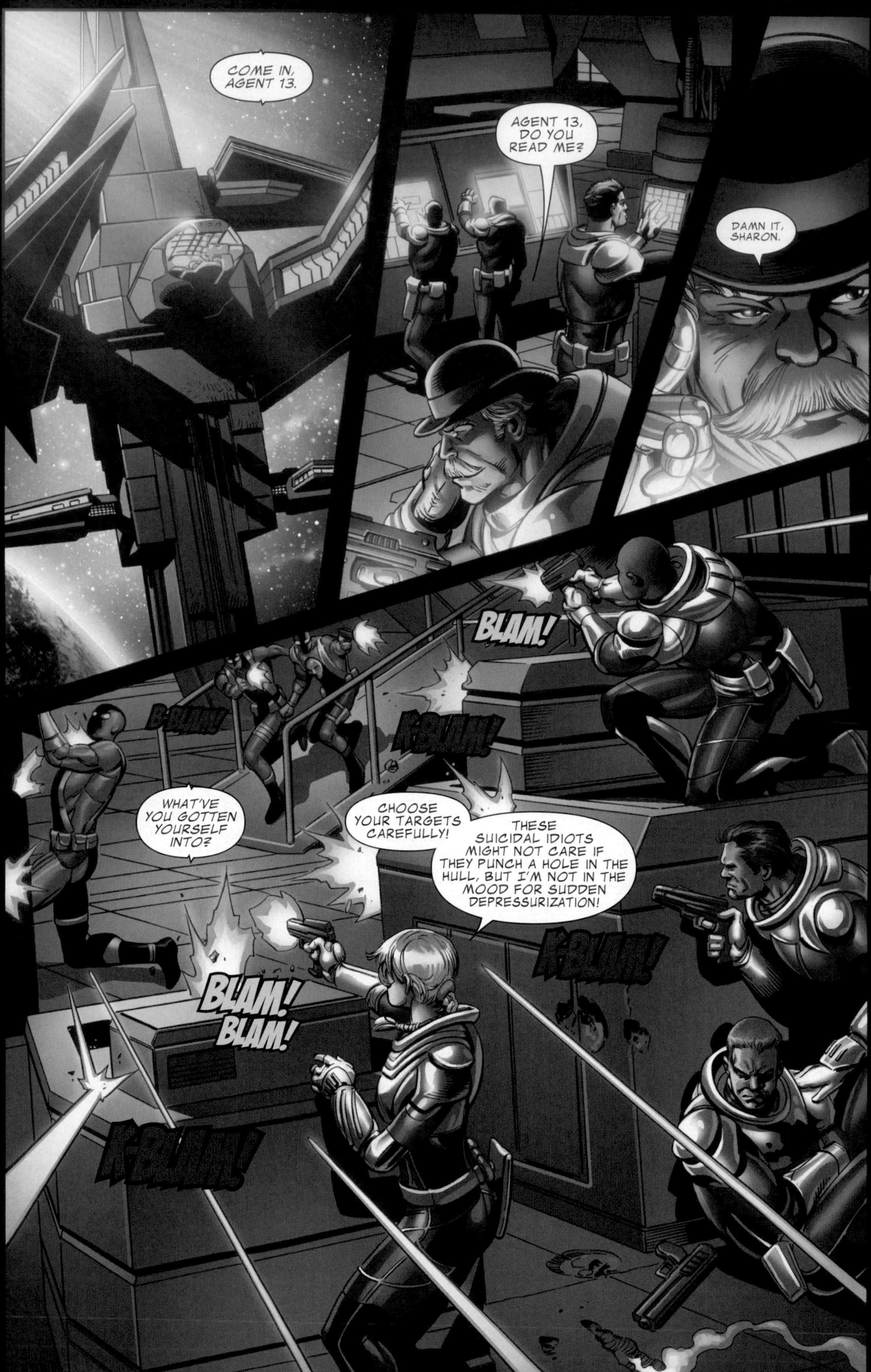
COME IN, AGENT 13.
AGENT 13, DO YOU READ ME?
DAMN IT, SHARON.
BLAM!
B-BLAM!
K-BLAM!
WHAT'VE YOU GOTTEN YOURSELF INTO?
CHOOSE YOUR TARGETS CAREFULLY!
THESE SUICIDAL IDIOTS MIGHT NOT CARE IF THEY PUNCH A HOLE IN THE HULL, BUT I'M NOT IN THE MOOD FOR SUDDEN DEPRESSURIZATION!
K-BLAM!
BLAM! BLAM!
K-BLAM!

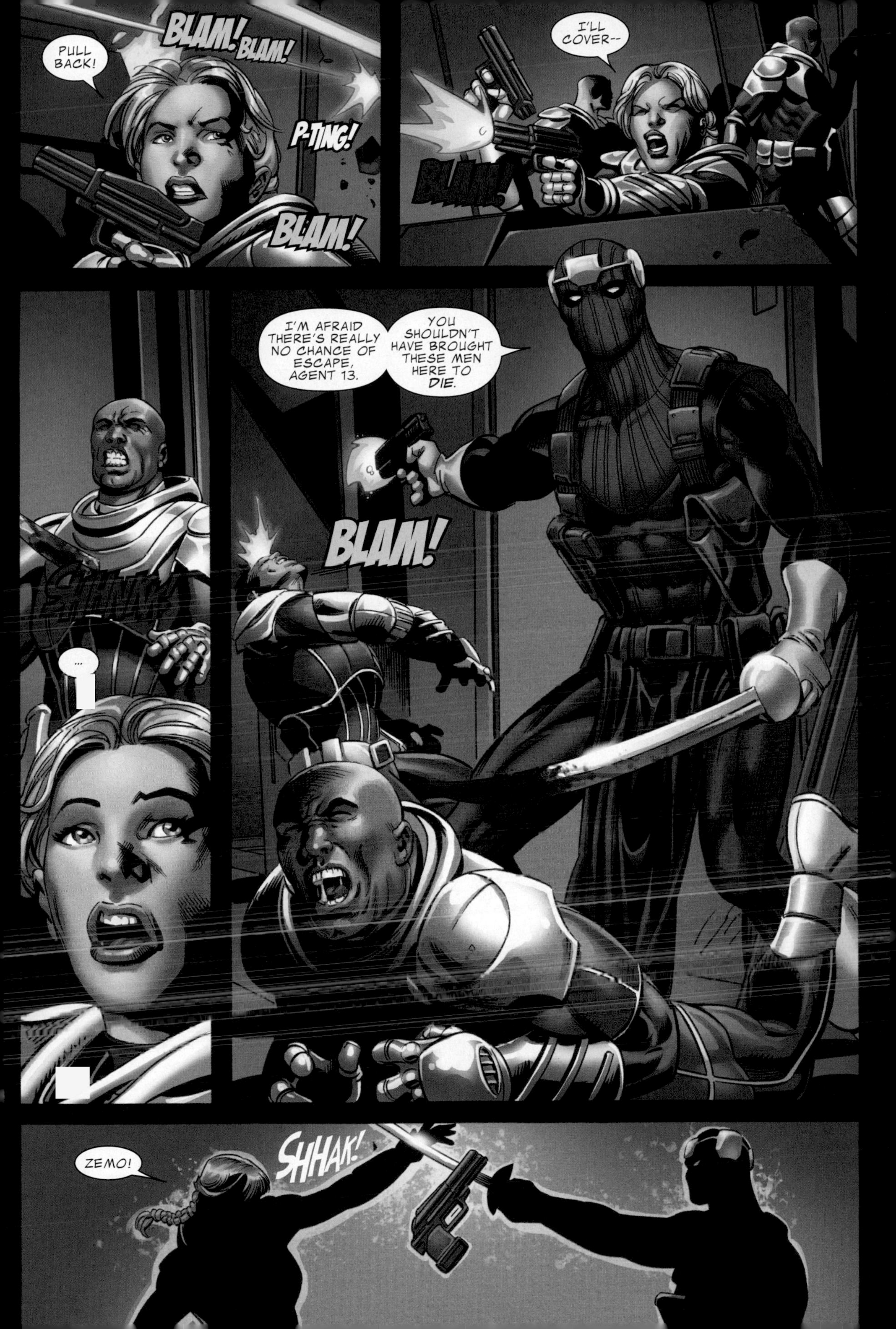
PULL BACK!
BLAM! BLAM!
P-TING!
BLAM!
I'LL COVER--
BLAM!
I'M AFRAID THERE'S REALLY NO CHANCE OF ESCAPE, AGENT 13.
YOU SHOULDN'T HAVE BROUGHT THESE MEN HERE TO DIE.
BLAM!
...
ZEMO!
SHHAK!

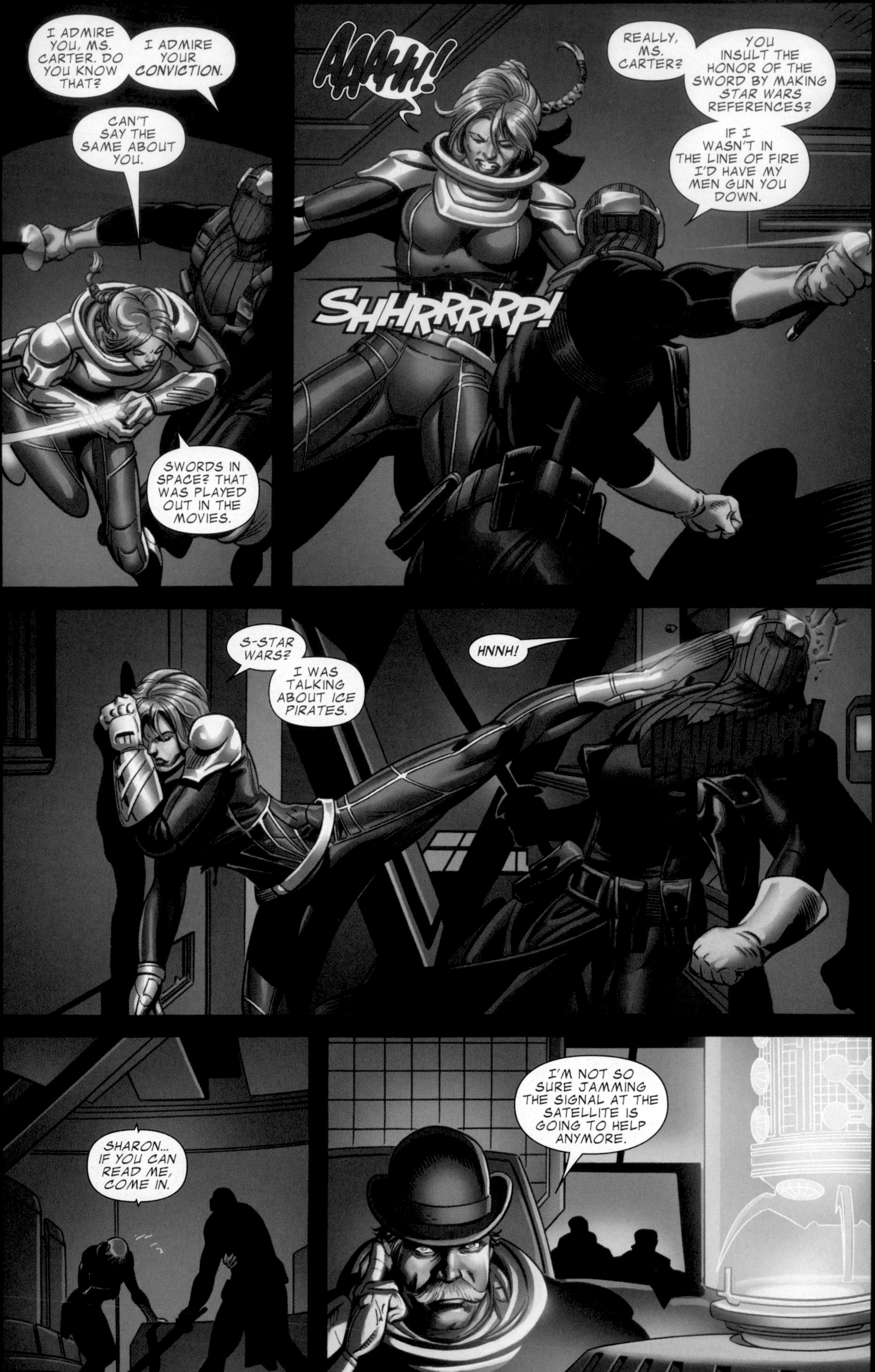
I ADMIRE YOU, MS. CARTER. DO YOU KNOW THAT?
I ADMIRE YOUR CONVICTION.
CAN'T SAY THE SAME ABOUT YOU.
SWORDS IN SPACE? THAT WAS PLAYED OUT IN THE MOVIES.
AAAHH!
SHHRRRRP!
REALLY, MS. CARTER?
YOU INSULT THE HONOR OF THE SWORD BY MAKING STAR WARS REFERENCES?
IF I WASN'T IN THE LINE OF FIRE I'D HAVE MY MEN GUN YOU DOWN.
S-STAR WARS?
I WAS TALKING ABOUT ICE PIRATES.
HNNH!
SHARON... IF YOU CAN READ ME, COME IN.
I'M NOT SO SURE JAMMING THE SIGNAL AT THE SATELLITE IS GOING TO HELP ANYMORE.

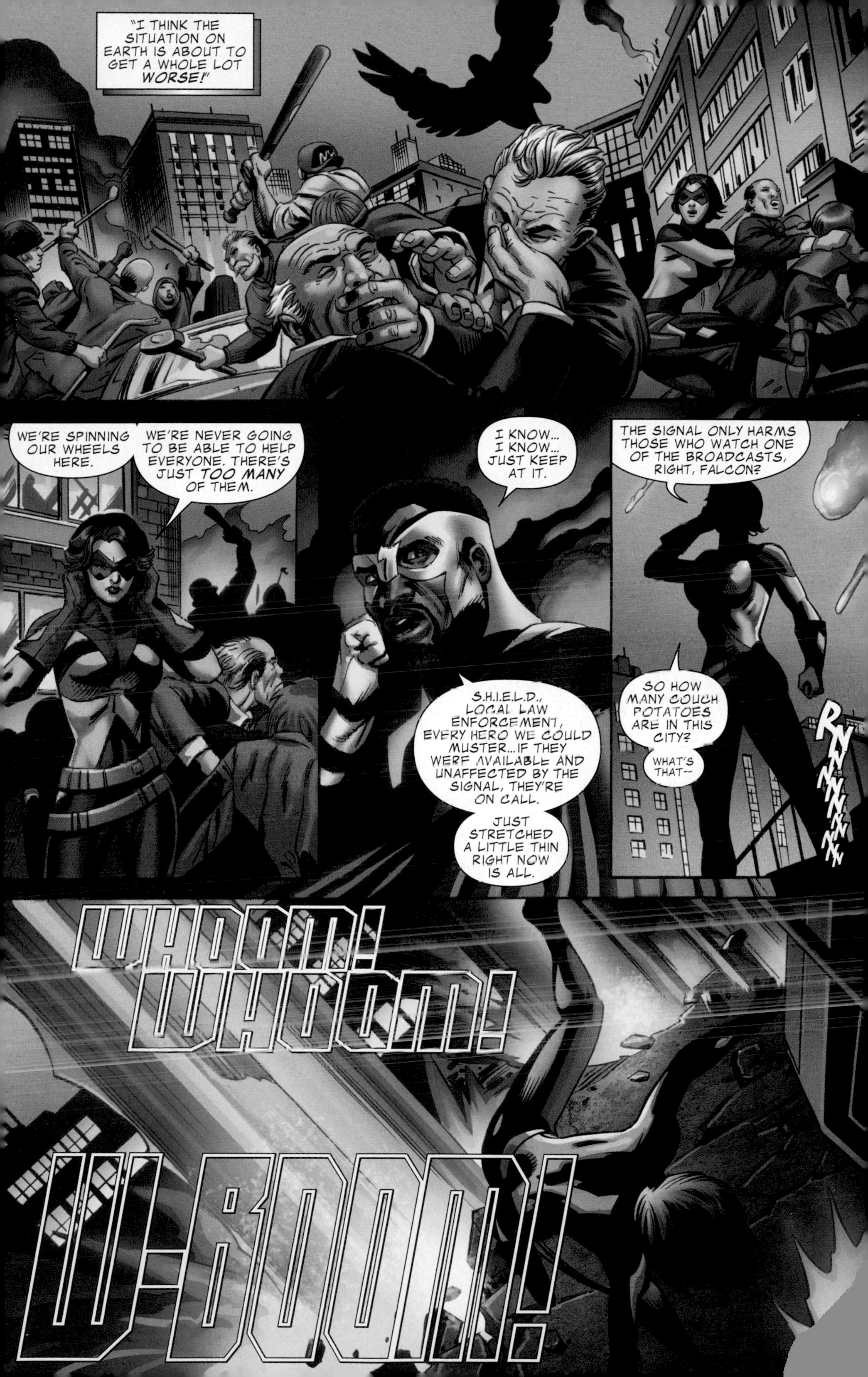
"I THINK THE SITUATION ON EARTH IS ABOUT TO GET A WHOLE LOT WORSE!"
WE'RE SPINNING OUR WHEELS HERE.
WE'RE NEVER GOING TO BE ABLE TO HELP EVERYONE. THERE'S JUST TOO MANY OF THEM.
I KNOW... I KNOW... JUST KEEP AT IT.
S.H.I.E.L.D., LOCAL LAW ENFORCEMENT, EVERY HERO WE COULD MUSTER...IF THEY WERE AVAILABLE AND UNAFFECTED BY THE SIGNAL, THEY'RE ON CALL.
JUST STRETCHED A LITTLE THIN RIGHT NOW IS ALL.
THE SIGNAL ONLY HARMS THOSE WHO WATCH ONE OF THE BROADCASTS, RIGHT, FALCON?
SO HOW MANY COUCH POTATOES ARE IN THIS CITY?
WHAT'S THAT--
RNNNNNNN
WHOOM! WHOOM!
W-BOOM!

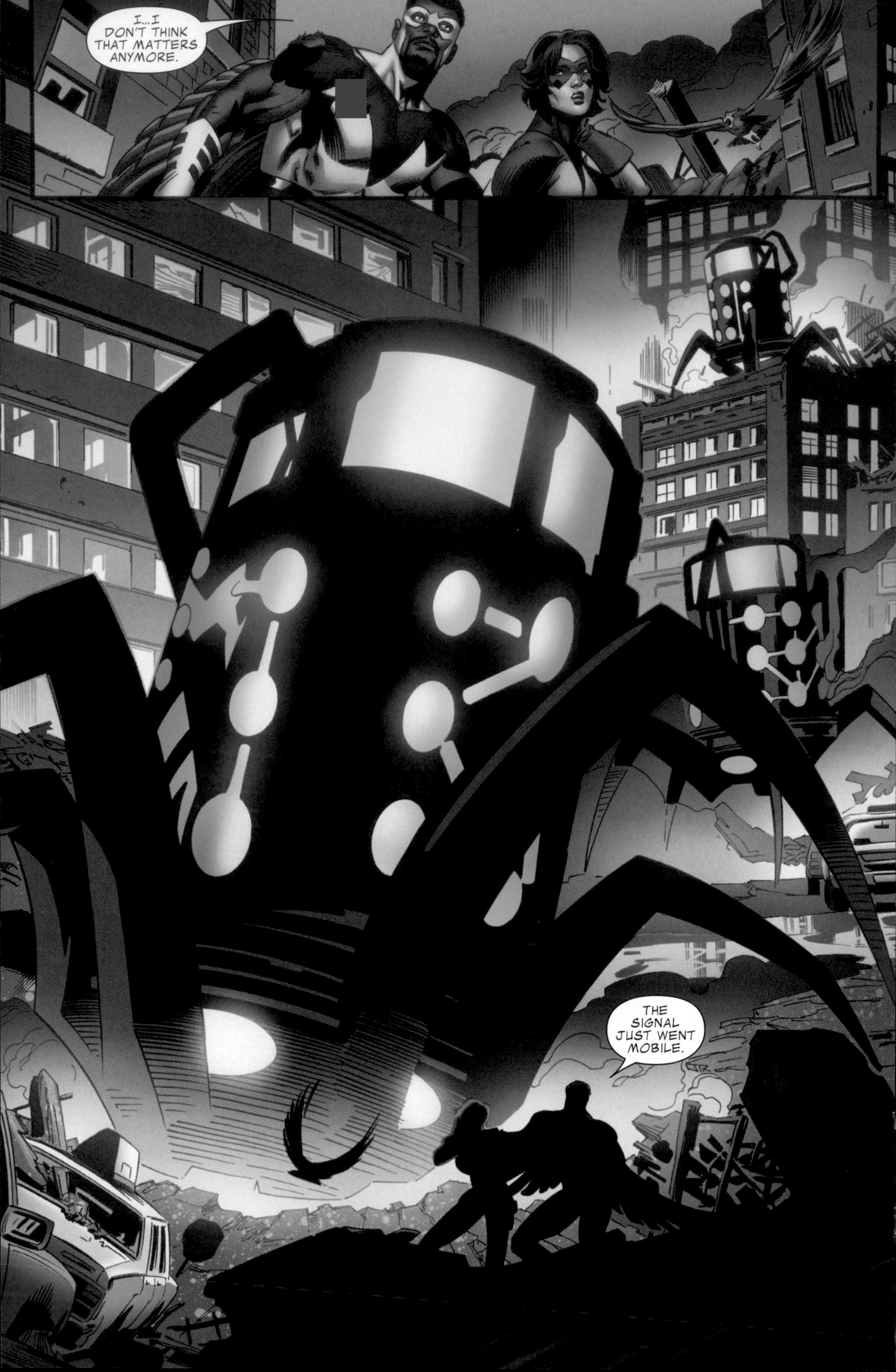
I...I DON'T THINK THAT MATTERS ANYMORE.
THE SIGNAL JUST WENT MOBILE.

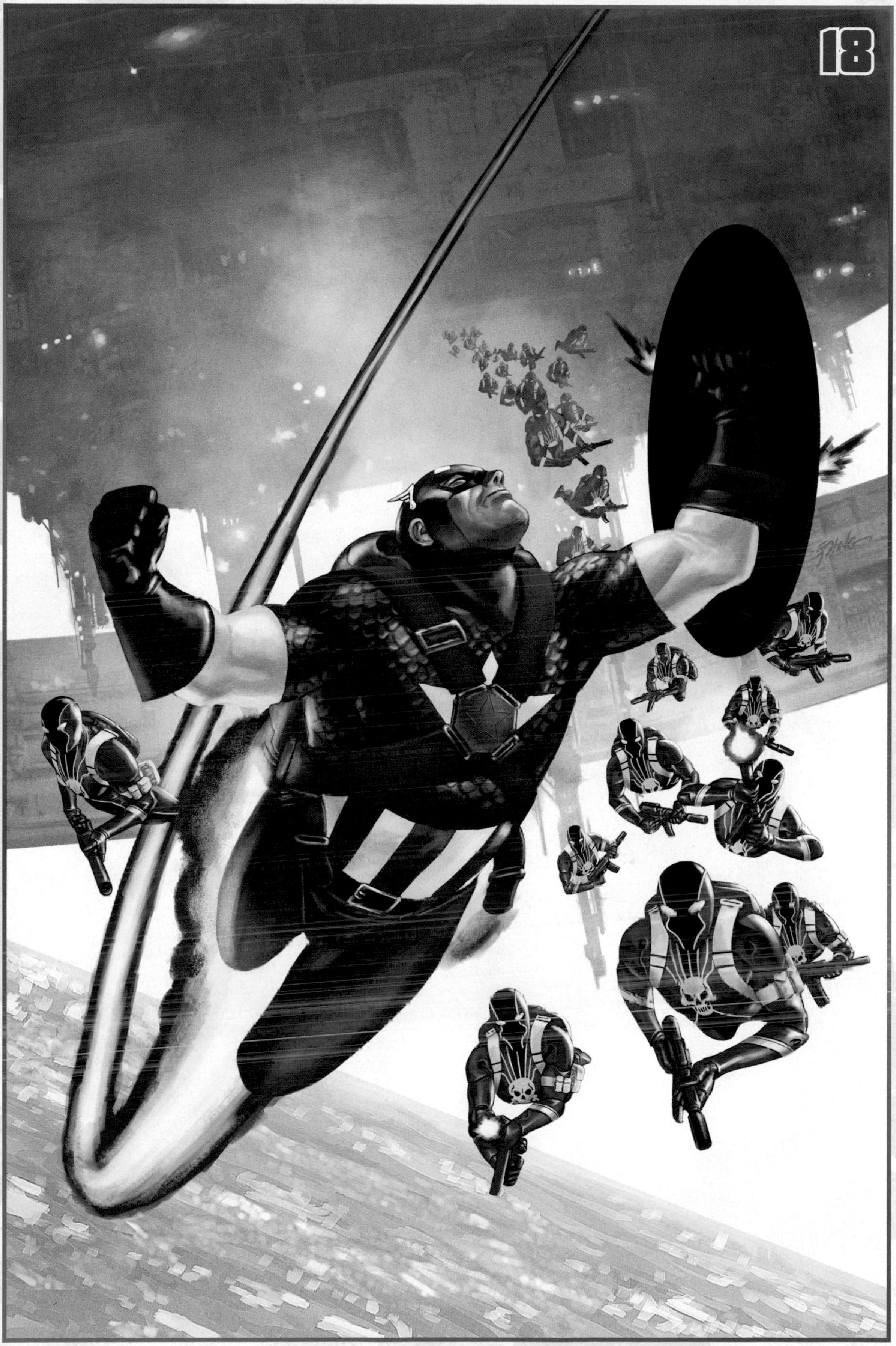
18

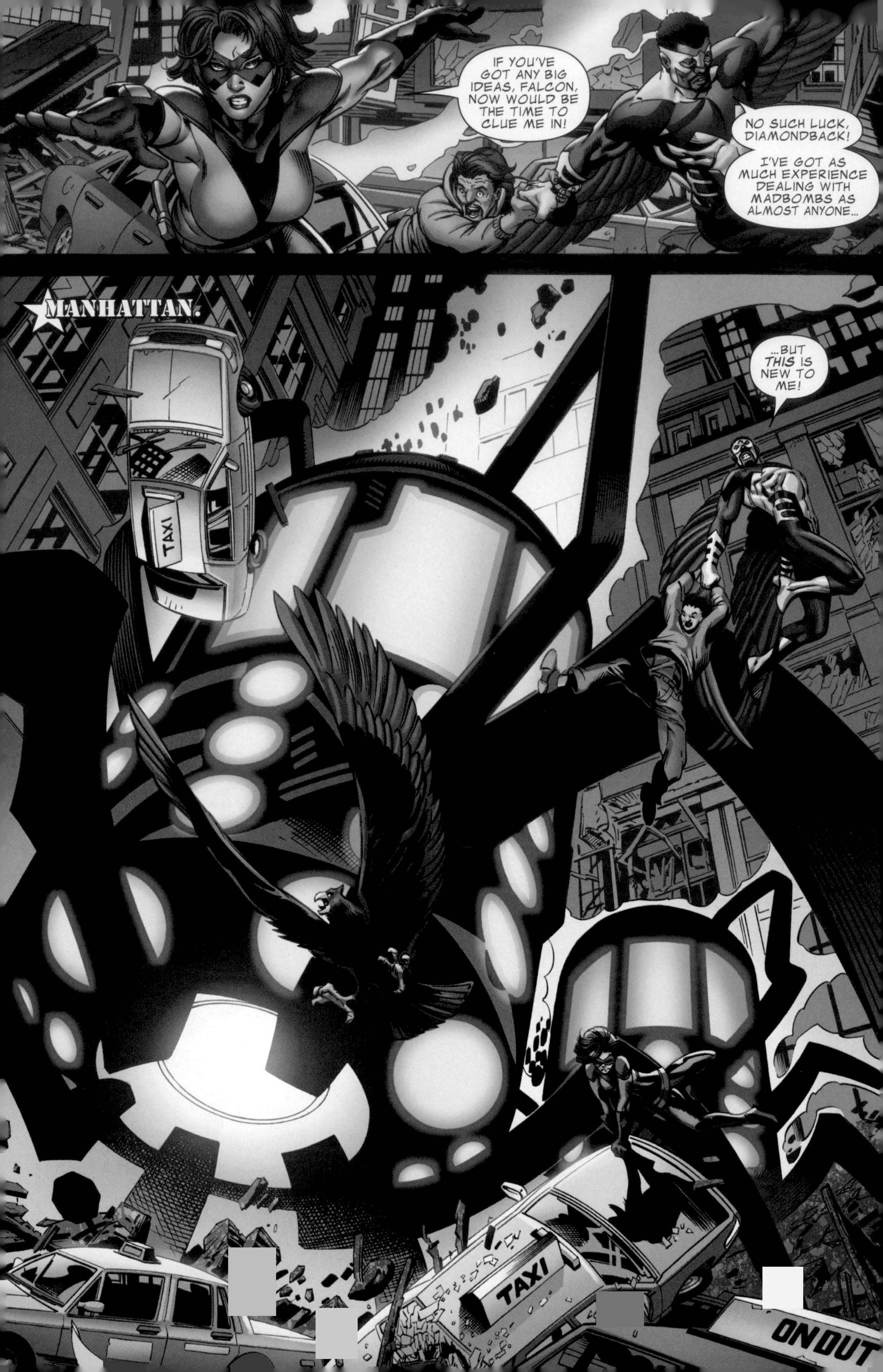
IF YOU'VE GOT ANY BIG IDEAS, FALCON, NOW WOULD BE THE TIME TO CLUE ME IN!
NO SUCH LUCK, DIAMONDBACK!
I'VE GOT AS MUCH EXPERIENCE DEALING WITH MADBOMBS AS ALMOST ANYONE...
MANHATTAN.
...BUT THIS IS NEW TO ME!
TAXI
TAXI
ONDUT

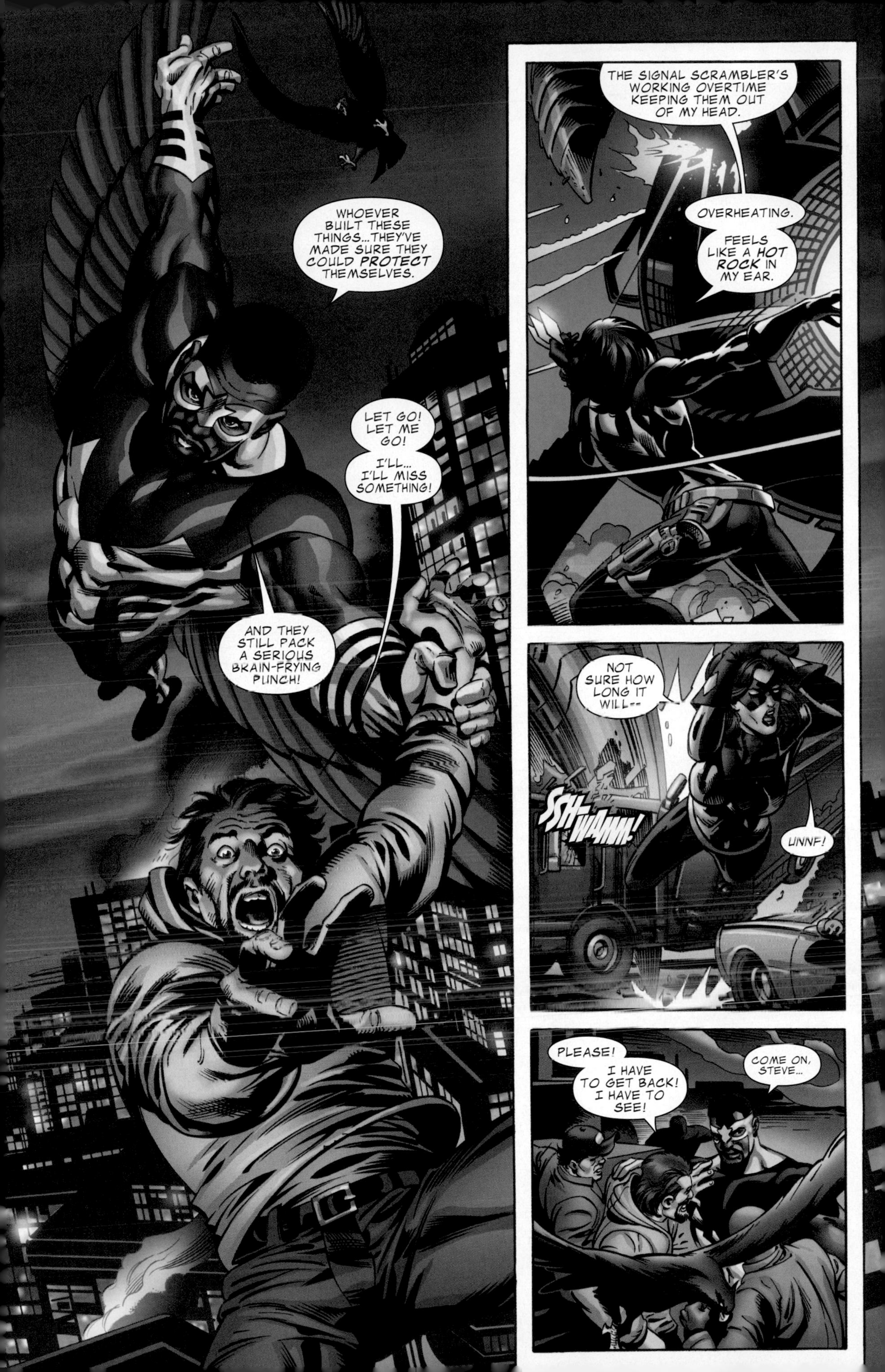
WHOEVER BUILT THESE THINGS...THEY'VE MADE SURE THEY COULD PROTECT THEMSELVES.
AND THEY STILL PACK A SERIOUS BRAIN-FRYING PUNCH!
LET GO! LET ME GO!
I'LL... I'LL MISS SOMETHING!
THE SIGNAL SCRAMBLER'S WORKING OVERTIME KEEPING THEM OUT OF MY HEAD.
OVERHEATING.
FEELS LIKE A HOT ROCK IN MY EAR.
NOT SURE HOW LONG IT WILL--
SSH-WAMM!
UNNF!
PLEASE!
I HAVE TO GET BACK! I HAVE TO SEE!
COME ON, STEVE...

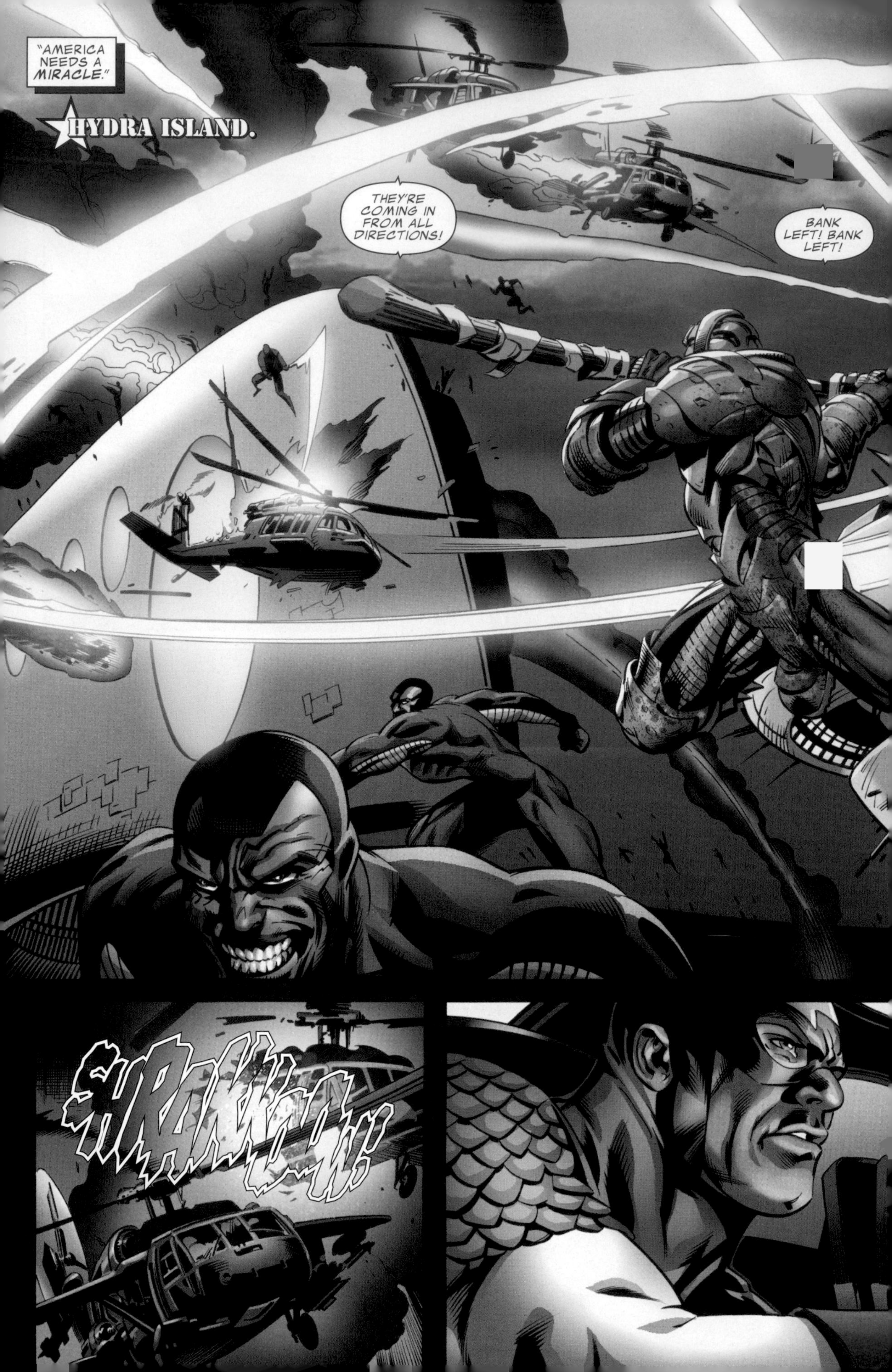
"AMERICA NEEDS A MIRACLE."
HYDRA ISLAND.
THEY'RE COMING IN FROM ALL DIRECTIONS!
BANK LEFT! BANK LEFT!

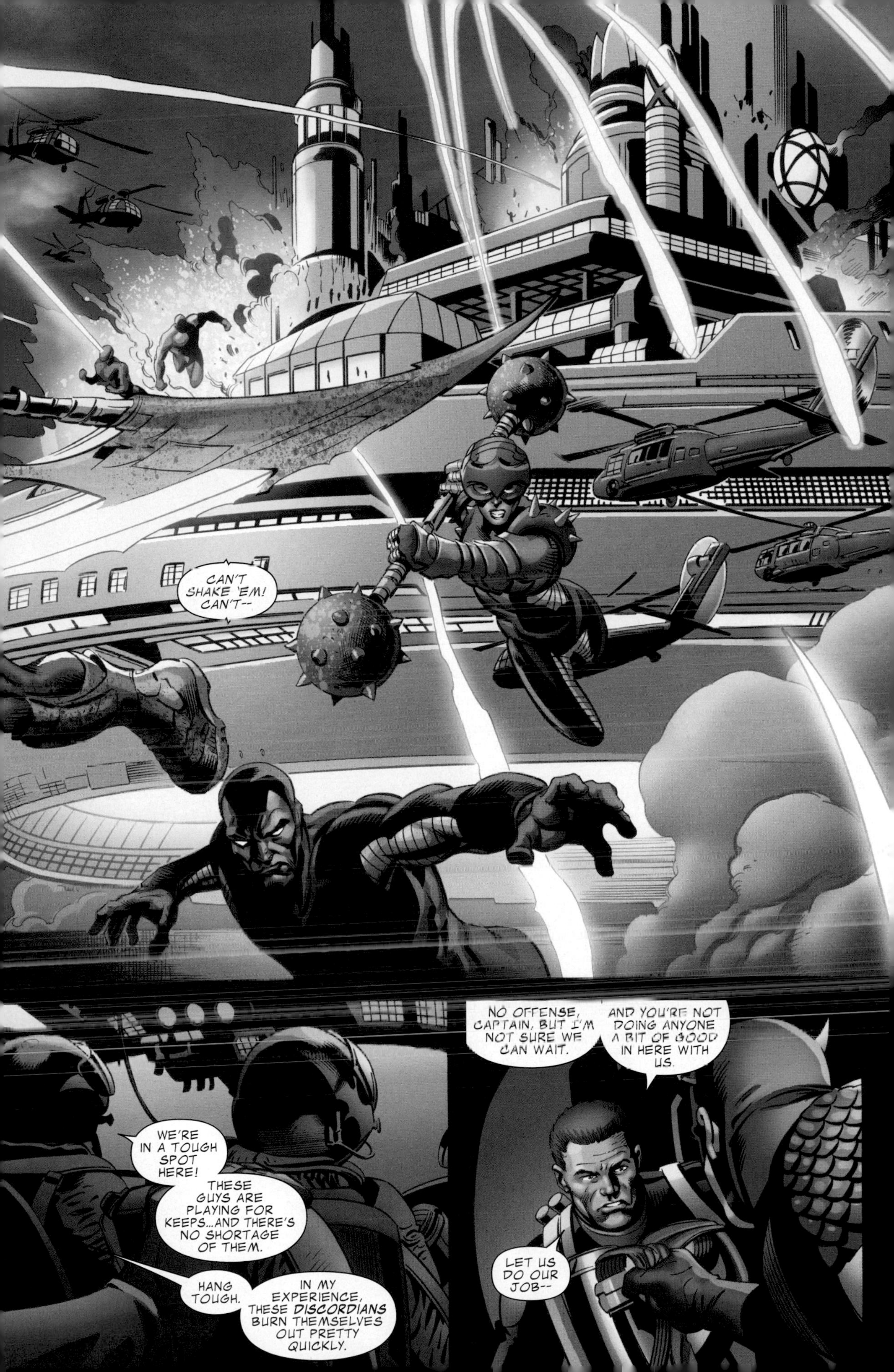
CAN'T SHAKE 'EM! CAN'T--
WE'RE IN A TOUGH SPOT HERE!
THESE GUYS ARE PLAYING FOR KEEPS...AND THERE'S NO SHORTAGE OF THEM.
HANG TOUGH.
IN MY EXPERIENCE, THESE DISCORDIANS BURN THEMSELVES OUT PRETTY QUICKLY.
NO OFFENSE, CAPTAIN, BUT I'M NOT SURE WE CAN WAIT.
AND YOU'RE NOT DOING ANYONE A BIT OF GOOD IN HERE WITH US.
LET US DO OUR JOB--

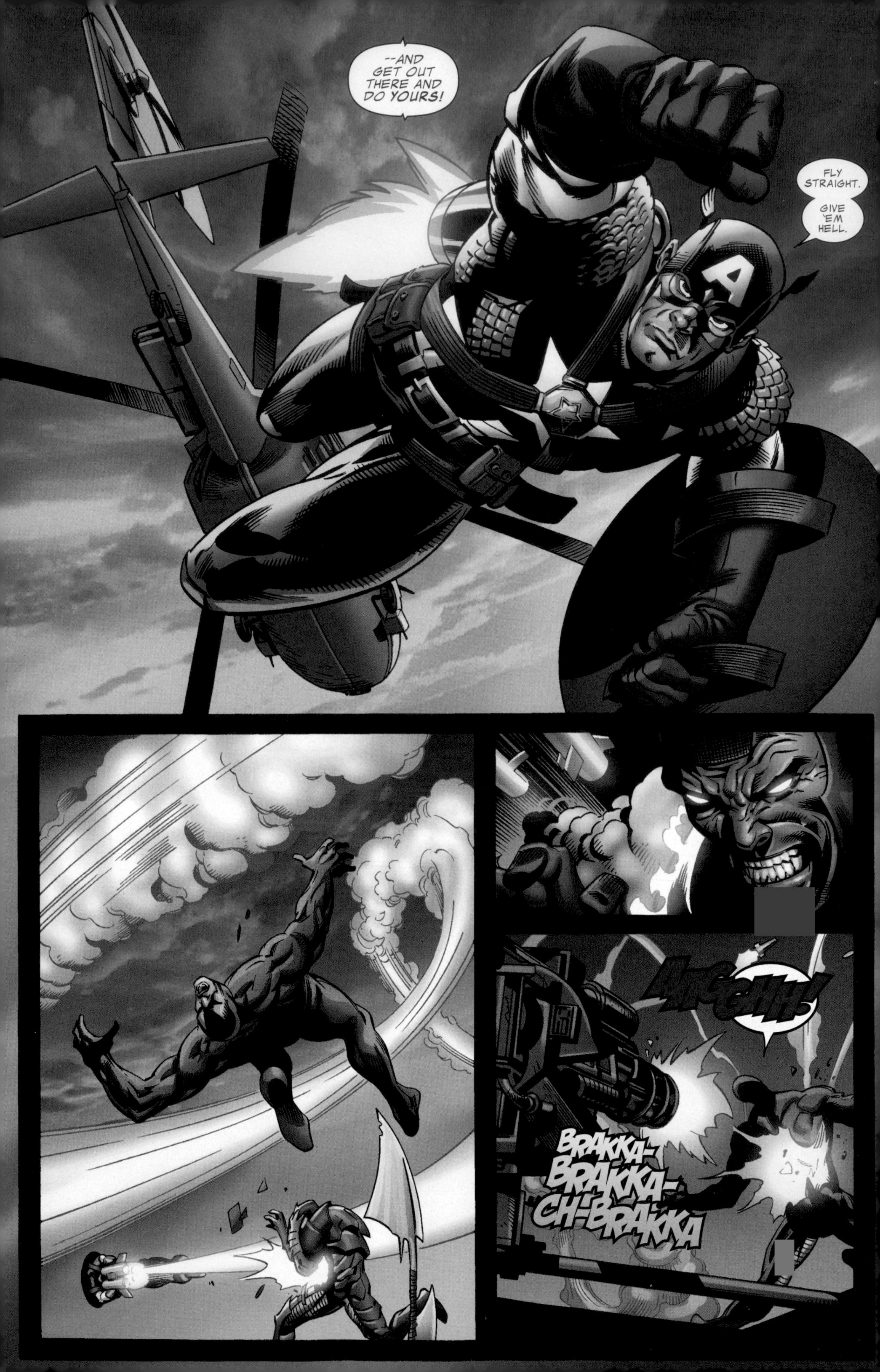
--AND GET OUT THERE AND DO YOURS!
FLY STRAIGHT.
GIVE 'EM HELL.
ARGGHH!
BRAKKA-BRAKKA-CH-BRAKKA

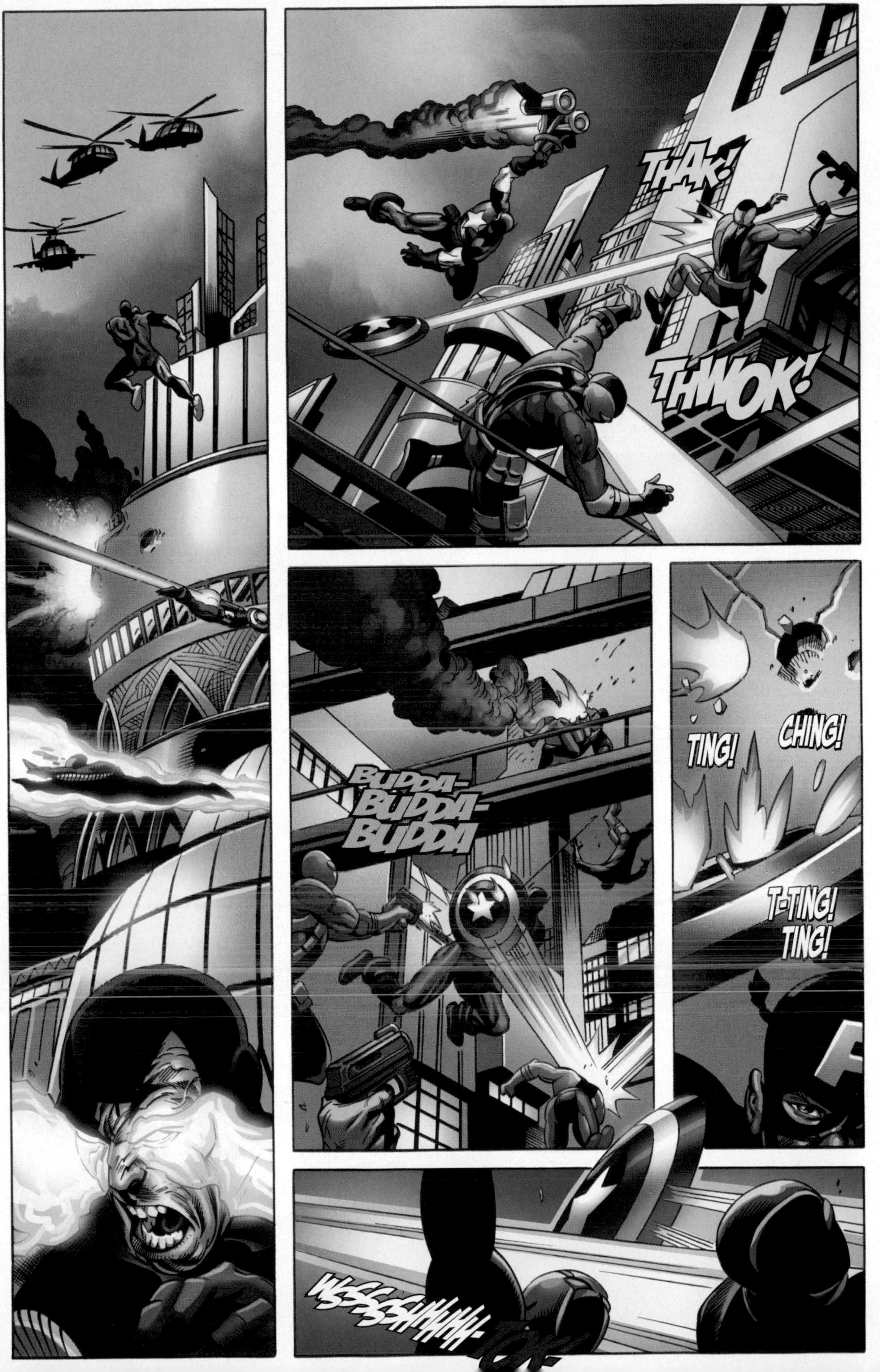
THAK!
THWOK!
BUDDA-BUDDA-BUDDA
TING!
CHING!
T-TING! TING!
WSSSHHHH-

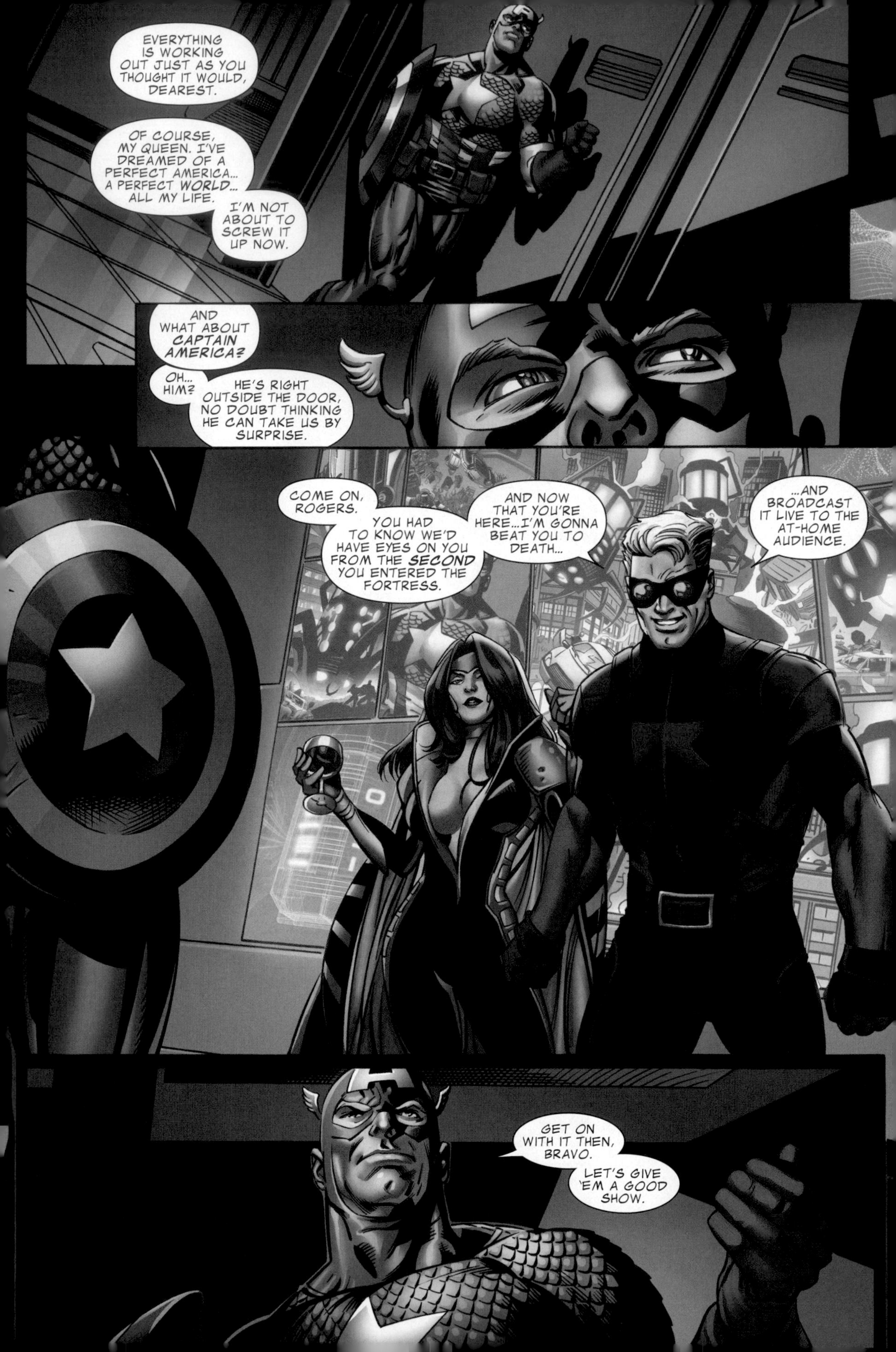
EVERYTHING IS WORKING OUT JUST AS YOU THOUGHT IT WOULD, DEAREST.
OF COURSE, MY QUEEN. I'VE DREAMED OF A PERFECT AMERICA... A PERFECT WORLD... ALL MY LIFE.
I'M NOT ABOUT TO SCREW IT UP NOW.
AND WHAT ABOUT CAPTAIN AMERICA?
OH... HIM?
HE'S RIGHT OUTSIDE THE DOOR, NO DOUBT THINKING HE CAN TAKE US BY SURPRISE.
COME ON, ROGERS.
YOU HAD TO KNOW WE'D HAVE EYES ON YOU FROM THE SECOND YOU ENTERED THE FORTRESS.
AND NOW THAT YOU'RE HERE...I'M GONNA BEAT YOU TO DEATH...
...AND BROADCAST IT LIVE TO THE AT-HOME AUDIENCE.
GET ON WITH IT THEN, BRAVO.
LET'S GIVE 'EM A GOOD SHOW.

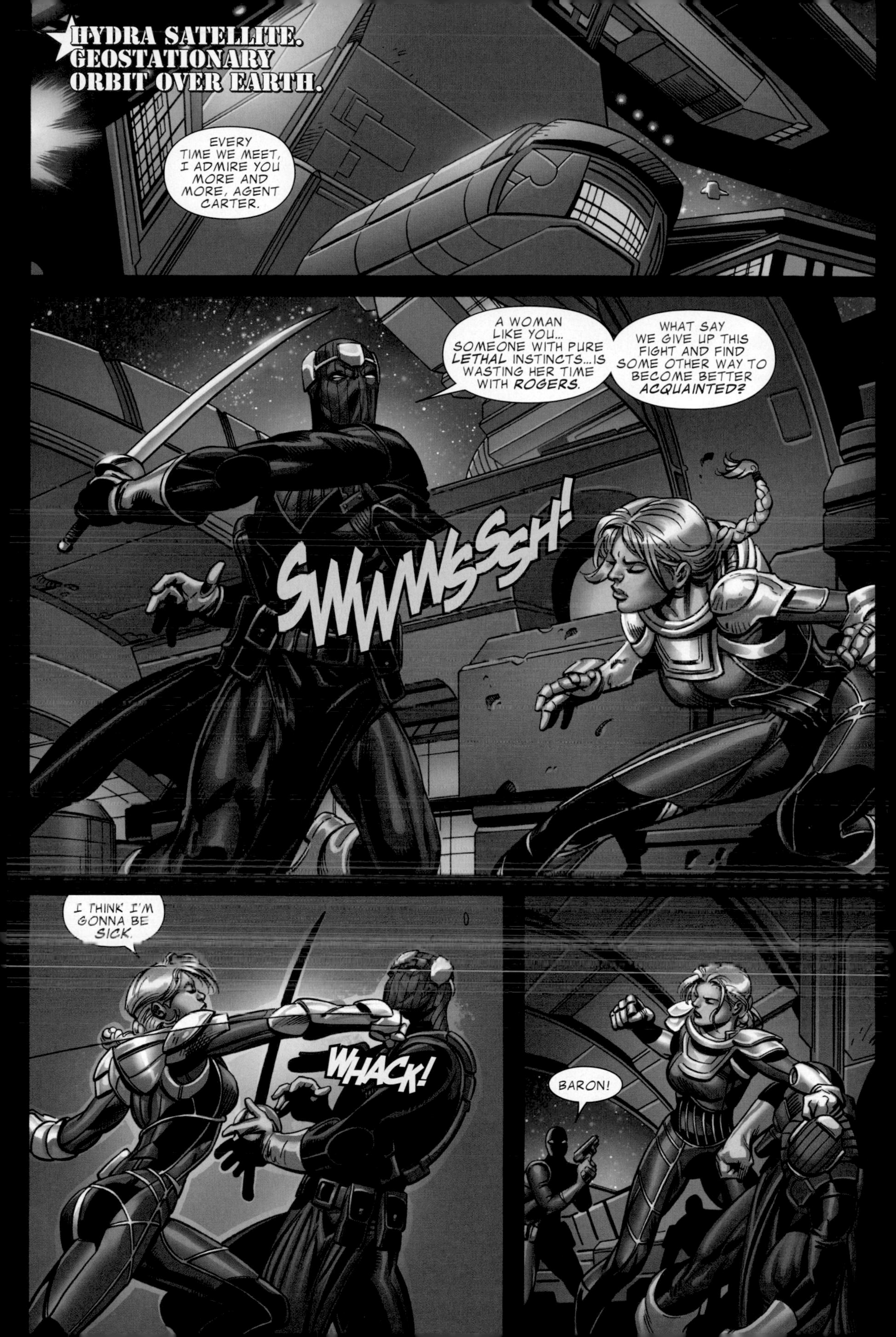
HYDRA SATELLITE. GEOSTATIONARY ORBIT OVER EARTH.
EVERY TIME WE MEET, I ADMIRE YOU MORE AND MORE, AGENT CARTER.
A WOMAN LIKE YOU... SOMEONE WITH PURE LETHAL INSTINCTS...IS WASTING HER TIME WITH ROGERS.
WHAT SAY WE GIVE UP THIS FIGHT AND FIND SOME OTHER WAY TO BECOME BETTER ACQUAINTED?
SWWWSSSH!
I THINK I'M GONNA BE SICK.
WHACK!
BARON!

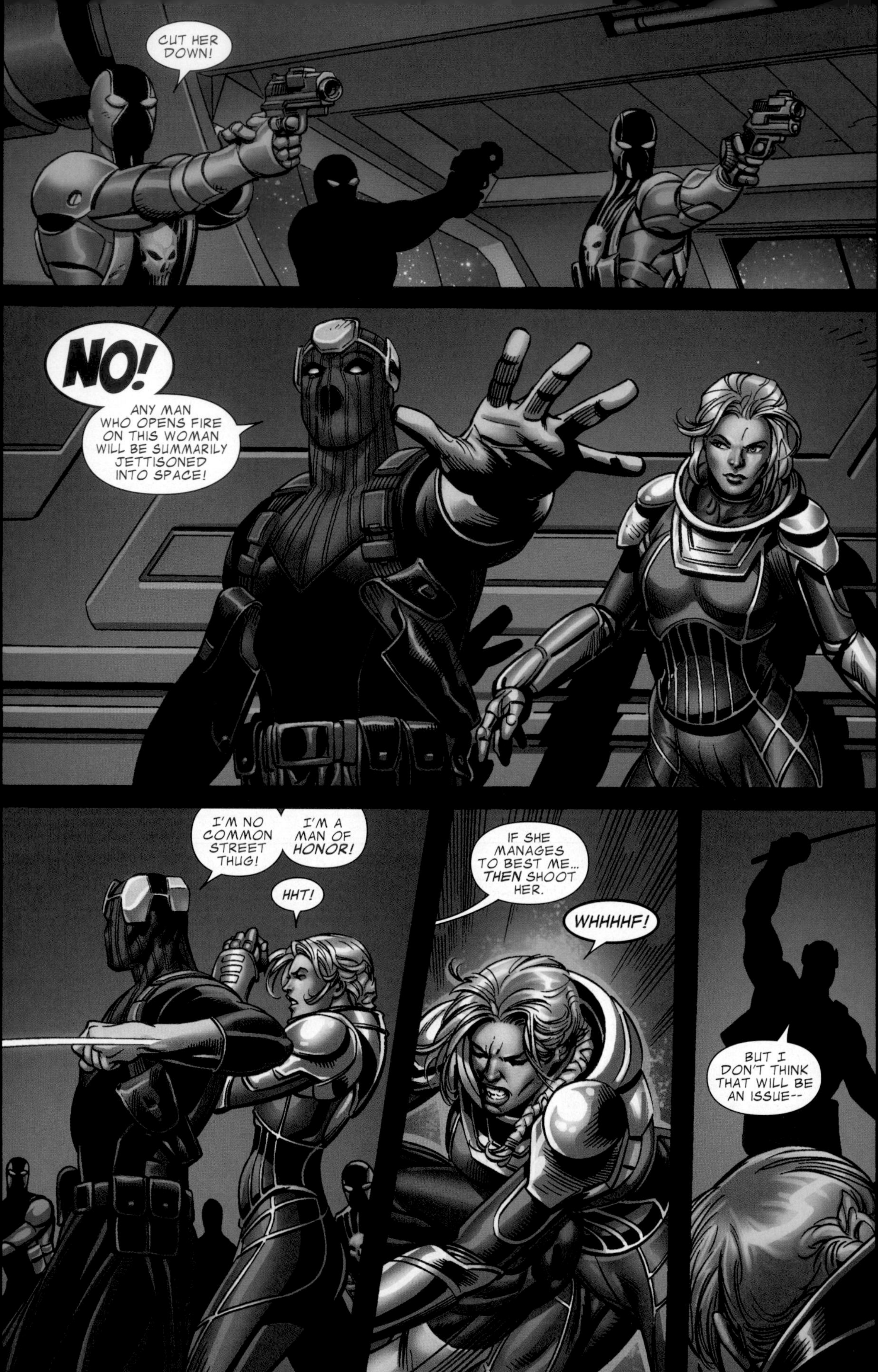
CUT HER DOWN!
NO!
ANY MAN WHO OPENS FIRE ON THIS WOMAN WILL BE SUMMARILY JETTISONED INTO SPACE!
I'M NO COMMON STREET THUG!
I'M A MAN OF HONOR!
HHT!
IF SHE MANAGES TO BEST ME... THEN SHOOT HER.
WHHHHF!
BUT I DON'T THINK THAT WILL BE AN ISSUE--

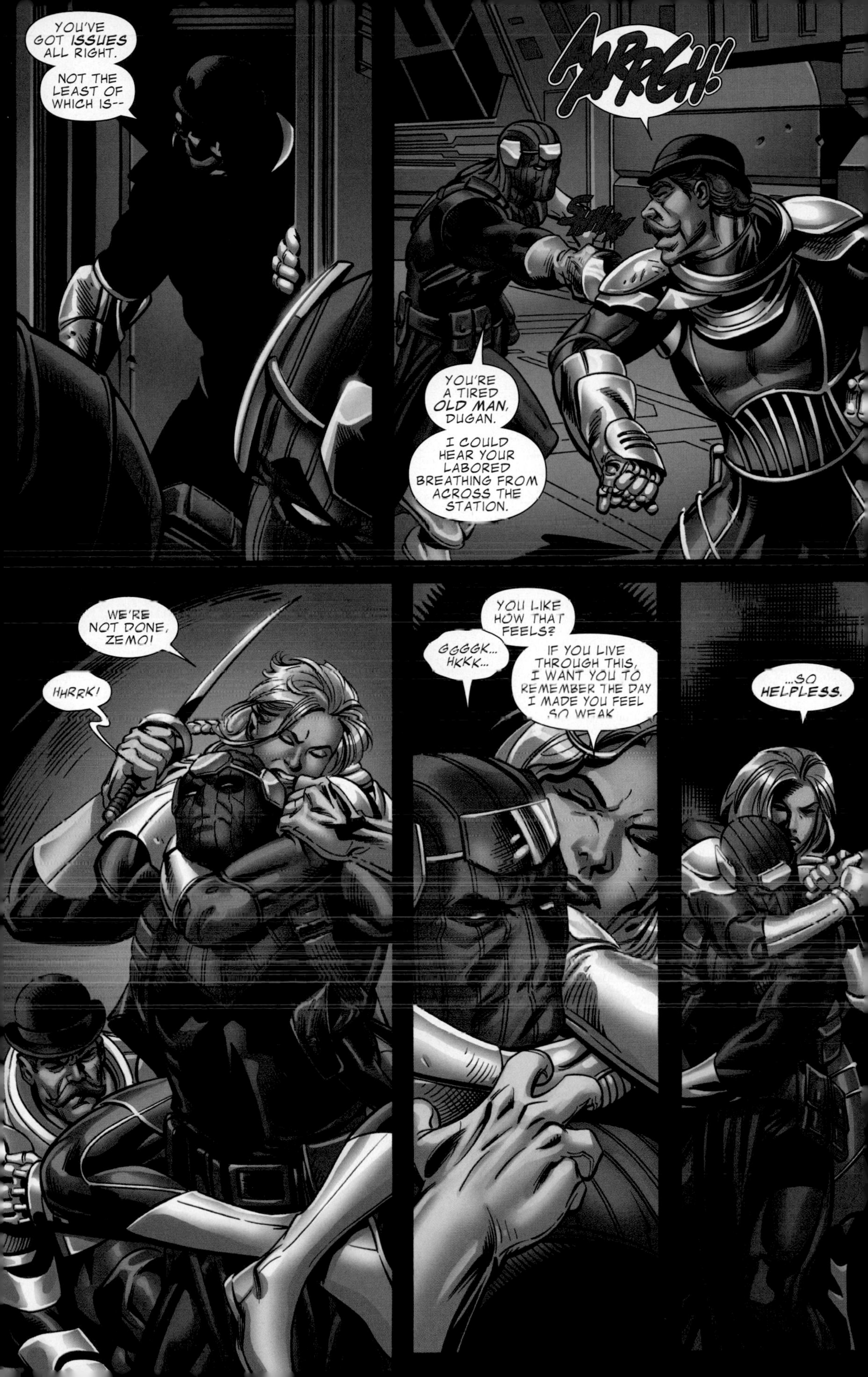
YOU'VE GOT ISSUES ALL RIGHT.
NOT THE LEAST OF WHICH IS--
AARGH!
YOU'RE A TIRED OLD MAN, DUGAN.
I COULD HEAR YOUR LABORED BREATHING FROM ACROSS THE STATION.
WE'RE NOT DONE, ZEMO!
HHRRK!
YOU LIKE HOW THAT FEELS?
GGGGK... HKKK...
IF YOU LIVE THROUGH THIS, I WANT YOU TO REMEMBER THE DAY I MADE YOU FEEL SO WEAK
...SO HELPLESS.

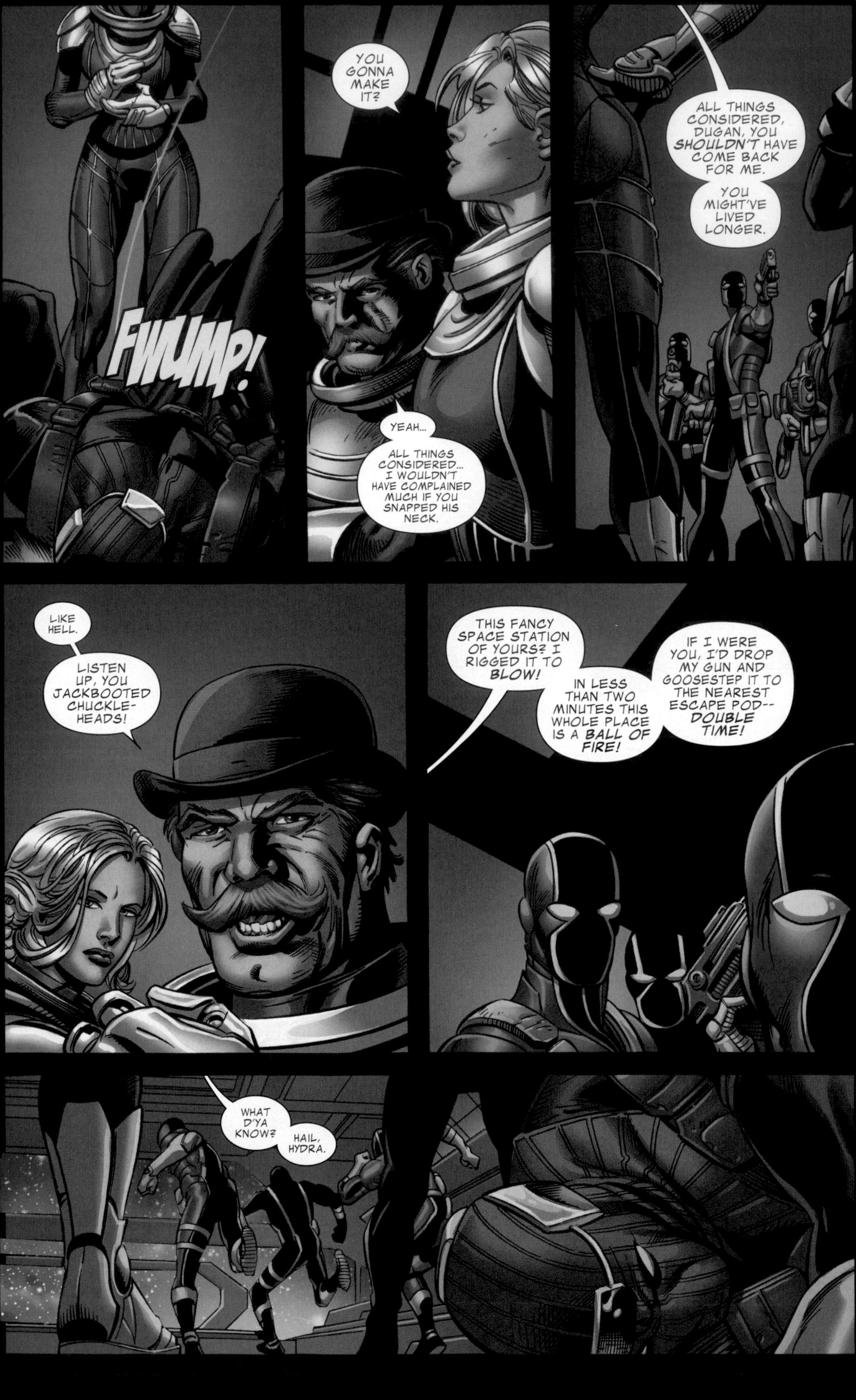
FWUMP!
YOU GONNA MAKE IT?
YEAH...
ALL THINGS CONSIDERED... I WOULDN'T HAVE COMPLAINED MUCH IF YOU SNAPPED HIS NECK.
ALL THINGS CONSIDERED, DUGAN, YOU SHOULDN'T HAVE COME BACK FOR ME.
YOU MIGHT'VE LIVED LONGER.
LIKE HELL.
LISTEN UP, YOU JACKBOOTED CHUCKLE-HEADS!
THIS FANCY SPACE STATION OF YOURS? I RIGGED IT TO BLOW!
IN LESS THAN TWO MINUTES THIS WHOLE PLACE IS A BALL OF FIRE!
IF I WERE YOU, I'D DROP MY GUN AND GOOSESTEP IT TO THE NEAREST ESCAPE POD-- DOUBLE TIME!
WHAT D'YA KNOW?
HAIL, HYDRA.

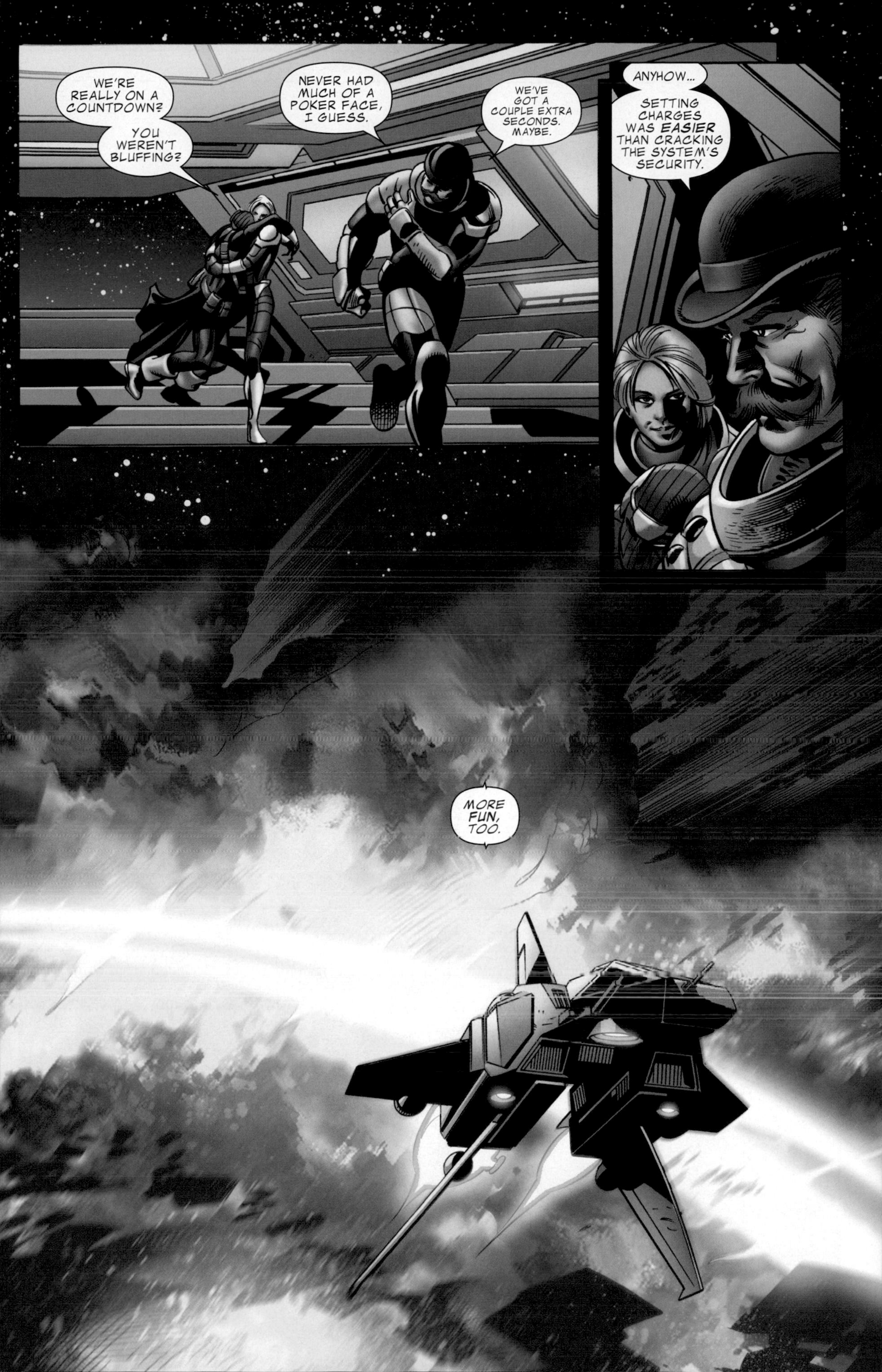
WE'RE REALLY ON A COUNTDOWN?
YOU WEREN'T BLUFFING?
NEVER HAD MUCH OF A POKER FACE, I GUESS.
WE'VE GOT A COUPLE EXTRA SECONDS. MAYBE.
ANYHOW...
SETTING CHARGES WAS EASIER THAN CRACKING THE SYSTEM'S SECURITY.
MORE FUN, TOO.

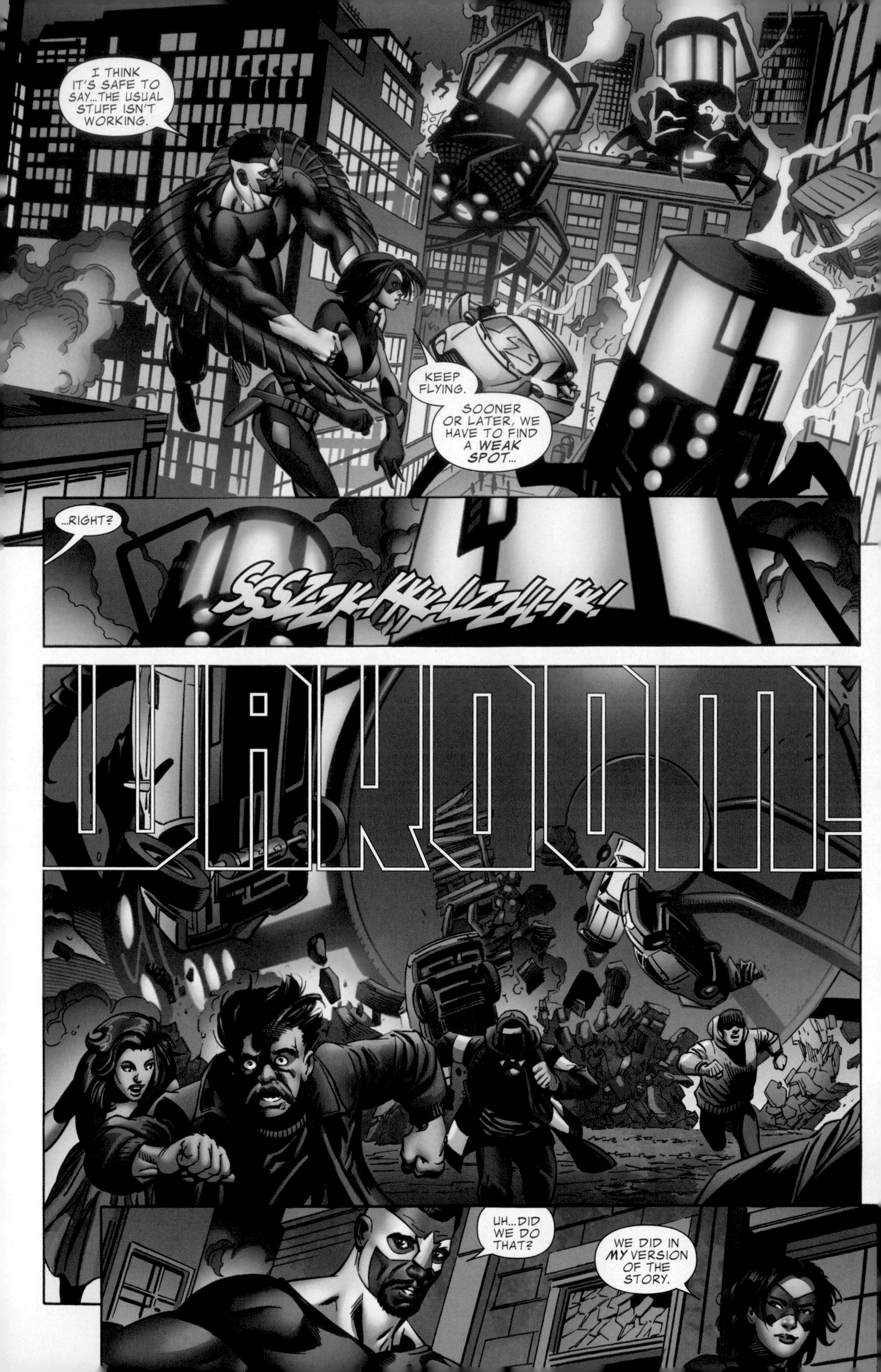
I THINK IT'S SAFE TO SAY...THE USUAL STUFF ISN'T WORKING.
KEEP FLYING.
SOONER OR LATER, WE HAVE TO FIND A WEAK SPOT...
...RIGHT?
SSSZZK-KK-LLZZLL-K!
UH...DID WE DO THAT?
WE DID IN MY VERSION OF THE STORY.

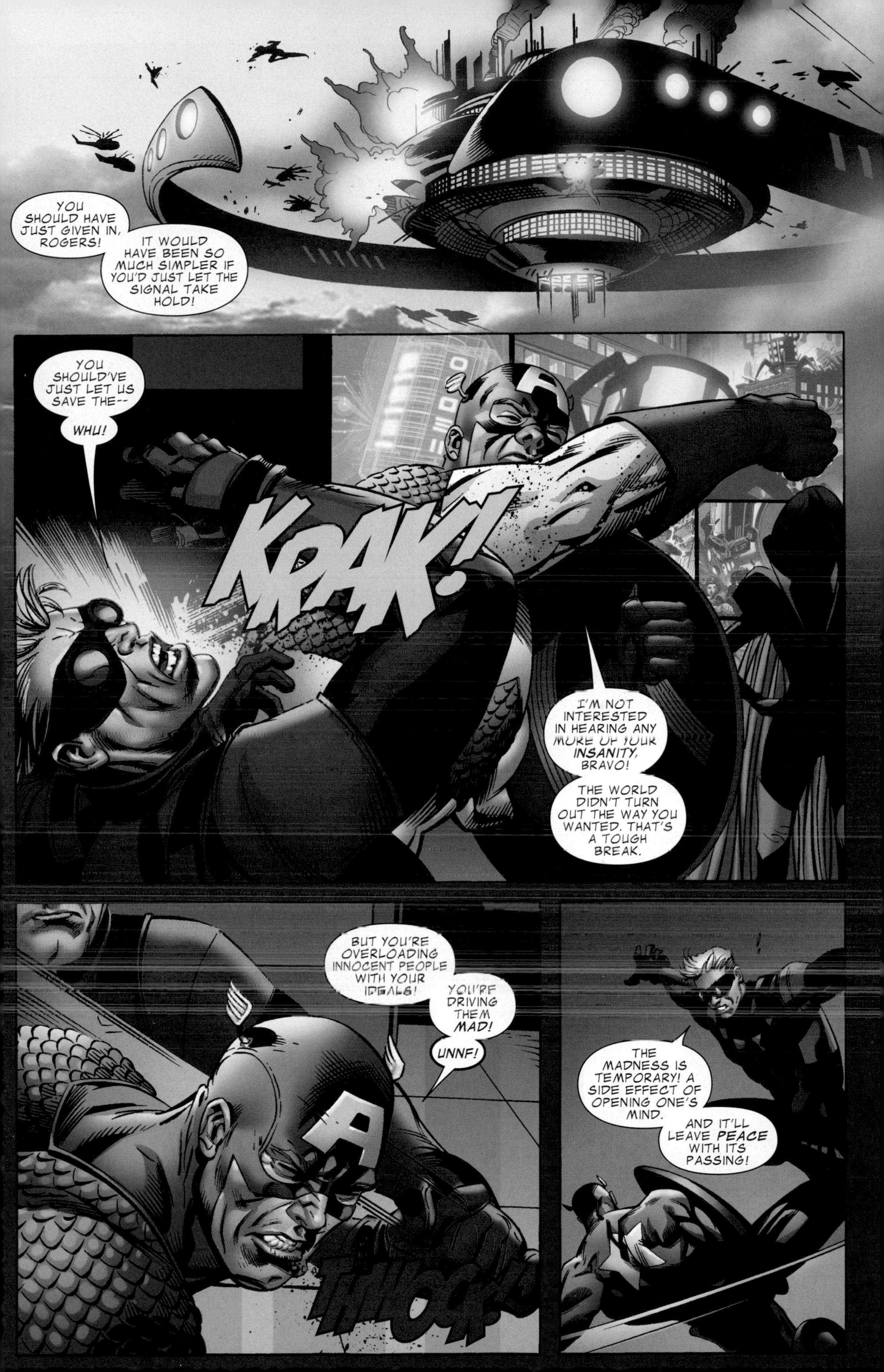

YOU SHOULD HAVE JUST GIVEN IN, ROGERS!
IT WOULD HAVE BEEN SO MUCH SIMPLER IF YOU'D JUST LET THE SIGNAL TAKE HOLD!
YOU SHOULD'VE JUST LET US SAVE THE--
WHU!
KRAK!
I'M NOT INTERESTED IN HEARING ANY MORE OF YOUR INSANITY, BRAVO!
THE WORLD DIDN'T TURN OUT THE WAY YOU WANTED. THAT'S A TOUGH BREAK.
BUT YOU'RE OVERLOADING INNOCENT PEOPLE WITH YOUR IDEALS!
YOU'RE DRIVING THEM MAD!
UNNF!
THE MADNESS IS TEMPORARY! A SIDE EFFECT OF OPENING ONE'S MIND.
AND IT'LL LEAVE PEACE WITH ITS PASSING!

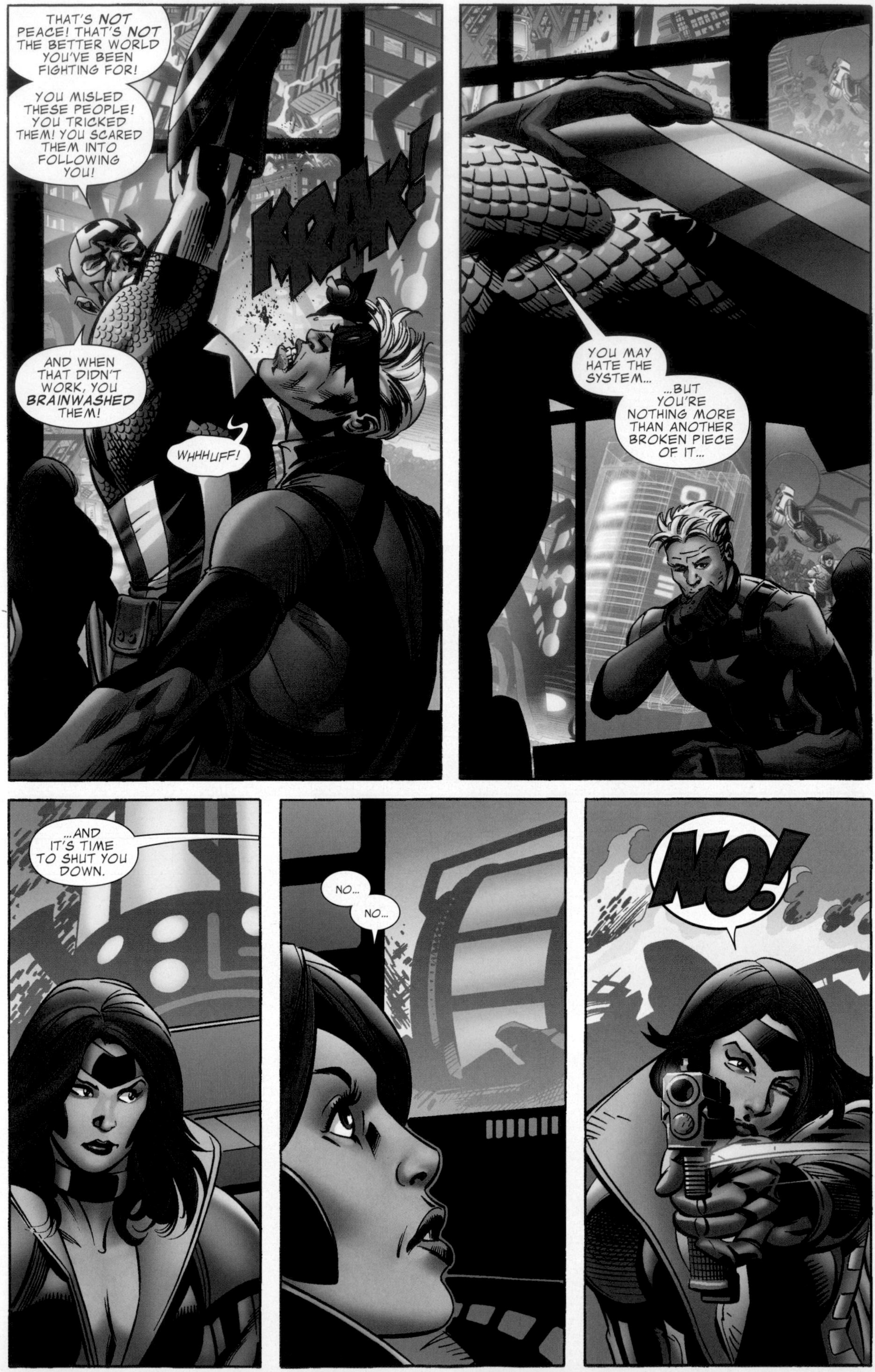
THAT'S NOT PEACE! THAT'S NOT THE BETTER WORLD YOU'VE BEEN FIGHTING FOR!
YOU MISLED THESE PEOPLE! YOU TRICKED THEM! YOU SCARED THEM INTO FOLLOWING YOU!
KRAK!
AND WHEN THAT DIDN'T WORK, YOU BRAINWASHED THEM!
WHHHUFF!
YOU MAY HATE THE SYSTEM...
...BUT YOU'RE NOTHING MORE THAN ANOTHER BROKEN PIECE OF IT...
...AND IT'S TIME TO SHUT YOU DOWN.
NO...
NO...
NO!

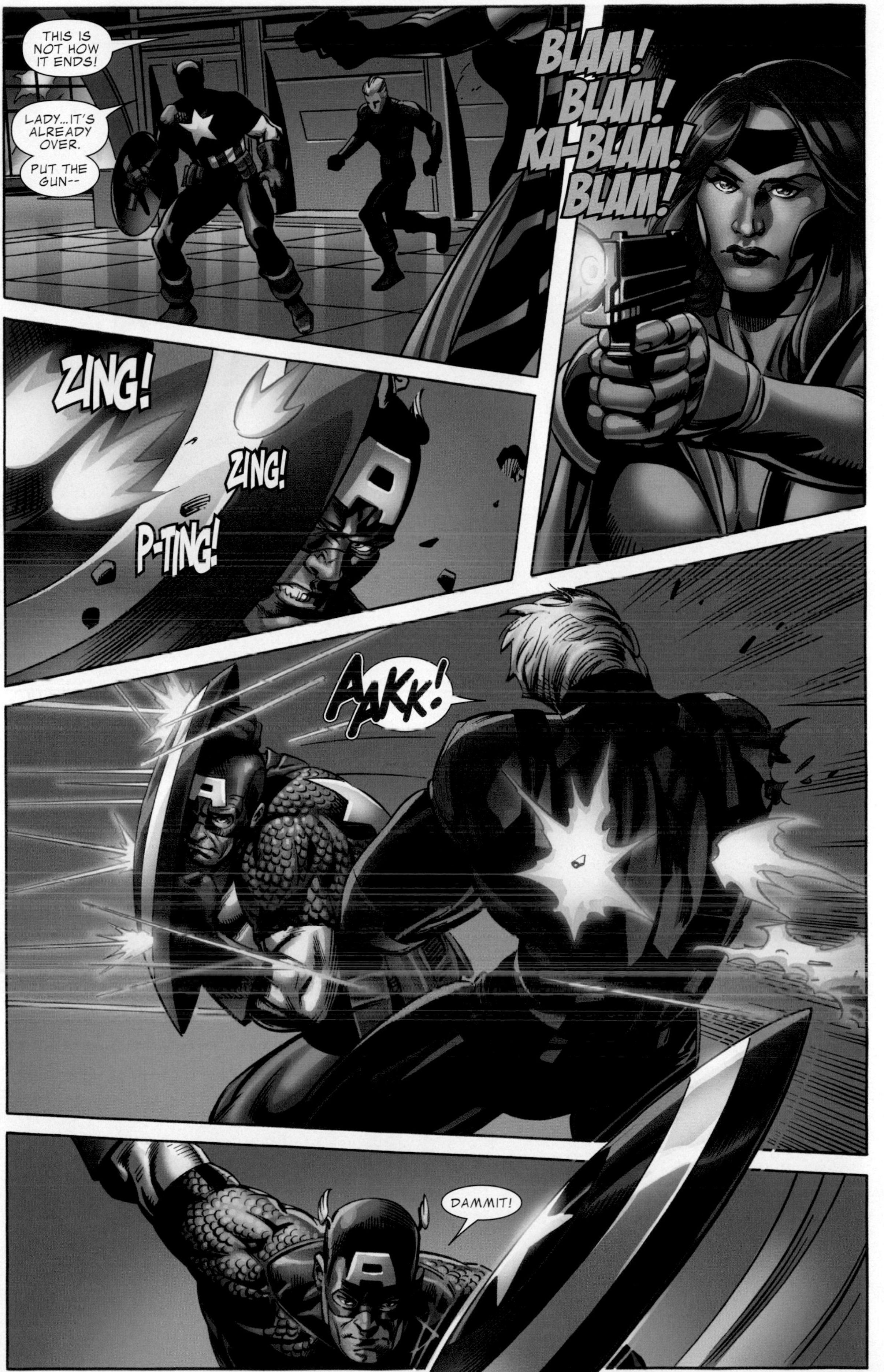
THIS IS NOT HOW IT ENDS!
LADY...IT'S ALREADY OVER.
PUT THE GUN--
BLAM! BLAM! KA-BLAM! BLAM!
ZING!
ZING!
P-TING!
AAKK!
DAMMIT!

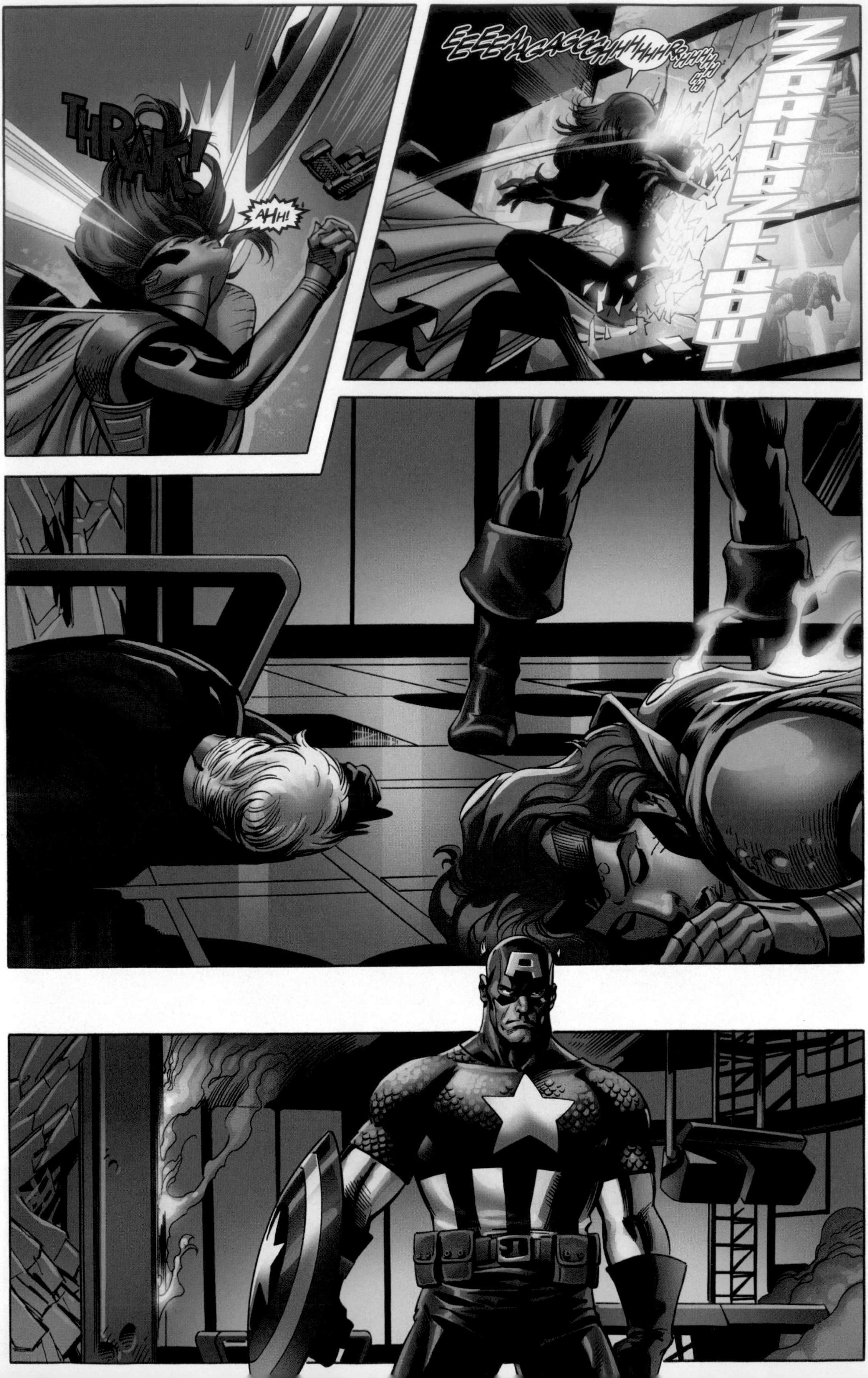
THRAK!
AHH!

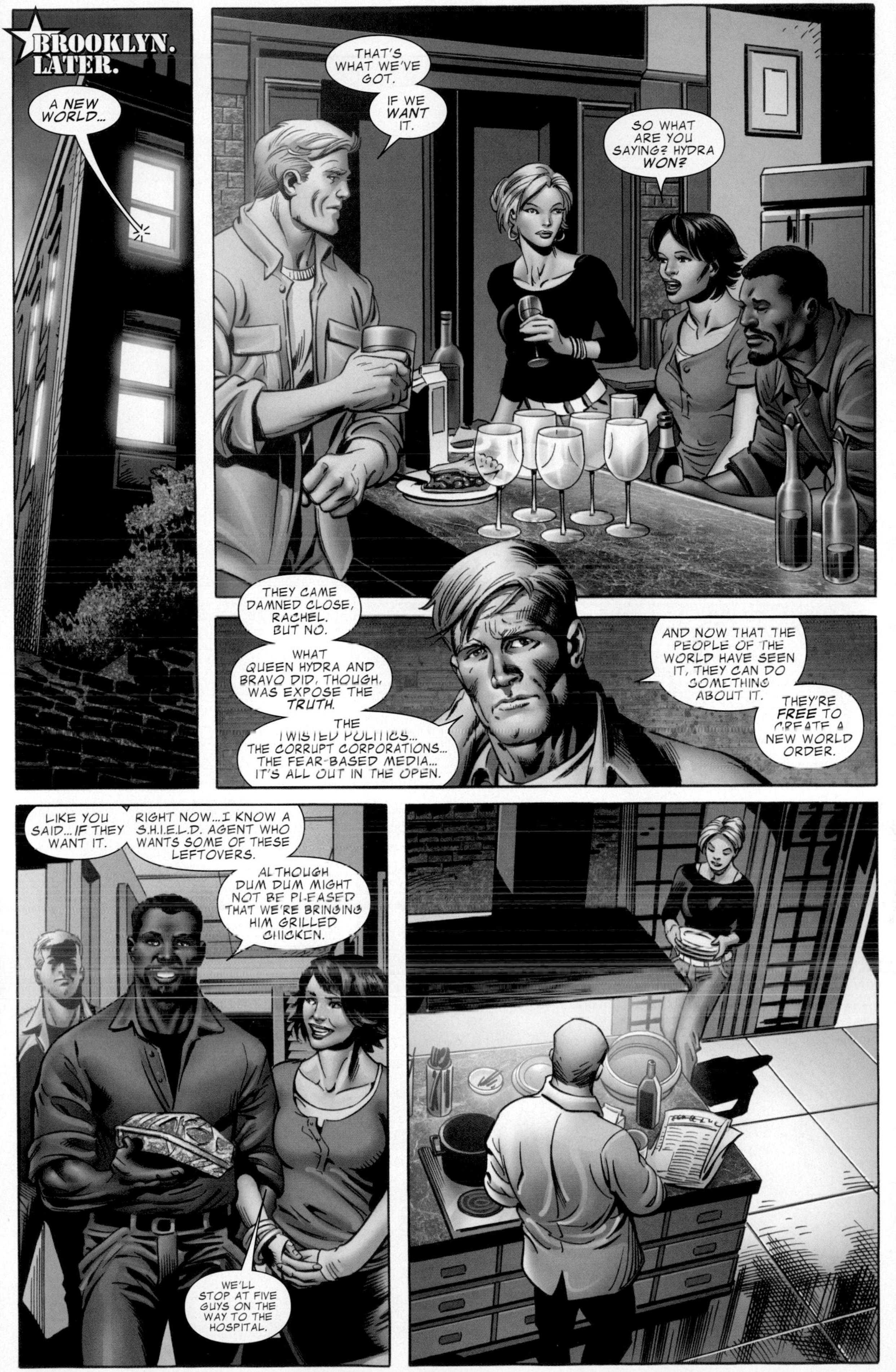
BROOKLYN. LATER.
A NEW WORLD...
THAT'S WHAT WE'VE GOT.
IF WE WANT IT.
SO WHAT ARE YOU SAYING? HYDRA WON?
THEY CAME DAMNED CLOSE, RACHEL. BUT NO.
WHAT QUEEN HYDRA AND BRAVO DID, THOUGH, WAS EXPOSE THE TRUTH.
THE TWISTED POLITICS... THE CORRUPT CORPORATIONS... THE FEAR-BASED MEDIA... IT'S ALL OUT IN THE OPEN.
AND NOW THAT THE PEOPLE OF THE WORLD HAVE SEEN IT, THEY CAN DO SOMETHING ABOUT IT.
THEY'RE FREE TO CREATE A NEW WORLD ORDER.
LIKE YOU SAID... IF THEY WANT IT.
RIGHT NOW...I KNOW A S.H.I.E.L.D. AGENT WHO WANTS SOME OF THESE LEFTOVERS.
ALTHOUGH DUM DUM MIGHT NOT BE PLEASED THAT WE'RE BRINGING HIM GRILLED CHICKEN.
WE'LL STOP AT FIVE GUYS ON THE WAY TO THE HOSPITAL.

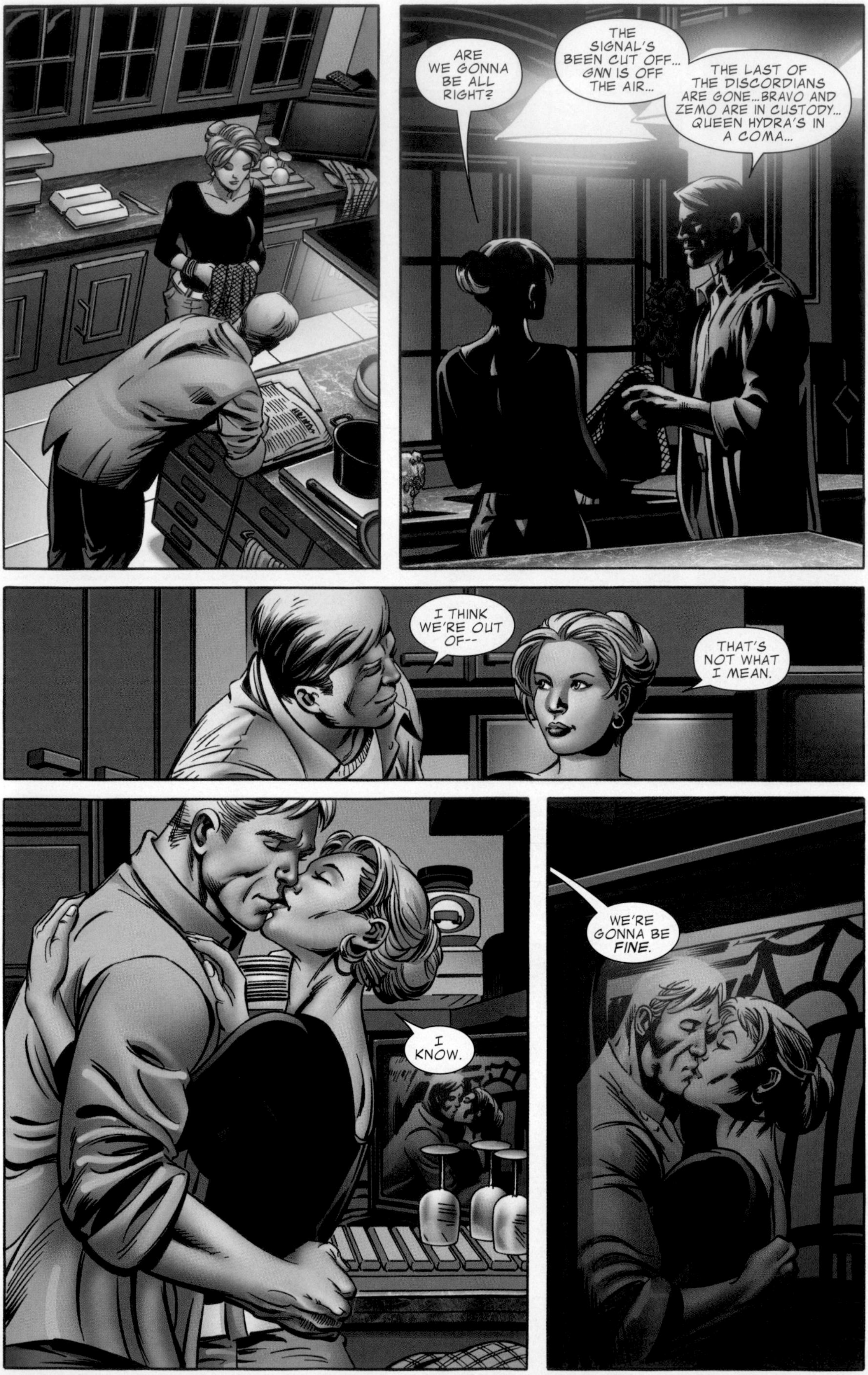

ARE WE GONNA BE ALL RIGHT?
THE SIGNAL'S BEEN CUT OFF... GNN IS OFF THE AIR...
THE LAST OF THE DISCORDIANS ARE GONE...BRAVO AND ZEMO ARE IN CUSTODY... QUEEN HYDRA'S IN A COMA...
I THINK WE'RE OUT OF--
THAT'S NOT WHAT I MEAN.
I KNOW.
WE'RE GONNA BE *FINE*.

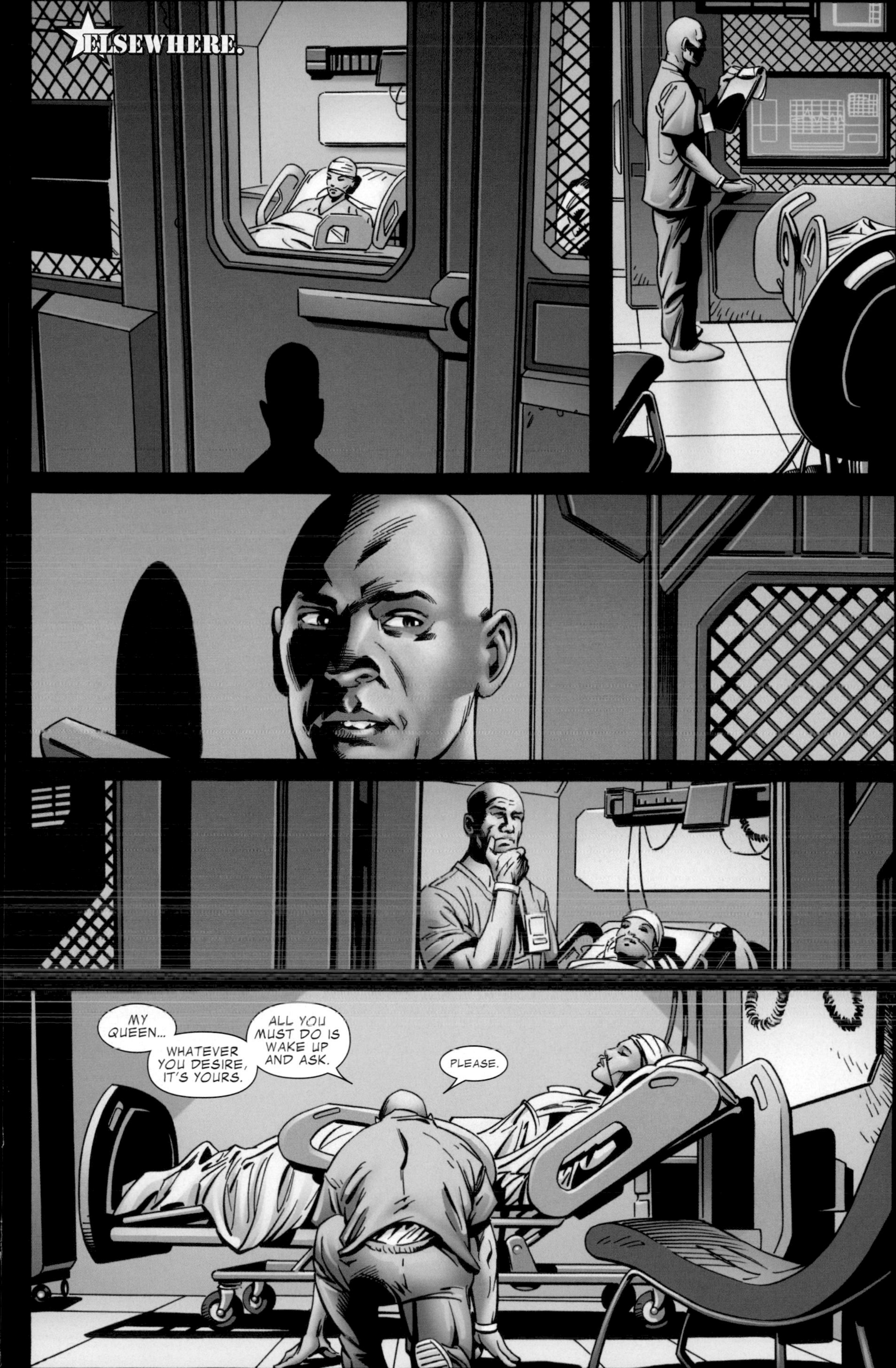
ELSEWHERE.
MY QUEEN...
WHATEVER YOU DESIRE, IT'S YOURS.
ALL YOU MUST DO IS WAKE UP AND ASK.
PLEASE.

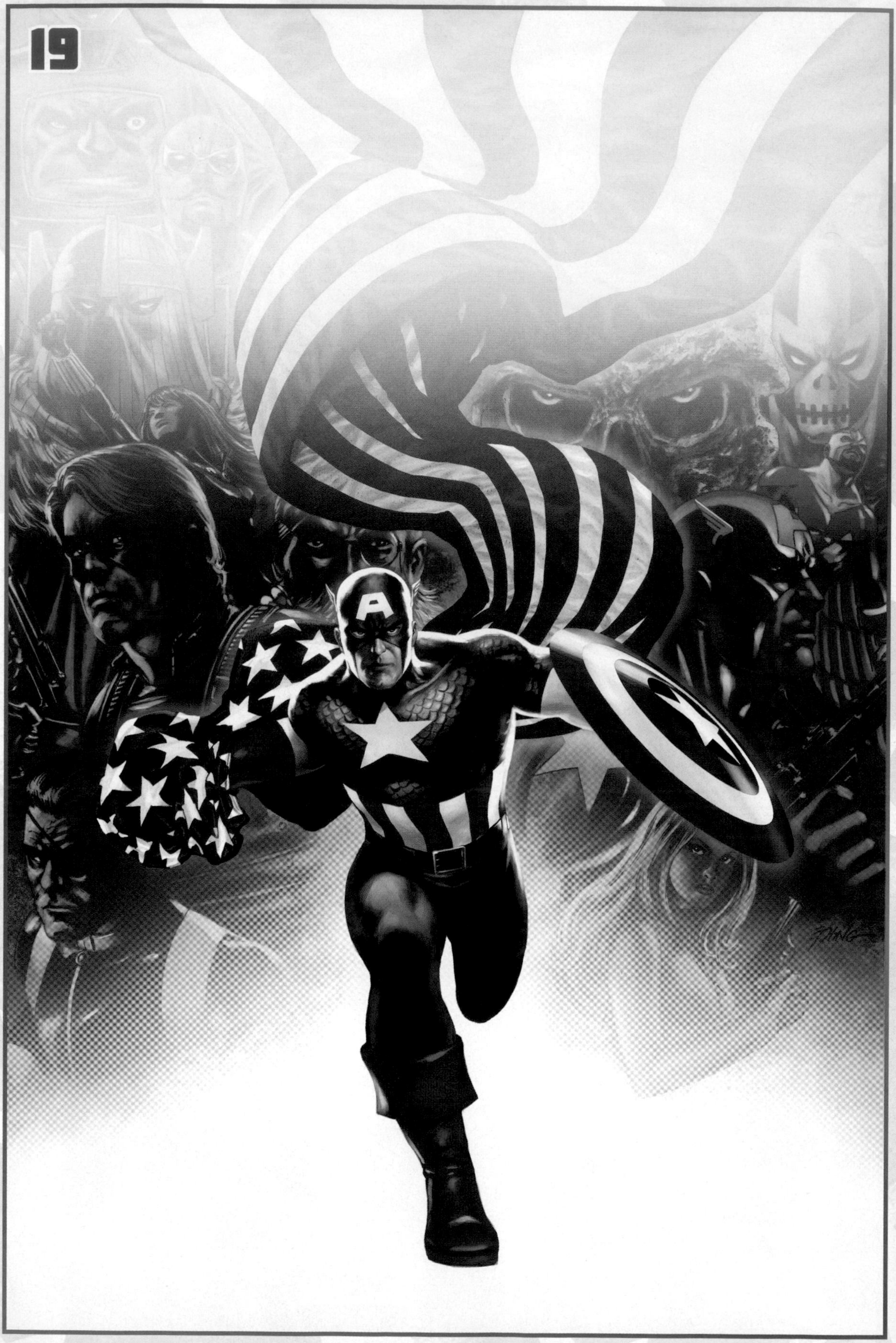
19

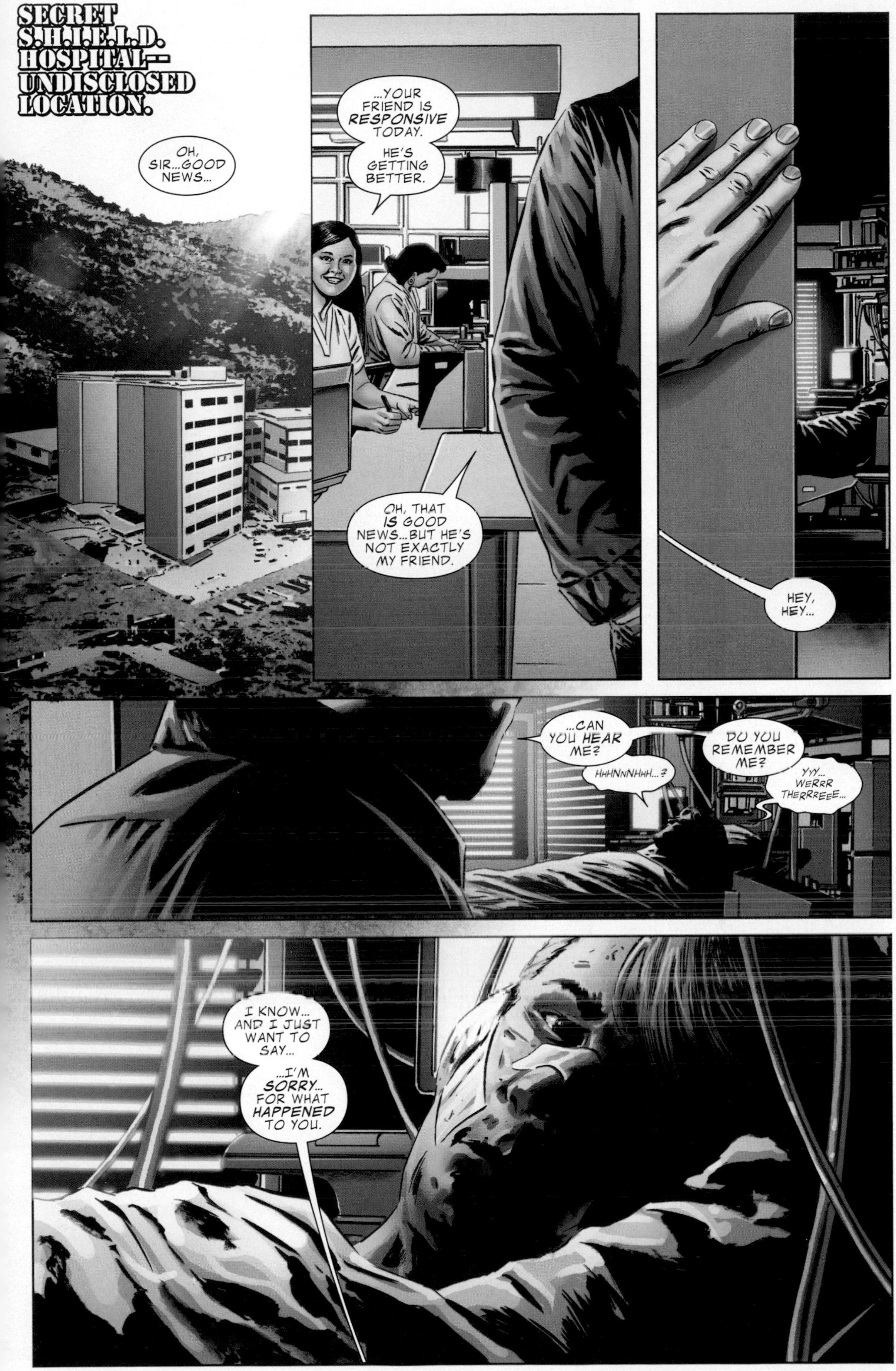
SECRET S.H.I.E.L.D. HOSPITAL-- UNDISCLOSED LOCATION.
OH, SIR...GOOD NEWS...
...YOUR FRIEND IS RESPONSIVE TODAY.
HE'S GETTING BETTER.
OH, THAT IS GOOD NEWS...BUT HE'S NOT EXACTLY MY FRIEND.
HEY, HEY...
...CAN YOU HEAR ME?
HHHNNHHH...?
DO YOU REMEMBER ME?
YYY... WERRR THERRREEE...
I KNOW... AND I JUST WANT TO SAY...
...I'M SORRY... FOR WHAT HAPPENED TO YOU.

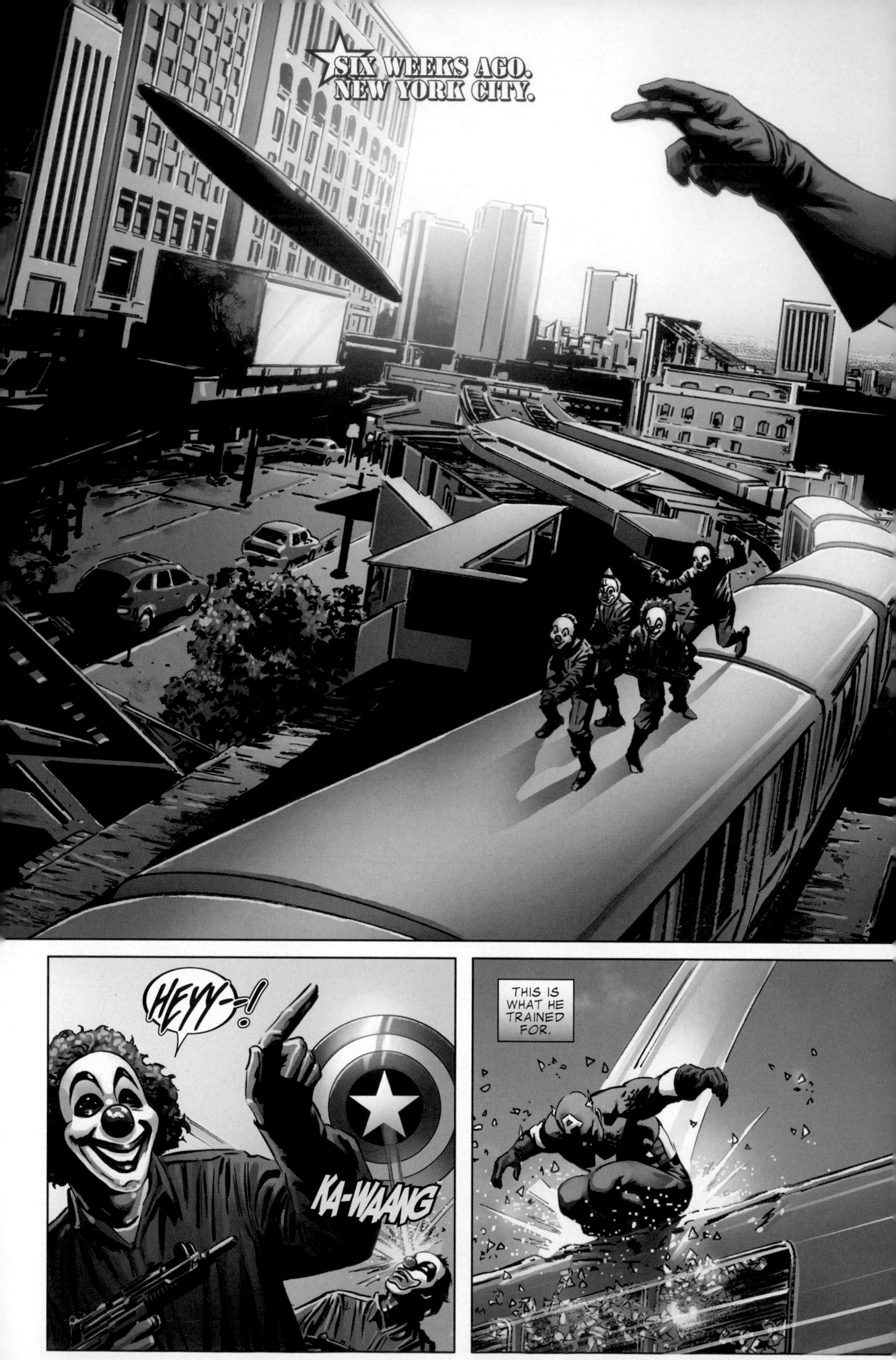
SIX WEEKS AGO.
NEW YORK CITY.
HEYY--!
KA-WAANG
THIS IS WHAT HE TRAINED FOR.

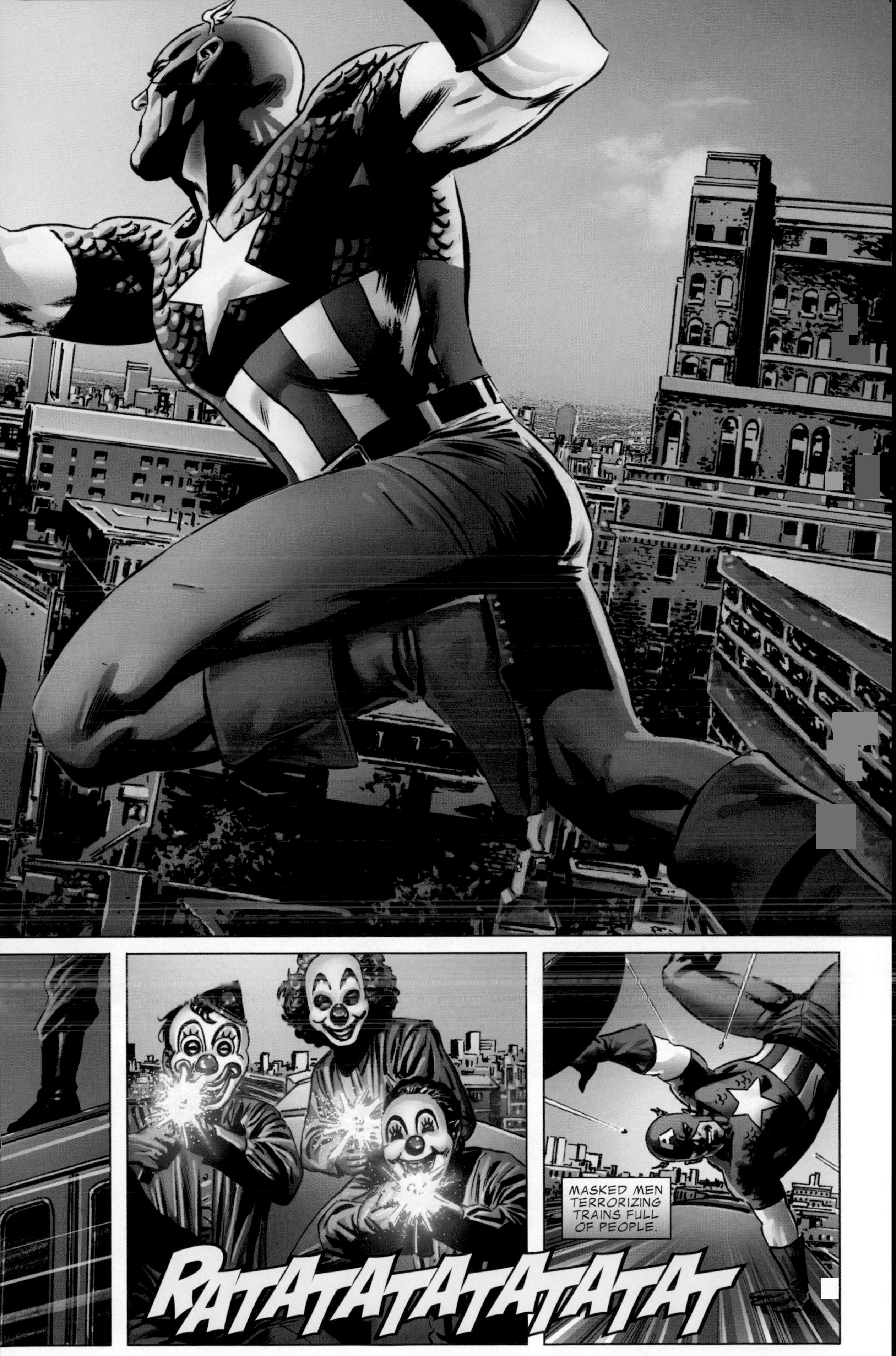
MASKED MEN TERRORIZING TRAINS FULL OF PEOPLE.
RATATATATATATATAT

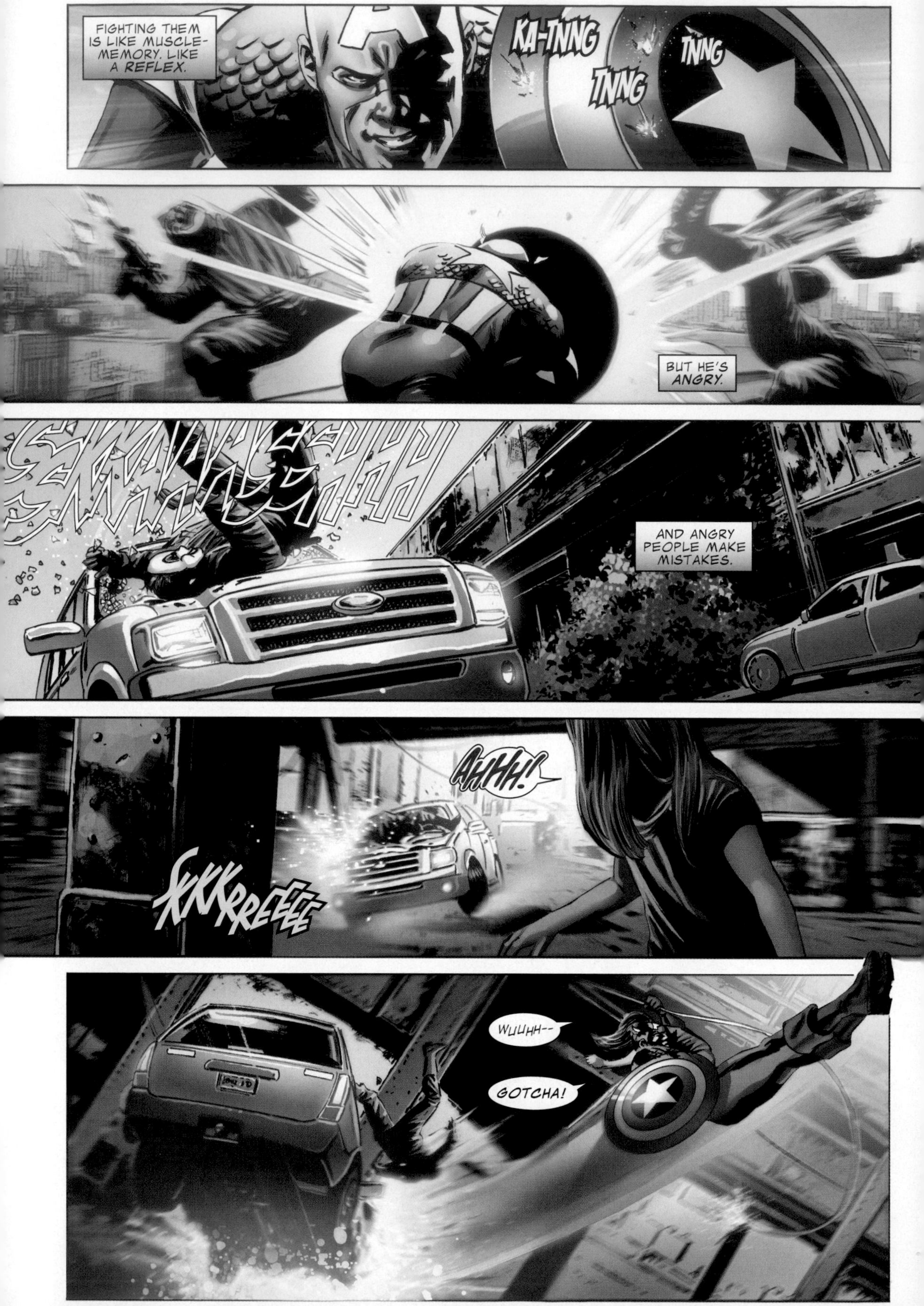
FIGHTING THEM IS LIKE MUSCLE-MEMORY. LIKE A REFLEX.
KA-TNNG
TNNG
TNNG
BUT HE'S ANGRY.
AND ANGRY PEOPLE MAKE MISTAKES.
AHHH!
SKKKRREEEEE
WUUHH--
GOTCHA!

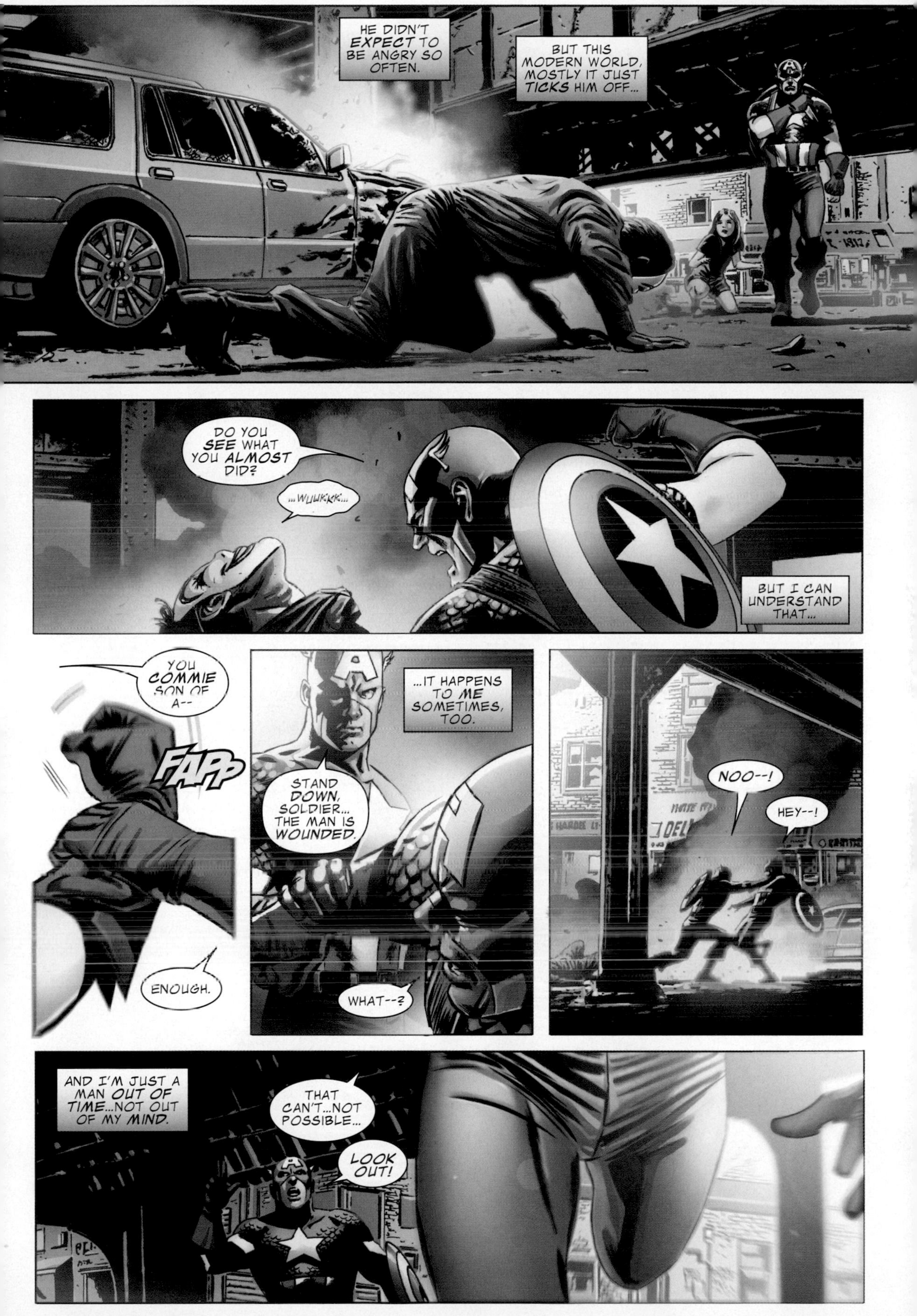

HE DIDN'T EXPECT TO BE ANGRY SO OFTEN.
BUT THIS MODERN WORLD, MOSTLY IT JUST TICKS HIM OFF...
DO YOU SEE WHAT YOU ALMOST DID?
...WUUKKK...
BUT I CAN UNDERSTAND THAT...
YOU COMMIE SON OF A--
FAPP
ENOUGH.
...IT HAPPENS TO ME SOMETIMES, TOO.
STAND DOWN, SOLDIER... THE MAN IS WOUNDED.
WHAT--?
NOO--!
HEY--!
AND I'M JUST A MAN OUT OF TIME...NOT OUT OF MY MIND.
THAT CAN'T...NOT POSSIBLE...
LOOK OUT!

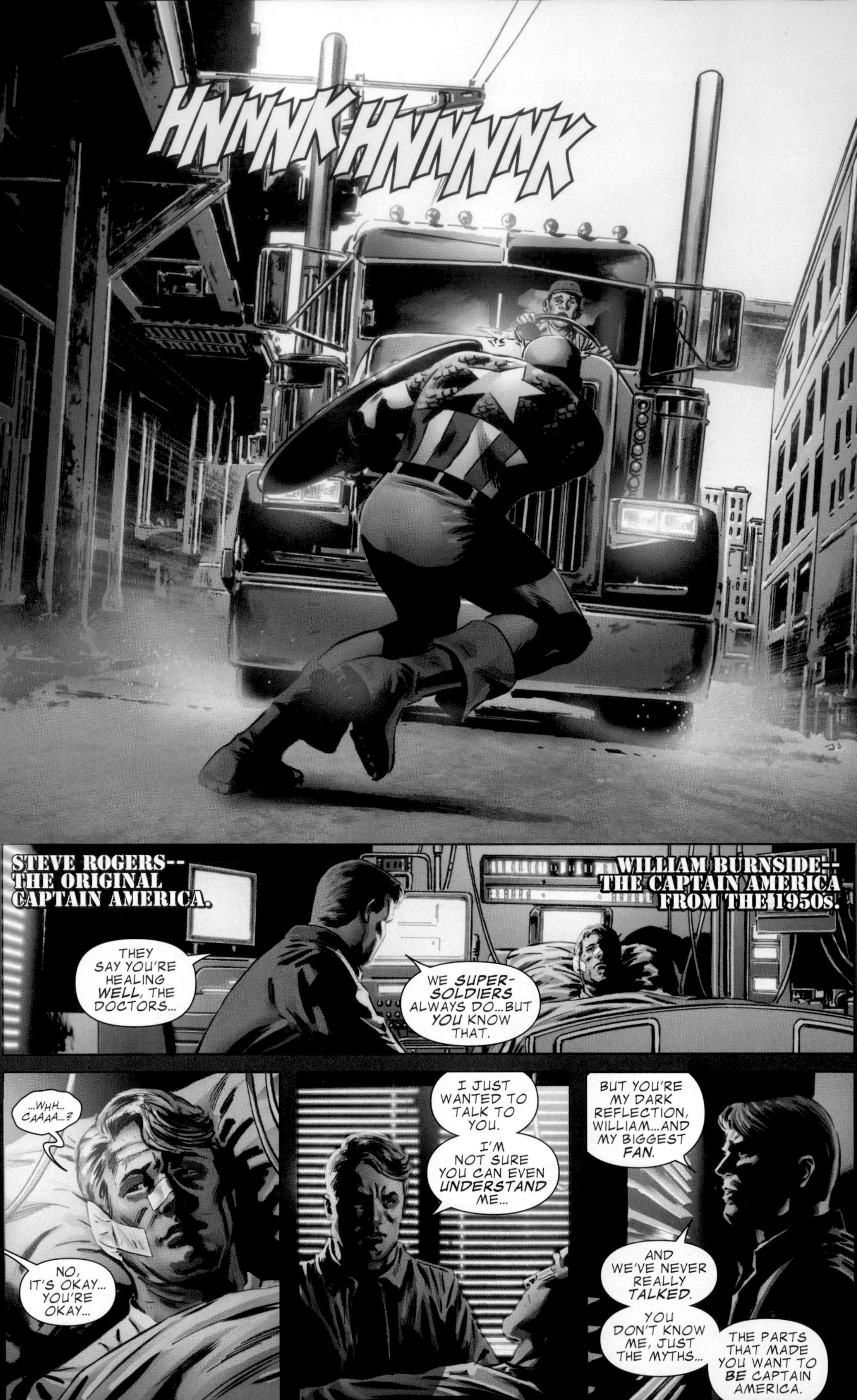
HNNNK HNNNNK
STEVE ROGERS-- THE ORIGINAL CAPTAIN AMERICA.
WILLIAM BURNSIDE-- THE CAPTAIN AMERICA FROM THE 1950s.
THEY SAY YOU'RE HEALING WELL, THE DOCTORS...
WE SUPER-SOLDIERS ALWAYS DO...BUT YOU KNOW THAT.
...WHH... CAAAA...?
NO, IT'S OKAY... YOU'RE OKAY...
I JUST WANTED TO TALK TO YOU.
I'M NOT SURE YOU CAN EVEN UNDERSTAND ME...
BUT YOU'RE MY DARK REFLECTION, WILLIAM...AND MY BIGGEST FAN.
AND WE'VE NEVER REALLY TALKED.
YOU DON'T KNOW ME, JUST THE MYTHS...
THE PARTS THAT MADE YOU WANT TO BE CAPTAIN AMERICA.

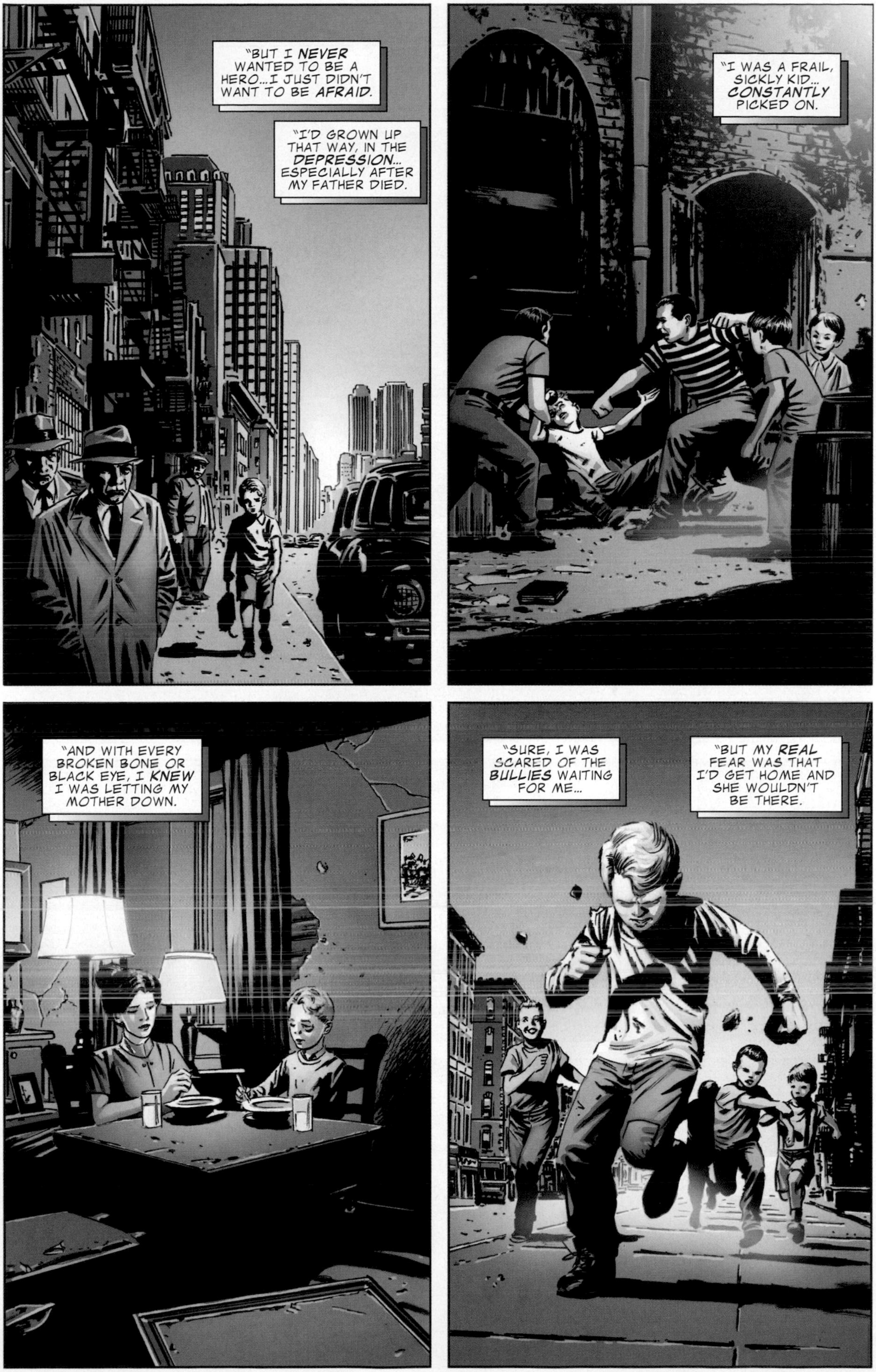
"BUT I NEVER WANTED TO BE A HERO...I JUST DIDN'T WANT TO BE AFRAID.
"I'D GROWN UP THAT WAY, IN THE DEPRESSION... ESPECIALLY AFTER MY FATHER DIED.
"I WAS A FRAIL, SICKLY KID... CONSTANTLY PICKED ON.
"AND WITH EVERY BROKEN BONE OR BLACK EYE, I KNEW I WAS LETTING MY MOTHER DOWN.
"SURE, I WAS SCARED OF THE BULLIES WAITING FOR ME...
"BUT MY REAL FEAR WAS THAT I'D GET HOME AND SHE WOULDN'T BE THERE.

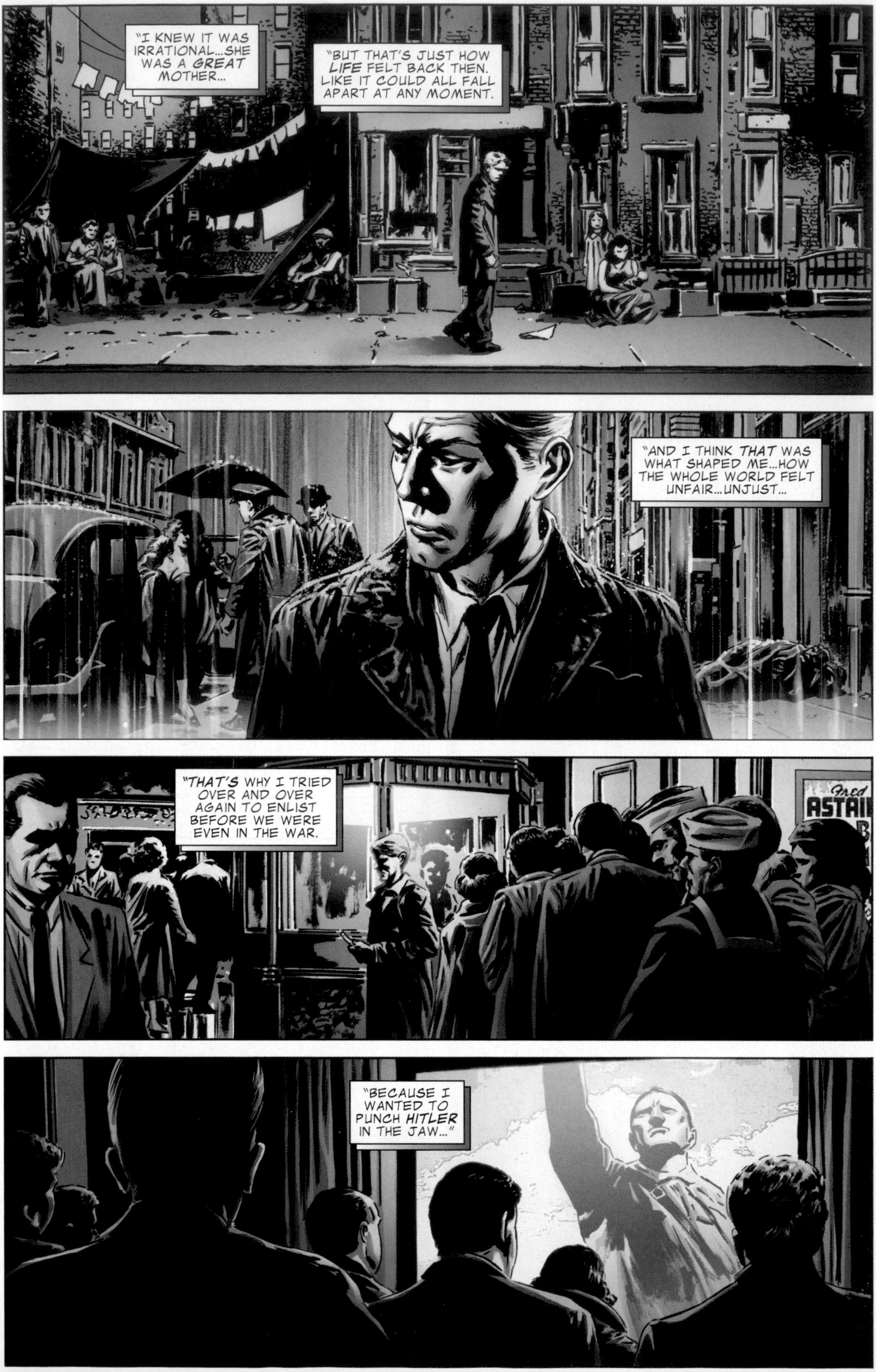
"I KNEW IT WAS IRRATIONAL...SHE WAS A *GREAT* MOTHER...
"BUT THAT'S JUST HOW *LIFE* FELT BACK THEN. LIKE IT COULD ALL FALL APART AT ANY MOMENT.
"AND I THINK *THAT* WAS WHAT SHAPED ME...HOW THE WHOLE WORLD FELT UNFAIR...UNJUST...
"*THAT'S* WHY I TRIED OVER AND OVER AGAIN TO ENLIST BEFORE WE WERE EVEN IN THE WAR.
"BECAUSE I WANTED TO PUNCH *HITLER* IN THE JAW..."

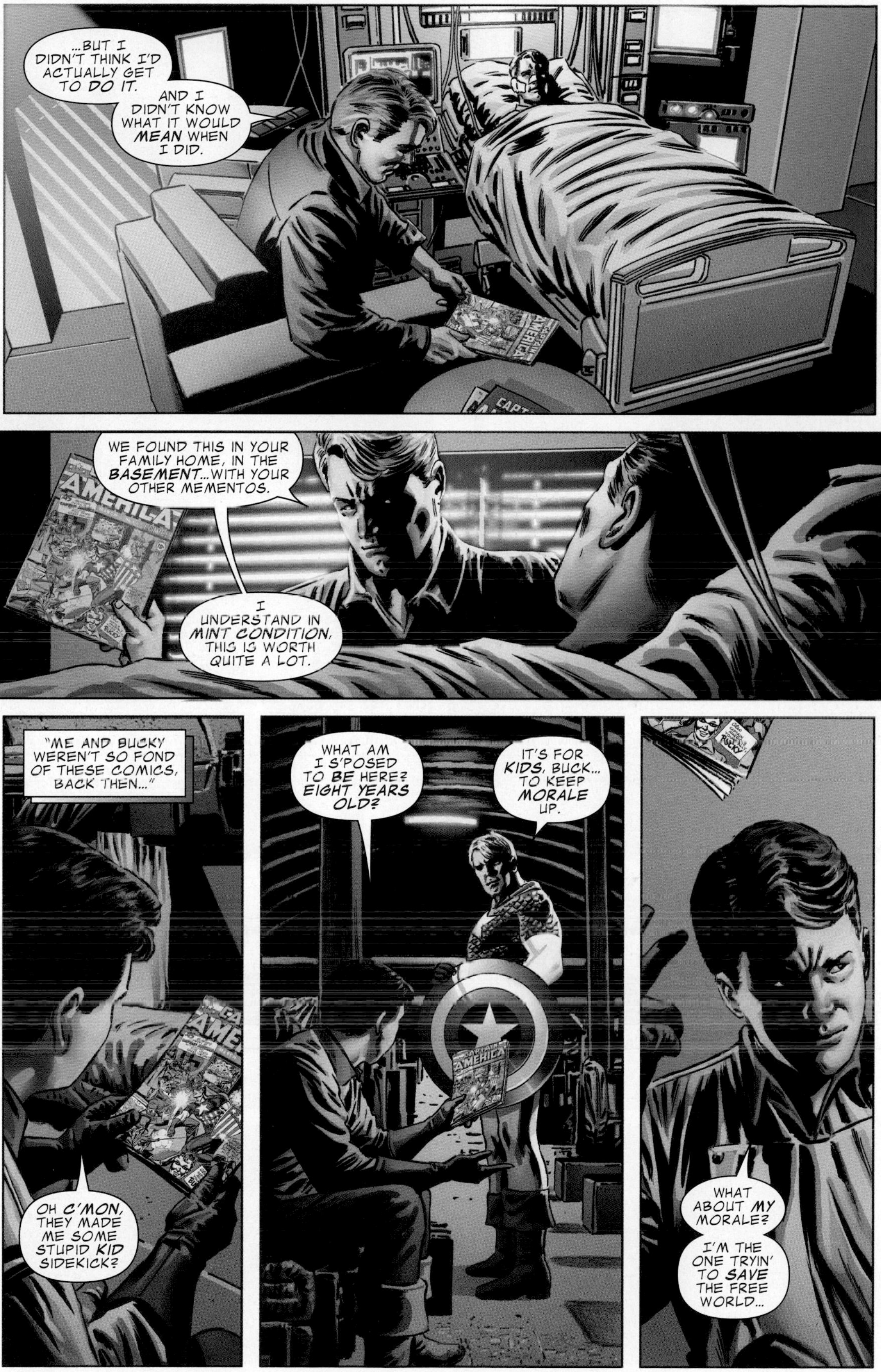
...BUT I DIDN'T THINK I'D ACTUALLY GET TO DO IT.
AND I DIDN'T KNOW WHAT IT WOULD MEAN WHEN I DID.
CAPTAIN AMERICA
WE FOUND THIS IN YOUR FAMILY HOME, IN THE BASEMENT...WITH YOUR OTHER MEMENTOS.
I UNDERSTAND IN MINT CONDITION, THIS IS WORTH QUITE A LOT.
"ME AND BUCKY WEREN'T SO FOND OF THESE COMICS, BACK THEN..."
OH C'MON, THEY MADE ME SOME STUPID KID SIDEKICK?
WHAT AM I S'POSED TO BE HERE? EIGHT YEARS OLD?
IT'S FOR KIDS, BUCK... TO KEEP MORALE UP.
WHAT ABOUT MY MORALE?
I'M THE ONE TRYIN' TO SAVE THE FREE WORLD...

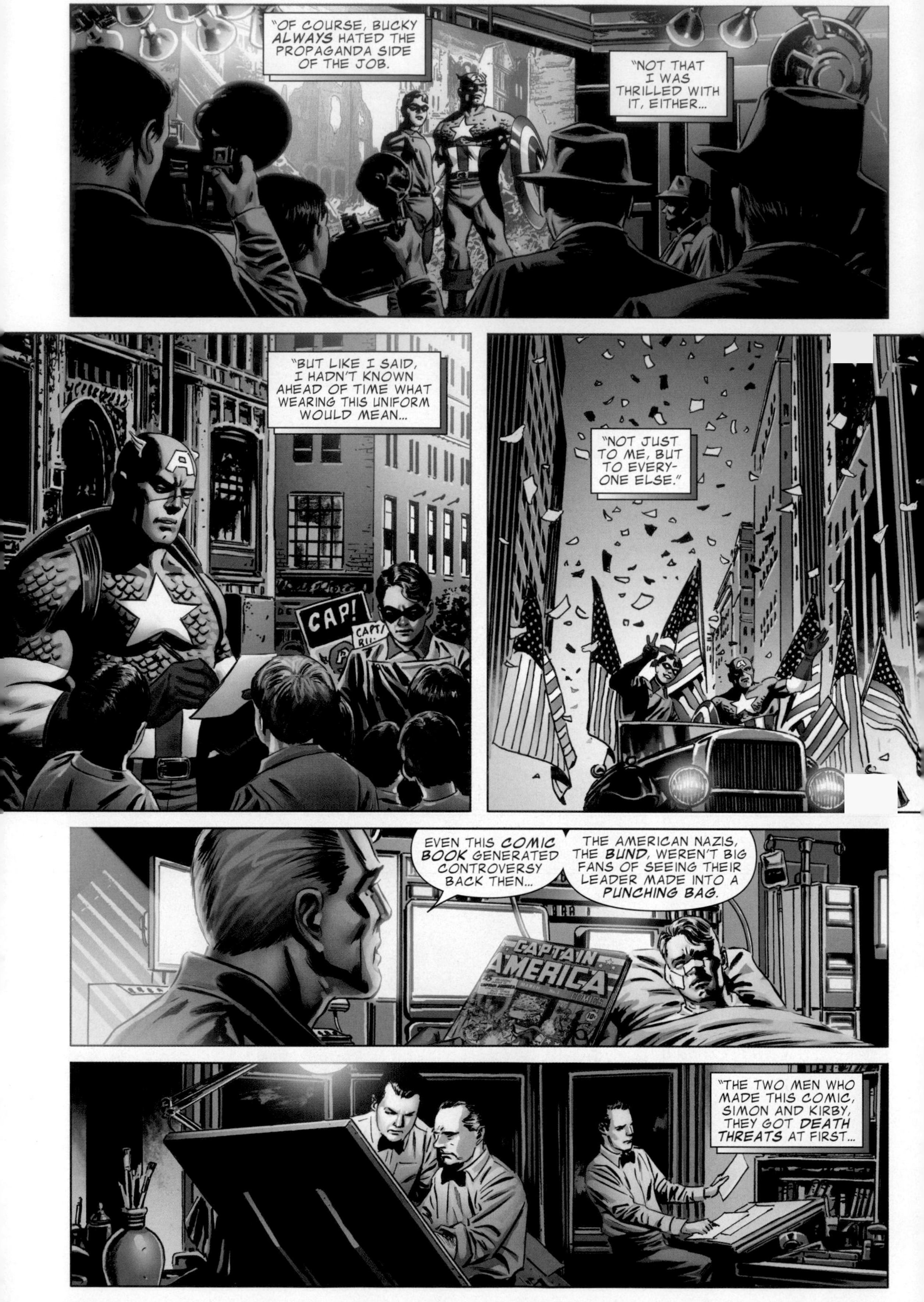
"OF COURSE, BUCKY ALWAYS HATED THE PROPAGANDA SIDE OF THE JOB.
"NOT THAT I WAS THRILLED WITH IT, EITHER...
"BUT LIKE I SAID, I HADN'T KNOWN AHEAD OF TIME WHAT WEARING THIS UNIFORM WOULD MEAN...
CAP!
"NOT JUST TO ME, BUT TO EVERY-ONE ELSE."
EVEN THIS COMIC BOOK GENERATED CONTROVERSY BACK THEN...
THE AMERICAN NAZIS, THE BUND, WEREN'T BIG FANS OF SEEING THEIR LEADER MADE INTO A PUNCHING BAG.
CAPTAIN AMERICA COMICS
"THE TWO MEN WHO MADE THIS COMIC, SIMON AND KIRBY, THEY GOT DEATH THREATS AT FIRST...

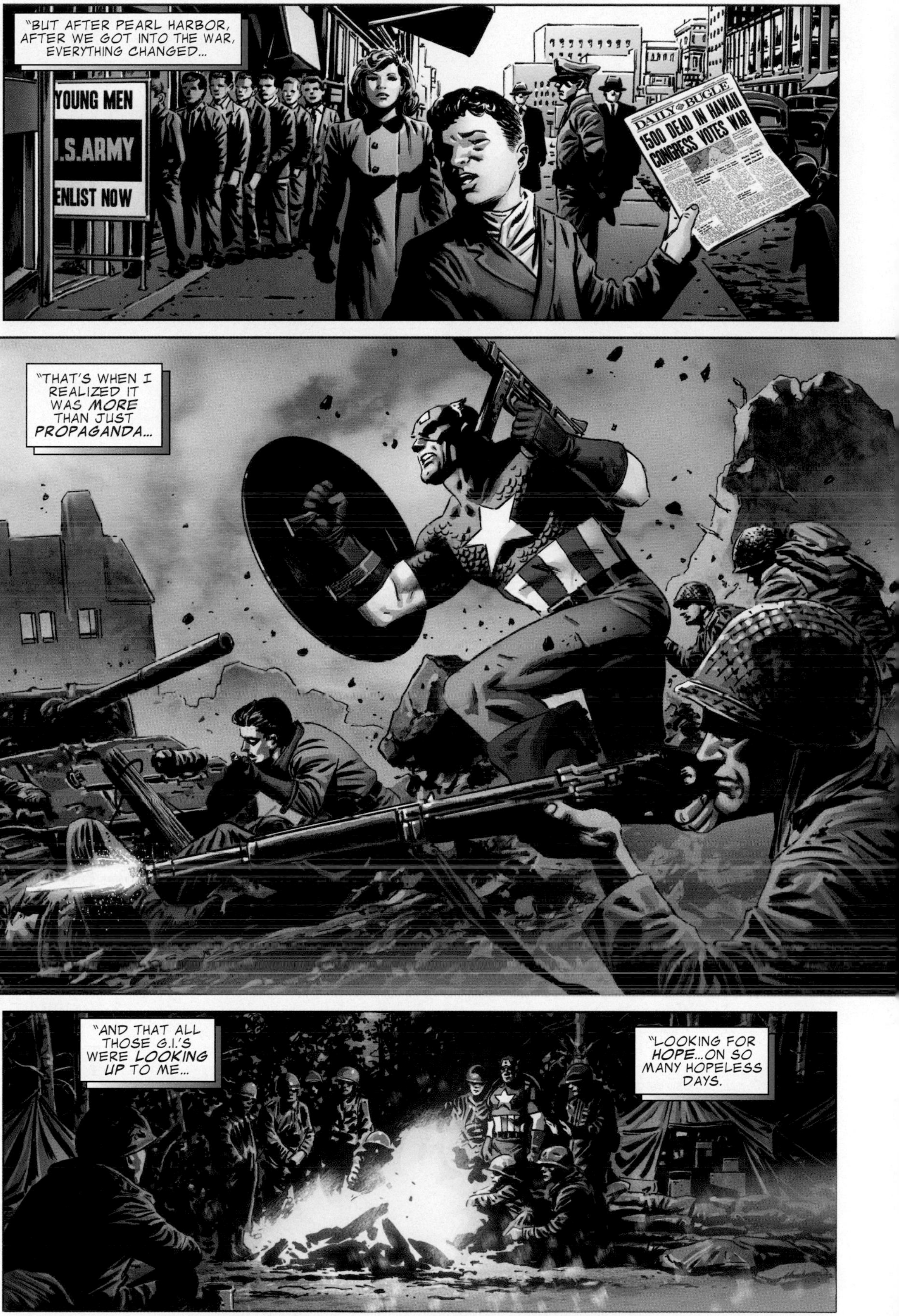
"BUT AFTER PEARL HARBOR, AFTER WE GOT INTO THE WAR, EVERYTHING CHANGED...
YOUNG MEN
ENLIST NOW
DAILY BUGLE
1500 DEAD IN HAWAII
CONGRESS VOTES WAR
"THAT'S WHEN I REALIZED IT WAS *MORE* THAN JUST *PROPAGANDA*...
"AND THAT ALL THOSE G.I.'S WERE *LOOKING UP* TO ME...
"LOOKING FOR *HOPE*...ON SO MANY HOPELESS DAYS.

"AND THAT SCARED ME MORE THAN ANYTHING IN MY WHOLE LIFE EVER HAD.

"BECAUSE I'D NEVER BEEN A LEADER.

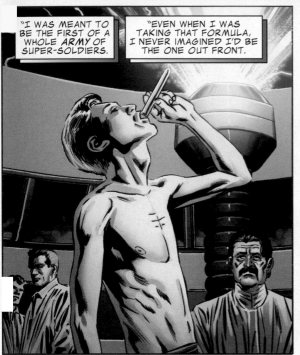

"I WAS MEANT TO BE THE FIRST OF A WHOLE *ARMY* OF SUPER-SOLDIERS.

"EVEN WHEN I WAS TAKING THAT FORMULA, I NEVER IMAGINED I'D BE THE ONE OUT FRONT.

"I HADN'T WANTED TO WEAR THE FLAG AND CARRY THAT BURDEN...

"I JUST WANTED TO DO THE RIGHT THING.

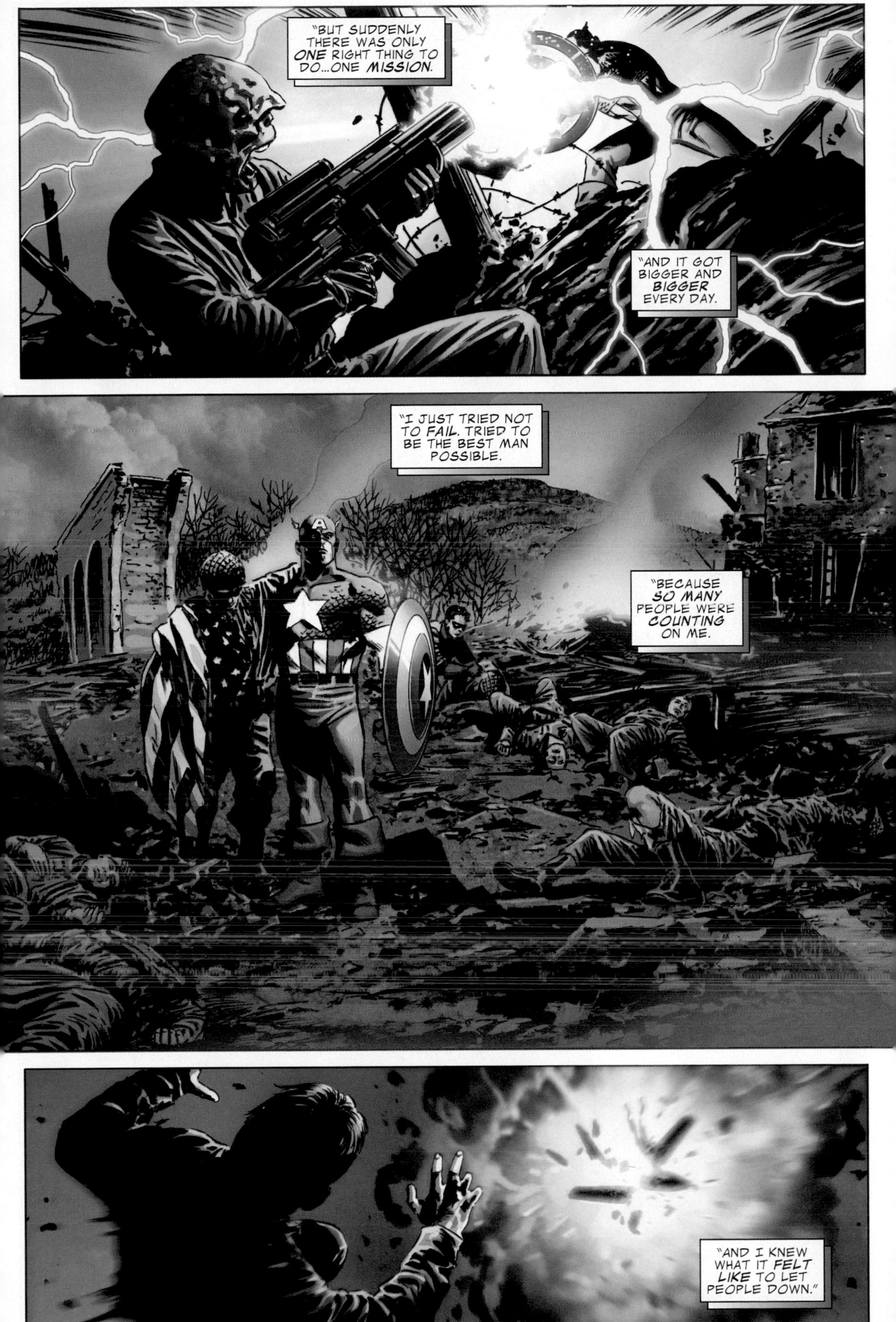
"BUT SUDDENLY THERE WAS ONLY *ONE* RIGHT THING TO DO...ONE *MISSION*.
"AND IT GOT BIGGER AND *BIGGER* EVERY DAY.
"I JUST TRIED NOT TO *FAIL*. TRIED TO BE THE BEST MAN POSSIBLE.
"BECAUSE *SO MANY* PEOPLE WERE *COUNTING* ON ME.
"AND I KNEW WHAT IT *FELT LIKE* TO LET PEOPLE DOWN."

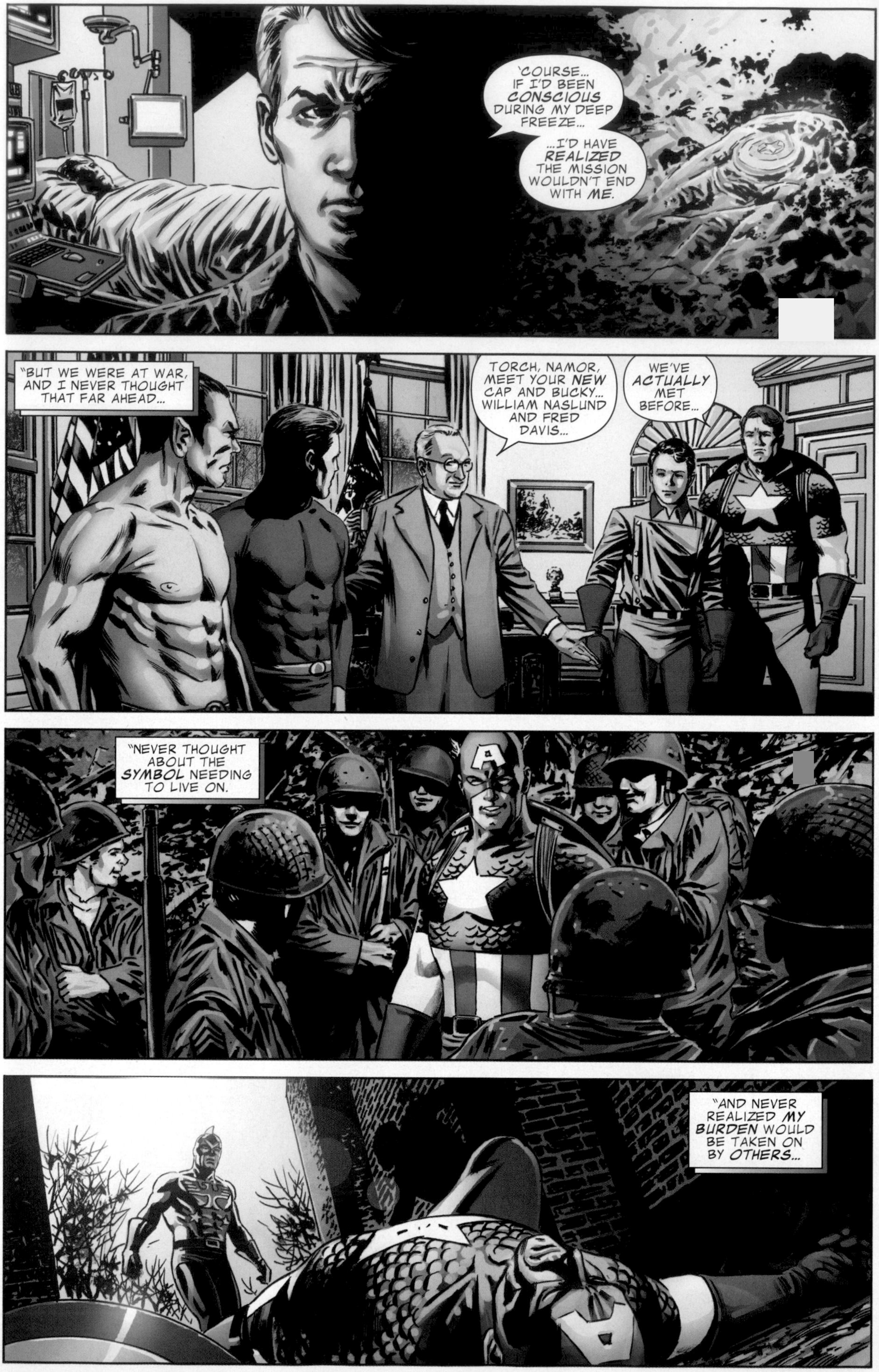
'COURSE... IF I'D BEEN CONSCIOUS DURING MY DEEP FREEZE...
...I'D HAVE REALIZED THE MISSION WOULDN'T END WITH ME.
"BUT WE WERE AT WAR, AND I NEVER THOUGHT THAT FAR AHEAD...
TORCH, NAMOR, MEET YOUR NEW CAP AND BUCKY... WILLIAM NASLUND AND FRED DAVIS...
WE'VE ACTUALLY MET BEFORE...
"NEVER THOUGHT ABOUT THE SYMBOL NEEDING TO LIVE ON.
"AND NEVER REALIZED MY BURDEN WOULD BE TAKEN ON BY OTHERS...

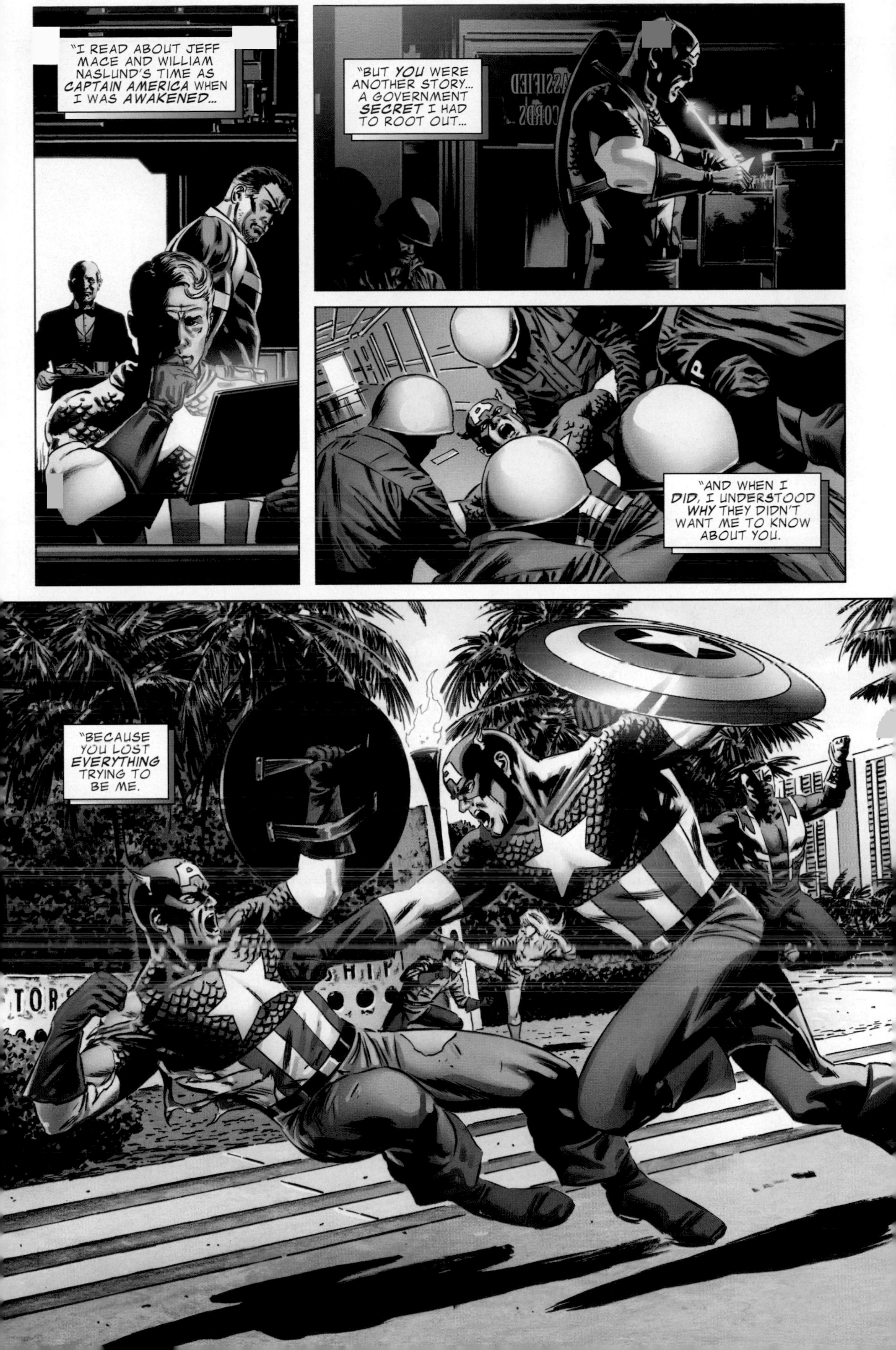
"I READ ABOUT JEFF MACE AND WILLIAM NASLUND'S TIME AS CAPTAIN AMERICA WHEN I WAS AWAKENED...
"BUT YOU WERE ANOTHER STORY... A GOVERNMENT SECRET I HAD TO ROOT OUT...
"AND WHEN I DID, I UNDERSTOOD WHY THEY DIDN'T WANT ME TO KNOW ABOUT YOU.
"BECAUSE YOU LOST EVERYTHING TRYING TO BE ME.

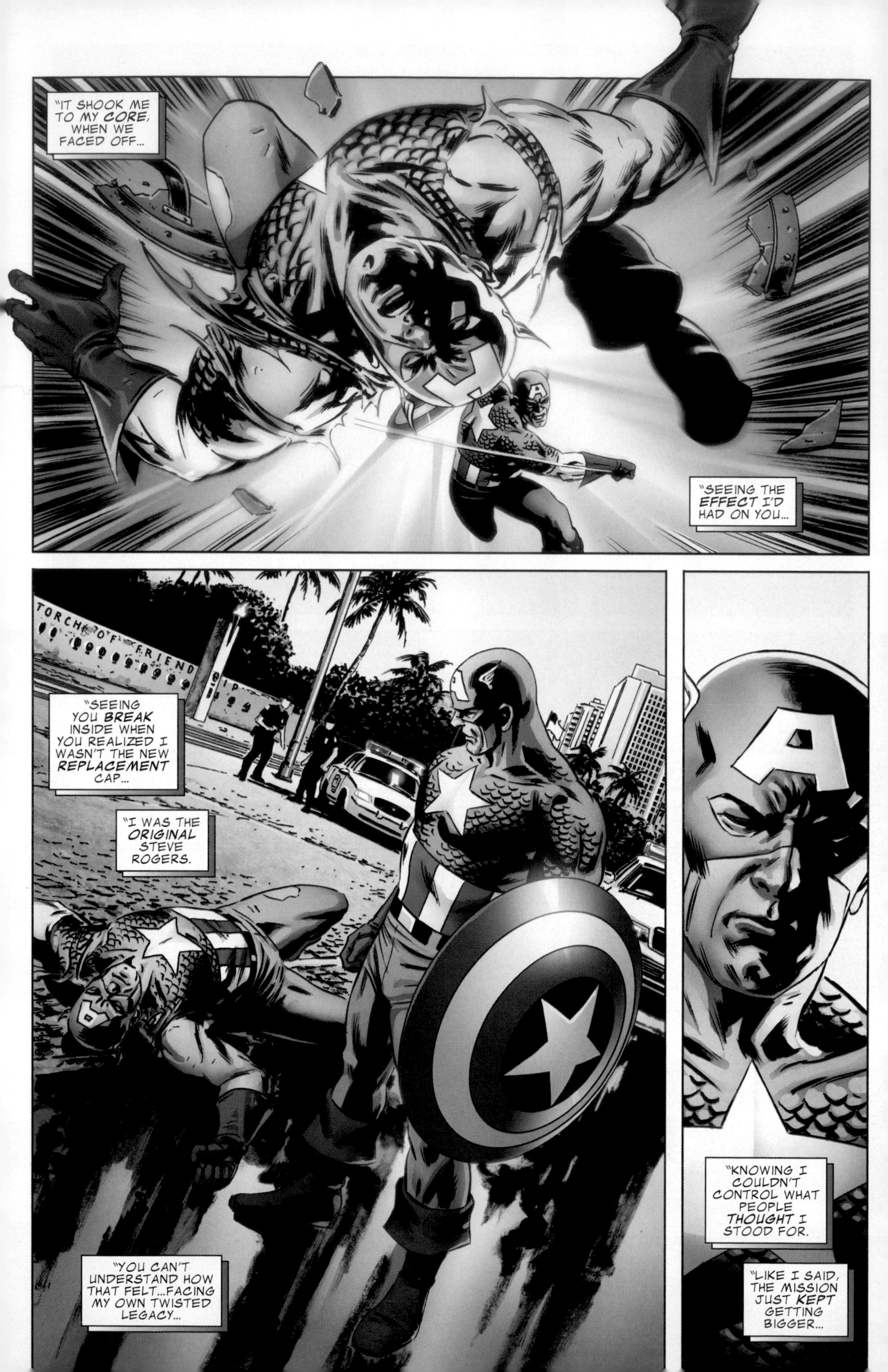
"IT SHOOK ME TO MY **CORE**, WHEN WE FACED OFF...
"SEEING THE **EFFECT** I'D HAD ON YOU...
"SEEING YOU **BREAK** INSIDE WHEN YOU REALIZED I WASN'T THE NEW **REPLACEMENT** CAP...
"I WAS THE **ORIGINAL** STEVE ROGERS.
"YOU CAN'T UNDERSTAND HOW THAT FELT...FACING MY OWN TWISTED LEGACY...
"KNOWING I COULDN'T CONTROL WHAT PEOPLE **THOUGHT** I STOOD FOR.
"LIKE I SAID, THE MISSION JUST **KEPT** GETTING BIGGER...

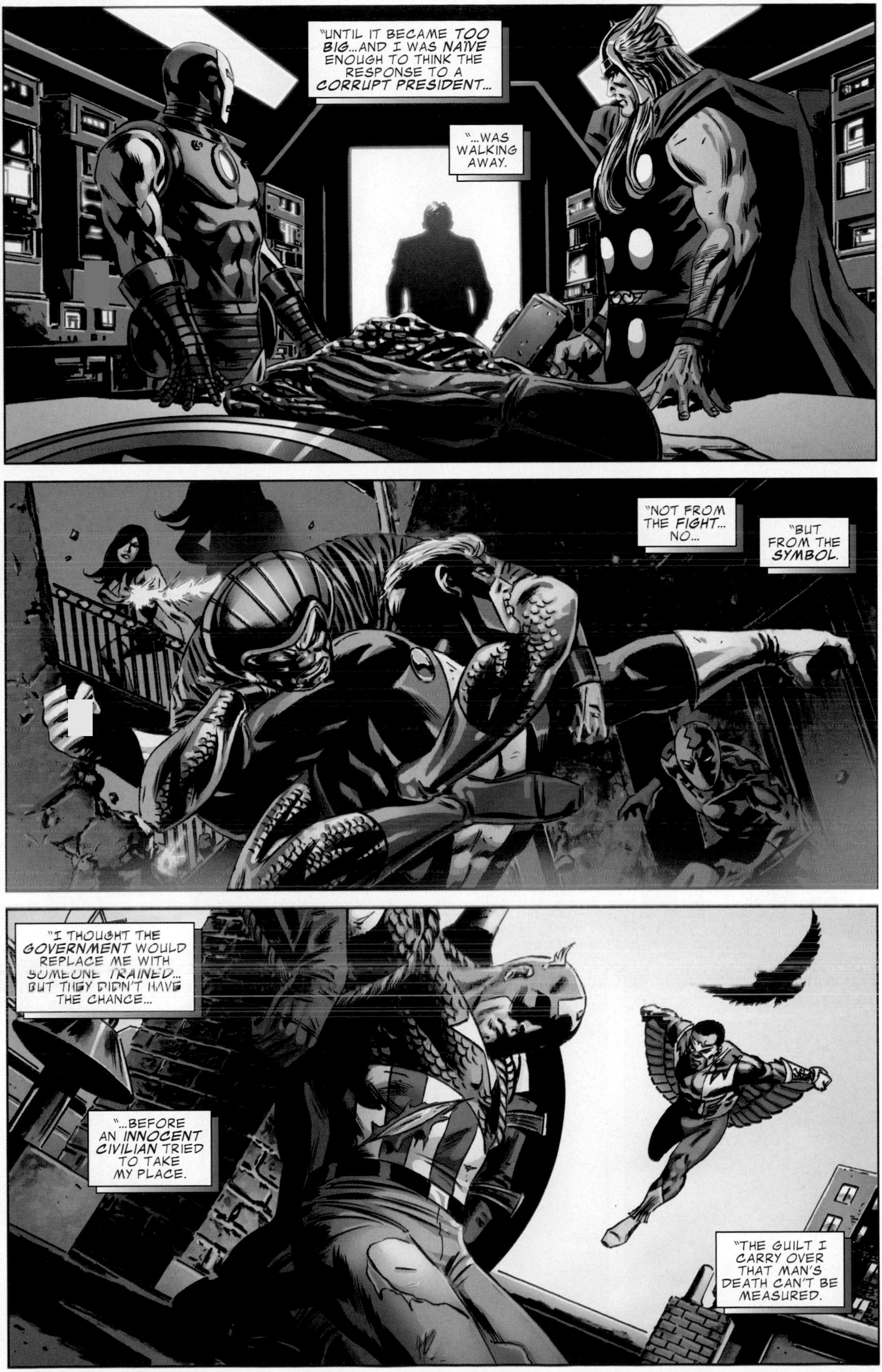
"UNTIL IT BECAME TOO BIG...AND I WAS NAÏVE ENOUGH TO THINK THE RESPONSE TO A CORRUPT PRESIDENT...
"...WAS WALKING AWAY.
"NOT FROM THE FIGHT... NO...
"BUT FROM THE SYMBOL.
"I THOUGHT THE GOVERNMENT WOULD REPLACE ME WITH SOMEONE TRAINED... BUT THEY DIDN'T HAVE THE CHANCE...
"...BEFORE AN INNOCENT CIVILIAN TRIED TO TAKE MY PLACE.
"THE GUILT I CARRY OVER THAT MAN'S DEATH CAN'T BE MEASURED.

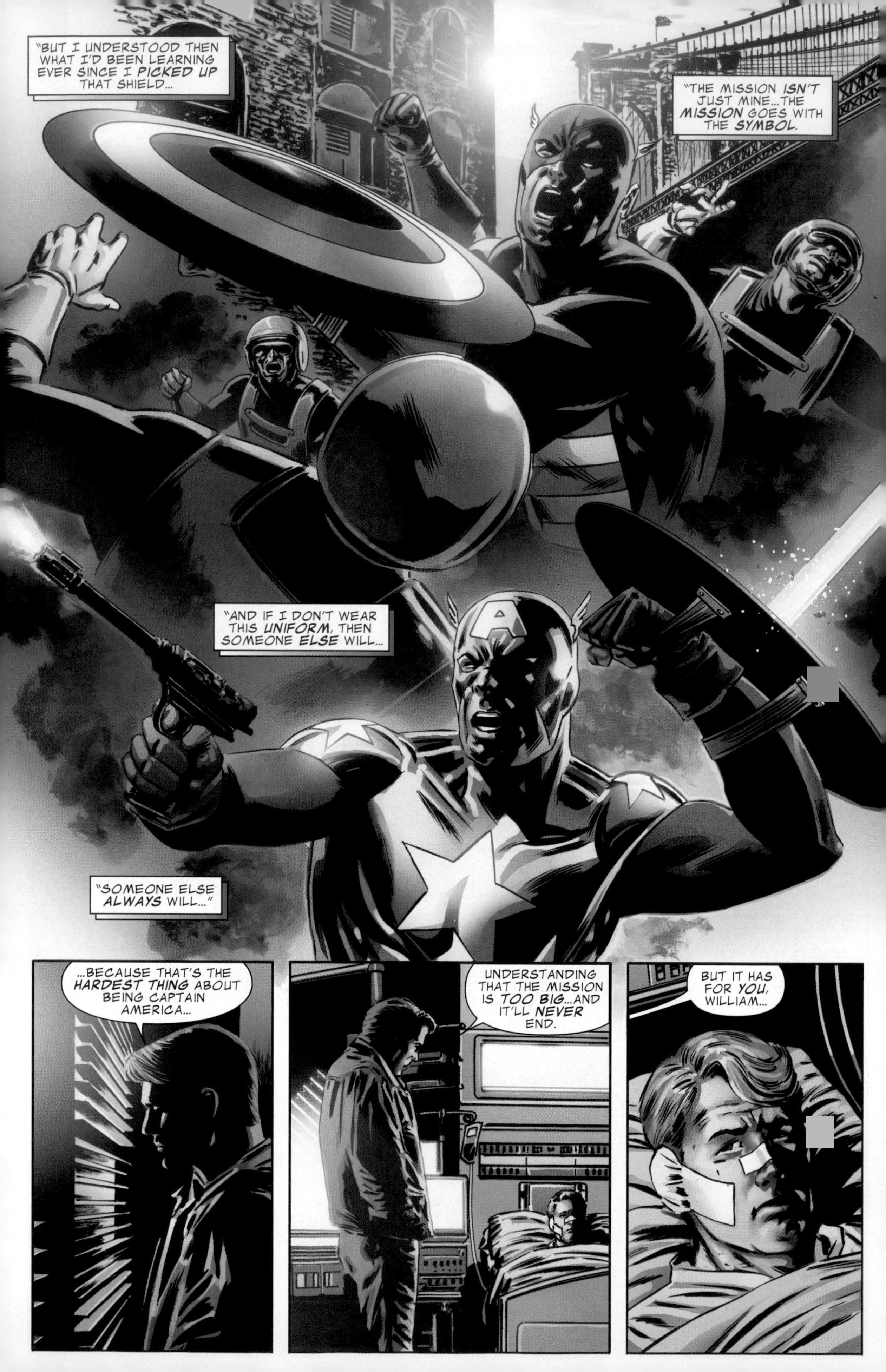
"BUT I UNDERSTOOD THEN WHAT I'D BEEN LEARNING EVER SINCE I PICKED UP THAT SHIELD...
"THE MISSION ISN'T JUST MINE...THE MISSION GOES WITH THE SYMBOL.
"AND IF I DON'T WEAR THIS UNIFORM, THEN SOMEONE ELSE WILL...
"SOMEONE ELSE ALWAYS WILL..."
...BECAUSE THAT'S THE HARDEST THING ABOUT BEING CAPTAIN AMERICA...
UNDERSTANDING THAT THE MISSION IS TOO BIG...AND IT'LL NEVER END.
BUT IT HAS FOR YOU, WILLIAM...

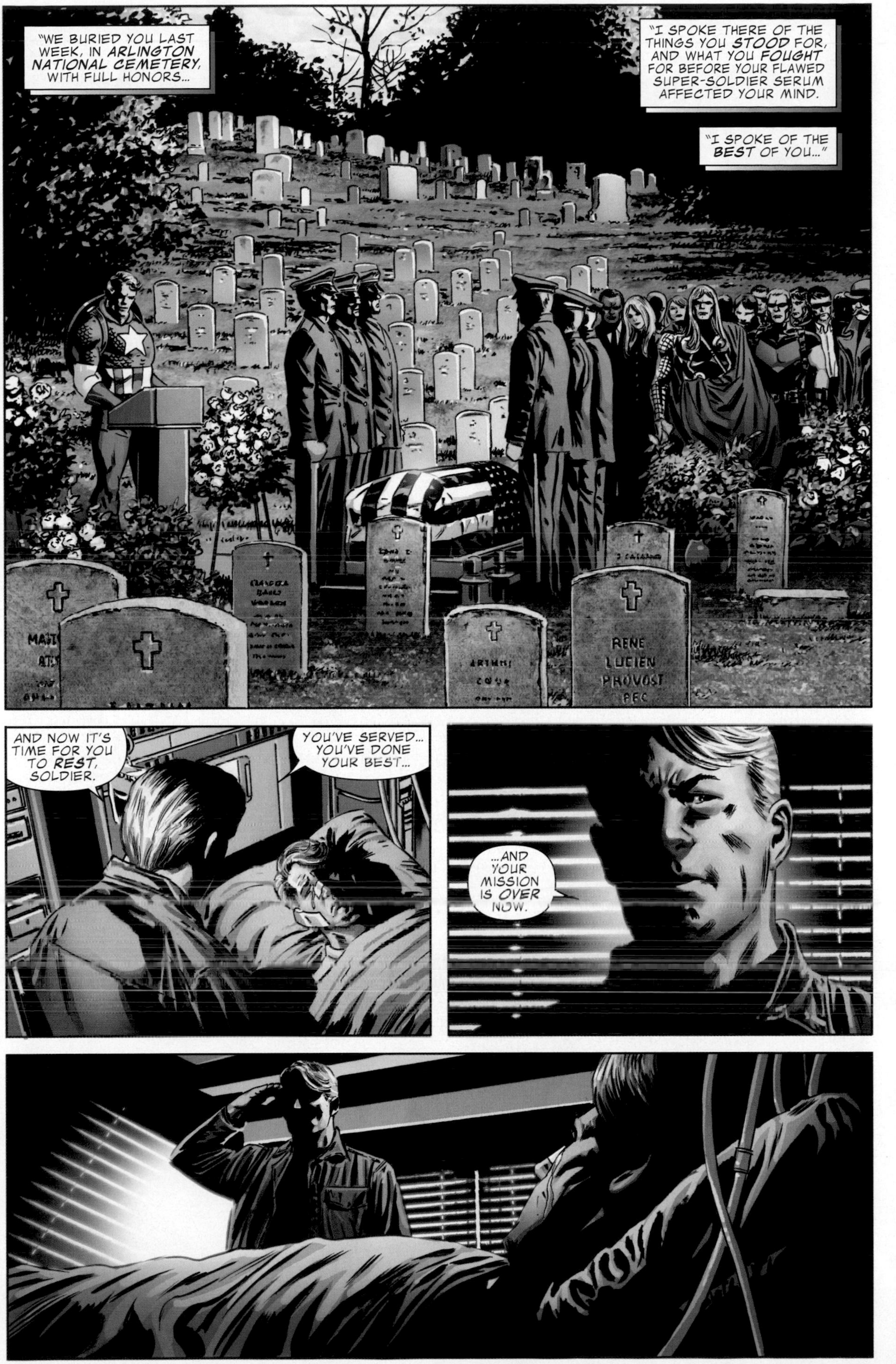
"WE BURIED YOU LAST WEEK, IN ARLINGTON NATIONAL CEMETERY, WITH FULL HONORS...
"I SPOKE THERE OF THE THINGS YOU STOOD FOR, AND WHAT YOU FOUGHT FOR BEFORE YOUR FLAWED SUPER-SOLDIER SERUM AFFECTED YOUR MIND.
"I SPOKE OF THE BEST OF YOU..."
RENE LUCIEN PROVOST PFC
AND NOW IT'S TIME FOR YOU TO REST, SOLDIER.
YOU'VE SERVED... YOU'VE DONE YOUR BEST...
...AND YOUR MISSION IS OVER NOW.

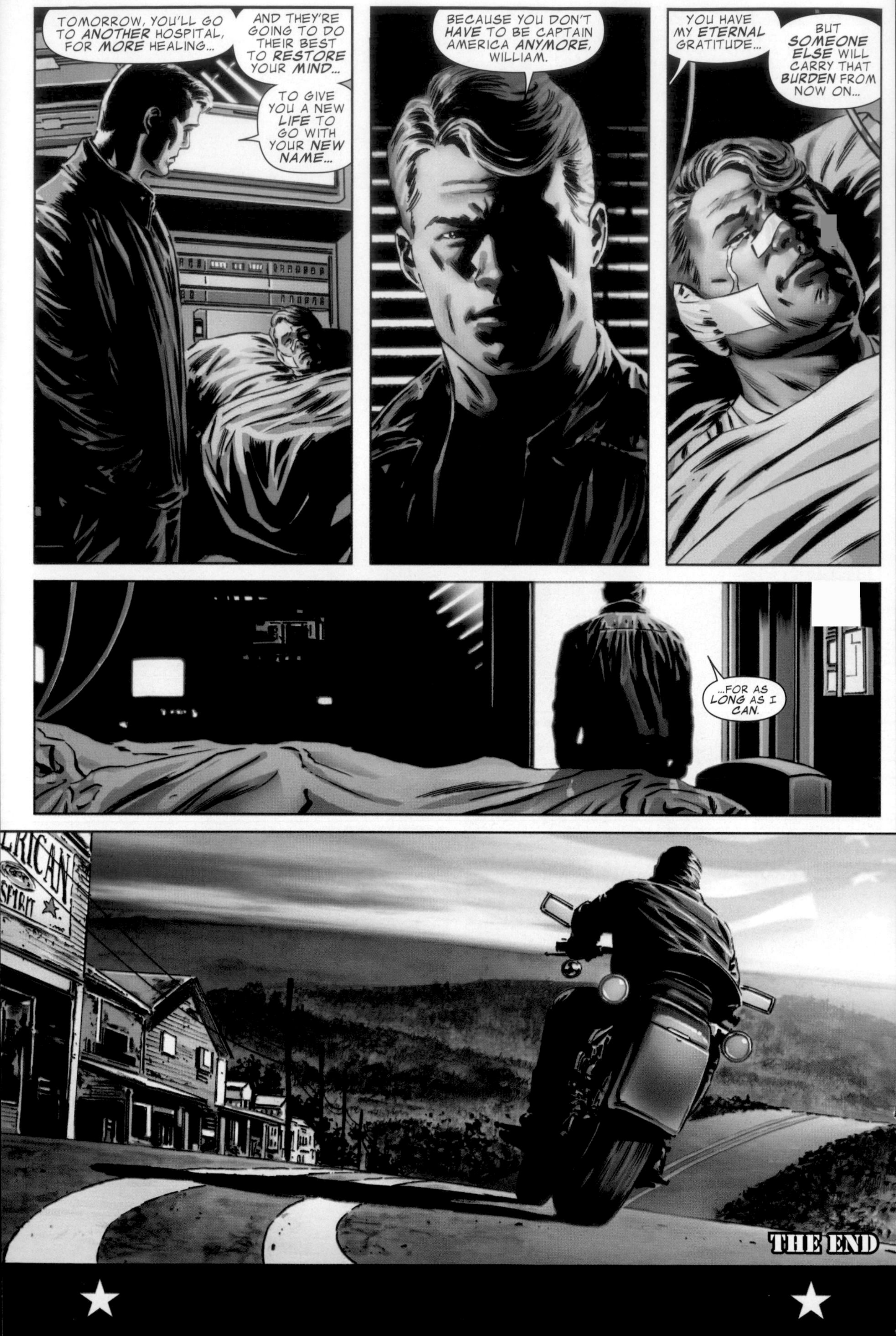

TOMORROW, YOU'LL GO TO ANOTHER HOSPITAL, FOR MORE HEALING...
AND THEY'RE GOING TO DO THEIR BEST TO RESTORE YOUR MIND...
TO GIVE YOU A NEW LIFE TO GO WITH YOUR NEW NAME...
BECAUSE YOU DON'T HAVE TO BE CAPTAIN AMERICA ANYMORE, WILLIAM.
YOU HAVE MY ETERNAL GRATITUDE...
BUT SOMEONE ELSE WILL CARRY THAT BURDEN FROM NOW ON...
...FOR AS LONG AS I CAN.
THE END

A GOOD-BYE TO CAP...
BY ED BRUBAKER

It was almost exactly eight years ago I started writing Captain America, and here we are, over 100 issues later. Amazing. And something I never thought possible.

Because I've been a lifelong Cap fan, ever since I first saw him and Bucky in one of the Marvel cartoons from the '60s, the one that adapted the origin story. So by the time I saw Cap #156 on the stands at the PX down the street, Cap had already leaped right past Spider-Man as my favorite comic, and a big part of that was because of Cap's sidekick in the cartoon, Bucky. I probably liked Bucky because, like me, he was a military brat, but I also just liked the idea that next to Captain America, the super-soldier, there was just this well-trained kid with a machine gun and an attitude.

I can still vividly recall the days I spent as a kid reading Cap comics and searching back issue bins for the Tales of Suspense issues with the stories I liked the best — Cap and Bucky in World War Two. Those Lee-Kirby tales, and the Jim Steranko "Cap vs. Madame Hydra" issues, were always my favorites. But even when I started writing comics for a living, even when I was doing Batman at DC, I never imagined I'd be writing Cap one day, trying to make it the book I'd always wanted it to be…and I never in my wildest dreams imagined anyone would actually let me bring Bucky back.

So I'd like to take a moment to thank everyone I can remember…Brian Bendis, who asked me, "What do you want to write at Marvel?" and Joe Quesada, who called me the next day to offer me this book, and who already wanted to bring back Bucky when I suggested it. Tom Brevoort, who gave me the list of questions to answer that helped me figure out how the Winter Soldier storyline would work, and who always had my back on this book even if he disagreed with me. Dan Buckley, who is an unsung hero of this era of Marvel Comics, and who helped me feel like this book was my home as long as I wanted it. That's a rare thing in any field, but I got the freedom to tell my stories my way and never felt like the rug was going to be pulled out from under me. Molly Lazer, who was the glue keeping our crazy ship together the first few years. And Lauren Sankovitch, who inherited the thankless task of cracking the whip on me to get pages written, and who's never acted like it's been a hassle.

To our artists — Steve Epting, who was my first choice for this book, and who I was lucky enough to get, and Michael Lark, who did much of our flashback work to help Steve out on the schedule at first. I think Steve and Michael learned from and inspired each other that first year, and I couldn't have made my ideas for this book work without their sense of gravity and reality, and their style. "Gentleman" Gene Colan, who gave me the honor of writing his final comic. Mike Perkins, Butch Guice and Luke Ross all did excellent work, as did Chris Samnee on the Cap and Bucky arc, and Bryan Hitch on Cap: Reborn, and it's been a dream to work with Steve McNiven, Alan Davis and Patrick Zircher on this more recent run. I've been blessed with great collaborators, and it was amazing to have Steve Epting and Frank D'Armata return for my final issue. Frank D'Armata was the other glue, always getting the book in and looking beautiful on tight deadlines. And to Joe Caramagna, who has lettered nearly all our issues, under those same tight schedules.

And finally, thanks to our readers, who made us one of the most popular books on the stands for a long time, and whose loyalty helped give me the freedom to write the book the way I did. I know it's time for both me and Cap to turn a new page, but I'm going to miss this.

— Ed

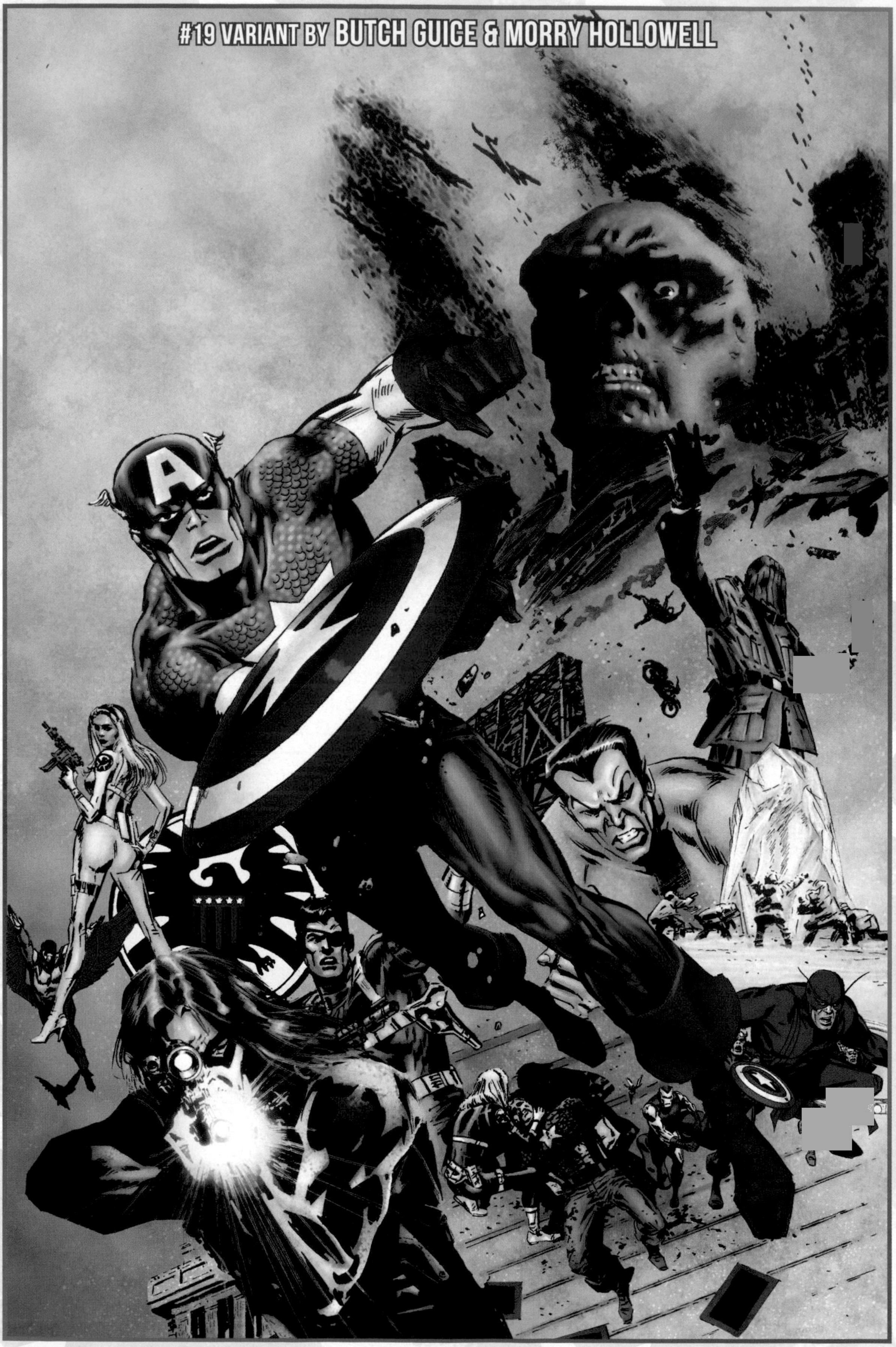

#19 VARIANT BY BUTCH GUICE & MORRY HOLLOWELL

#19 VARIANT BY MR GARCIN

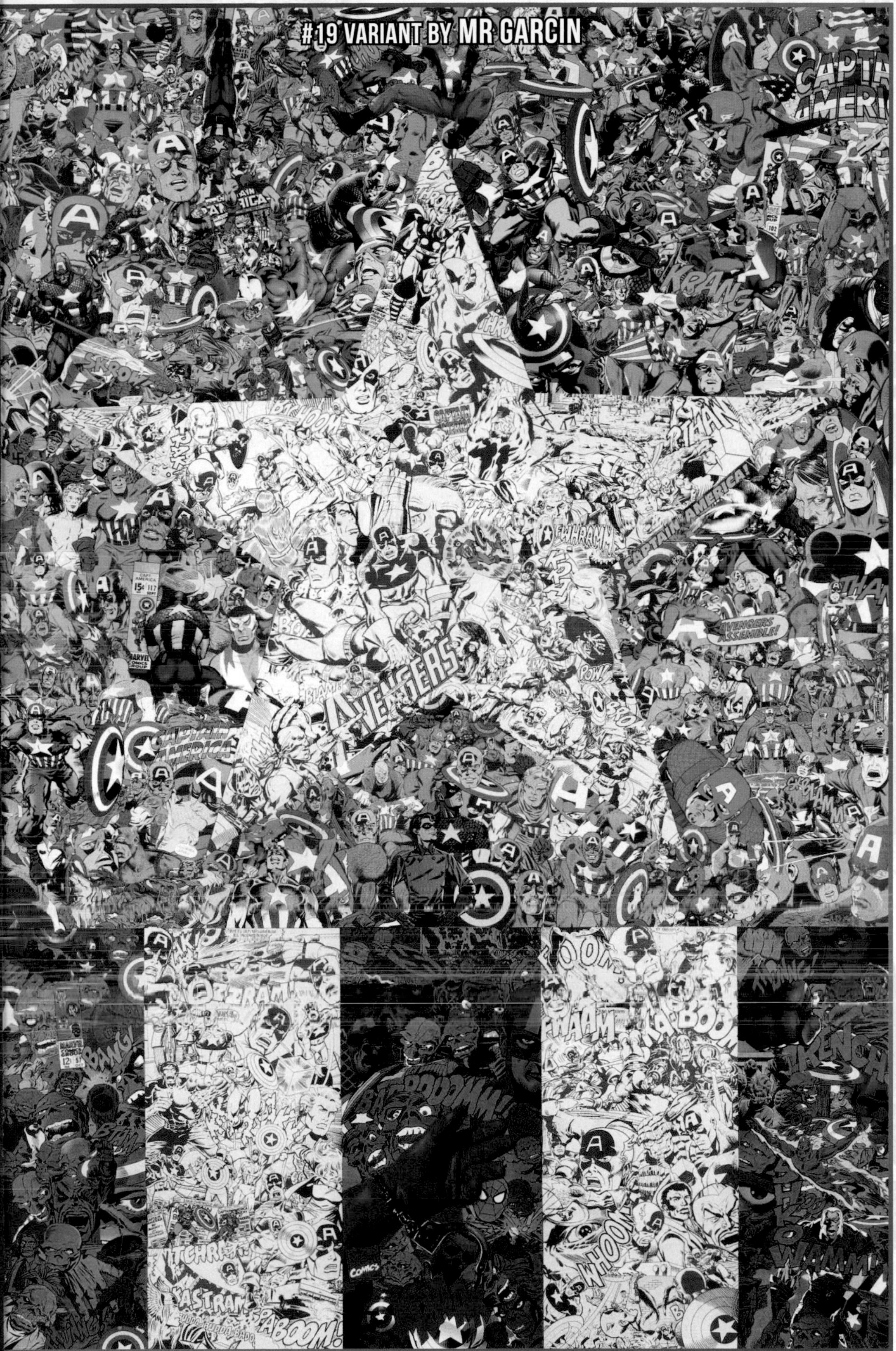
AVENGERS
AVENGERS ASSEMBLE!
KRANG

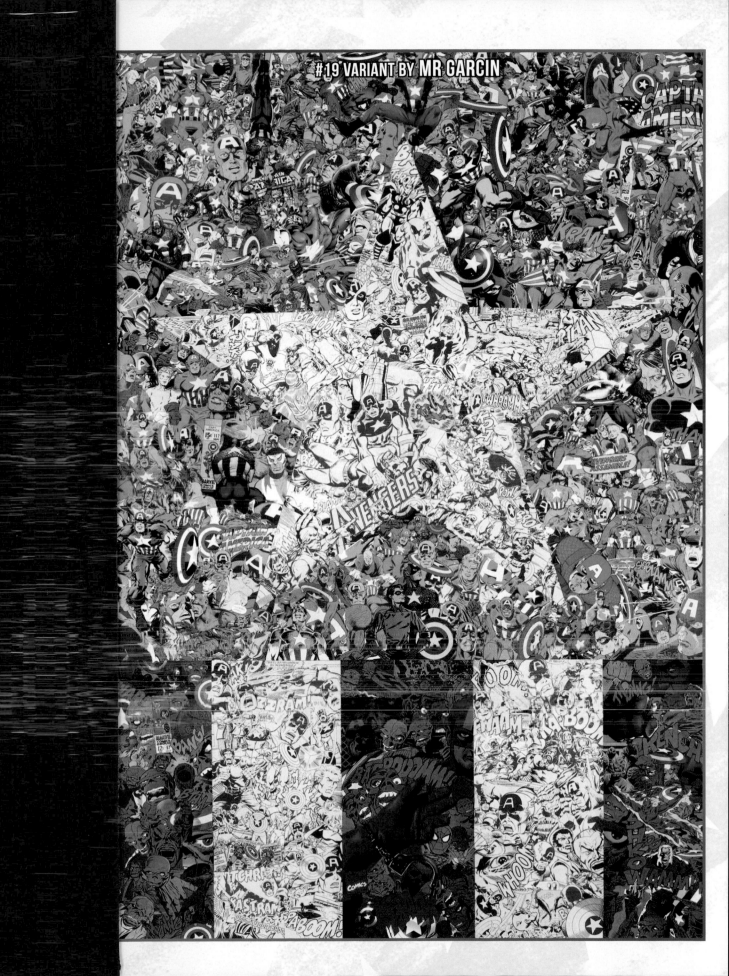

#19 VARIANT BY MR GARCIN

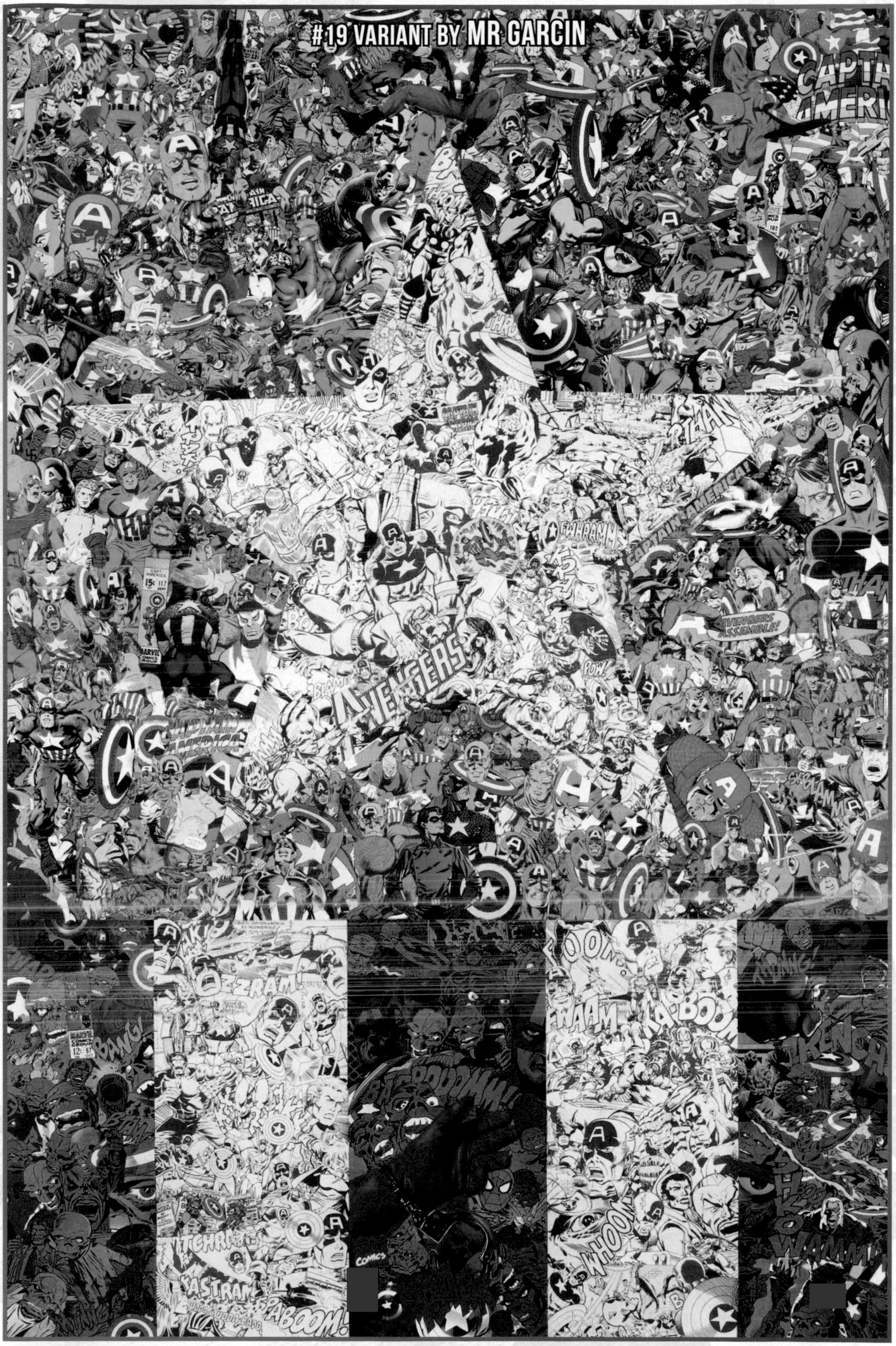
CAPTAIN AMERICA
KRANG
CAPTAIN AMERICA!
AVENGERS
AVENGERS ASSEMBLE!
CAPTAIN AMERICA
OZZRAM!
WAAM
BOOM
PABOOM!